Shakespeare's
More Than Words Can Witness

Shakespeare's
More Than Words Can Witness:

Essays on Visual and Nonverbal
Enactment in the Plays

Edited by Sidney Homan

Lewisburg
Bucknell University Press
London: Associated University Presses

LMS

Associated University Presses, Inc.
Cranbury, New Jersey 08512

Associated University Presses
Magdalen House
136-148 Tooley Street
London, SEI 2TT, England

Library of Congress Cataloging in Publication Data

Main entry under title:

Shakespeare's more than words can witness.

   Includes bibliographical references.
   1. Shakespeare, William, 1564-1616—Dramatic production—Addresses, essays,
lectures. 2. Nonverbal communication in literature—Addresses, essays,
lectures. I. Homan, Sidney, 1938-   II. Title: Visual and nonverbal enactment in the
plays.
PR2995.S5   822.3'3   79-19364
ISBN 0-8387-2153-2

PRINTED IN THE UNITED STATES OF AMERICA

To Beatrice

"What's new to speak, what now to register,
That may express my love, or thy dear merit?"
—Sonnet 108

Contents

Preface

SOME YEARS AGO AN ACTOR FRIEND TOLD ME OF A BIZARRE PERFOR-
mance. His troupe had agreed to do a benefit at a private school outside
Philadelphia, but in their hurry they had not bothered to check on the
exact nature of the school. Arriving minutes before the scheduled
performance, the actors raced onto a makeshift stage and started a play
that, fortunately, required no scenery or props, and that they had
performed countless times under all sorts of conditions. The problem lay
with the audience. It consisted of men and women of all ages who
absolutely baffled the actors. The audience would miss many lines,
respond enthusiastically to others, laugh when they weren't supposed
to, show great concern, even tears over moments that, according to the
script, were supposed to be happy. Clearly audience reaction was off
kilter with the performance. Yet in a curious sense the audience also
stimulated the actors, who were now frantically trying to break the
"code." Just what combination of voice, gesture, and words led to these
unpredictable reactions?

By the end of the one-act play the actors were exhausted. Somehow
the audience was *recreating* a drama below, or perhaps even above the
actors' conscious intentions. After numerous performances, indeed,
after routine performances where the actors knew just what line would
fetch a laugh, what gesture was needed to produce this or that emotion,
the actors were faced with an audience *alive* with its own semisecret
interpretation. What *was* their code, this special orientation to the
theater? It was only after the actual performance that the school principal
explained, with great apologies, that they had been performing before
two hundred students who were deaf and *dumb*—and only slowly
learning to read lips.

This book takes its title, *More Than Words Can Witness*, from
Tranio's line in *Taming of the Shrew* (2.1.337–38). Impersonating his
master while Lucentio pursues in disguise Kate's younger sister Bianca,
the fake suitor Tranio protests that his love for Bianca goes beyond that
of the aged Grumio, that he loves more than any words can witness. And
whereas Grumio's senses are now dead or dying, he, Tranio, has seen
Bianca with the eye of youth. This visually-inspired love dwarfs the

9

paltry words of his rival. The subtitle of this collection, "Visual and Nonverbal Enactment," does not imply the abandonment of words. Rather, the assumption is that Shakespeare's audience responds not just with the ears but with the eyes as well, that the playwright's glorious language is complemented, *enhanced*, indeed, totally dependent on the visual and nonverbal dimensions of a production.

These two terms, visual and nonverbal, receive a catholic interpretation in the twelve essays from fellow Shakespeareans. In general, "visual" means the *look* of a production, gestures, movements of the actors, even the physical fact of entrances and exits. The concluding essay expands the discussion by considering the aesthetic issues raised when attempts are made to "translate" a Shakespearean play to the movies. "Nonverbal" implies the "sound" or sounds of the play. This includes what we hear below the level of words, such as that cannon which, during Hamlet's interview with his father, booms in the background signaling Claudius's drinking. And also sounds beyond words, such as the music Prospero requires to still his beating soul after the successful staging of the wedding masque. The term will also accommodate things left unsaid or unseen, but that remain part of our experience with the play. And so one essay treats Shakespeare's sense of timing, the choreography of pace and rhythm felt by the characters and by the audience, while another essay cites examples in the Sonnets that expand on issues implied but left unsaid in the plays.

Shakespearean criticism, we all know, has been fascinated, sometimes properly, sometimes excessively so, with his language. Surely it is beating a dead horse to say that at times we treat his plays as if they were literary pieces not intended for the stage. There is probably no great harm in this, either, for in moving from a dramatic to a nondramatic medium we thereby only reverse what Shakespeare himself frequently did. Still, Shakespeare seemed more concerned with actual production than with literary publications—witness his going to print only for half the plays, and often to force a bad quarto off the market with an authorized edition. In its concern for the sight and sound of the plays this collection, then, tries to complement the numerous literary and textual studies.

The other extreme must also be avoided. I recall having my hackles raised recently when a graduate student in his oral examination for our Theater Department casually declared that in directing a production he would give "some attention" to the text, but that the words could just be one of his many priorities. There is a physical, visual dimension to Shakespeare's magnificent language, but I am talking about something far beyond spectacle.

And it was this very need that led to the present collection. Some years ago Maurice Charney and I chatted about a suitable theme for the Shakespeare session at a Chicago meeting of the Modern Language Association. Both of us had been thinking of a topic close to "Shakespeare without Words." The topic the year before had been "Shakespeare's Limitations," and the genial C. L. Barber reported to the meeting that since so few papers had been submitted he was forced—with happy results, as it turned out—to ask two of his colleagues at Buffalo to speak. Apparently not many Shakespeareans thought that the master had limitations. The response to Charney's invitation was just the opposite; he was overwhelmed with papers and proposals. Apparently, the limitation he set, a focus on something other than the words, was not so inhibiting. Two of the three papers (those of Professors Alan C. Dessen and Terence Hawkes) delivered at that meeting are here; Bernard Beckerman's was committed elsewhere, but he has graciously included another, delivered at the Folger, expanding on his general topic at the MLA meeting.

Appropriately, Maurice Charney's own classic essay, "*Hamlet* without Words," leads off this collection. He does here, I believe, just what a responsible critic should do, working with noises, sound effects, music, costumes, all the nonverbal and visual resources of the play—but *in terms of* the text. Mr. Charney tries to recreate what the tragedy might have sounded like and looked like to its audience in a performance in the 1600s.

With his essay as a frame, there follows three related articles concerned with the issue of language as it moves from nondramatic poetry, or the prompt copy, to the stage. James Calderwood traces Shakespeare's early career as he takes words that in poetry have their own autonomy and then vitalizes them in stage action. Distinguishing between the script and the poem, Calderwood sees plays such as *Romeo and Juliet* and *Henry IV* as dramatizing Shakespeare's own struggles and venture into the seas of the public theater to create a language for the actors and the actions of the stage. Obligated to the stage's physical, spacial, and temporal requirements, language so threatened ultimately absorbs and transcends the limitations, or seeming limitations, of the theater.

Terence Hawkes complements Mr. Calderwood by focusing on the nature of stage language, an activity he defines as both oral and aural. The text is enhanced by a "whole world of expressive bodily movements that must be beyond the words themselves." For examples he cites Lear's appearance with Cordelia in his arms, where the linguistic "something" offers no forms adequate for his situation, or Cleopatra's final posture on stage where, curled as in love at the feet of the victor Octavius, she wordlessly mocks the Roman. Mr. Hawkes's contention, in short, is that the words in the text are not all the "words" implied by the performed play. That play is ultimately speech, and speech is an oral-aural activity, not a literary one. Cordelia's response, "Nothing," admits the concept of "noting," being aware of meaning through eyes *and* ears. We must hear speech, rather than read texts. In a fascinating analogy, Mr. Hawkes argues that the difference between text and speech is that between written ragtime music and improvised New Orleans jazz.

Walter Herbert reverses the process, as he considers passages from four sonnets that enlarge on themes or ideas only suggested by a few words in the plays or that are born of brief, silent moments in the theater. Two important issues emerge from his essay. One is the ways in which the Sonnets serve as "source" or "reflector" for the plays. But there is a second question raised by Mr. Herbert: what does this verbalization of events in the plays tell us about the nature of the two media? Why does Shakespeare only imply things in the plays and then speak at length or, more properly, write at length about them in the Sonnets?

The next four articles by Alan Dessen, Alfred Harbage, Barbara Hodgdon, and Robert Hapgood form a third section. Each writer is concerned with the "look" of the plays. Mr. Dessen's paper treats what he calls "visual analogues" in the plays, those "sight" counterparts— and perhaps more immediate counterparts—to what literary critics mean by the "reiterative imagery" in the text. Mr. Dessen thus examines visual settings, or actions, which parallel and thereby comment on another earlier in the play: for example, the presence on stage of the Gadshill robbers and a later parallel arrangement of the conspirators, national crooks, if you will, calling to the mind's eye the earlier domestic crooks. Or consider Caliban carrying wood and, later, Ferdinand bearing logs as penance before he will be worthy of Miranda. The major part of his essay, however, examines the visual analogue provided by riding boots and their associations, especially in the history plays, with haste, commitment, blood, quiet, conscience—even with Cain.

In "Choral Juxtaposition in Shakespeare" Mr. Harbage takes up a similar subject as he concentrates on moments when a physical action or setting complements, indeed, determines or expands on the written text. He looks, for instance, at Macbeth's entrance immediately after Duncan's line "He was a gentleman on whom I built / An absolute trust," or the refutation to Jaques's cynical "Ages of Man" speech provided by the sudden appearance of Orlando carrying the aged Adam in his arms. With his account of the concluding visual image of *Lear*, "a pieta emblemizing all the heartaches of mankind" as a grieving father cradles the dead Cordelia in his arms, Mr. Harbage strikes a balance between the verbal and visual, satisfying, I believe, the very principles advocated in Mr. Charney's opening essay.

Barbara Hodgdon surveys the *Henry VI* plays, the two parts of *Henry IV*, and *Richard III* in terms of "Shakespeare's Directorial Eye." Her argument is that the playwright moves from large public scenes, embodying many characters and with broad visual perspectives, to an alternation between such scenes and more interior ones (as in the tavern scenes with Falstaff and Hal). In *Richard III* a malignant, but aesthetically pleasing usurper acts as Shakespeare's surrogate in directing our own "view" of what happens. Scenes in this play spring from Richard's interior, from his own imagination, and hence carry the concept of "private" scenes in *Henry IV* to an extreme. Richard is himself overwhelmed in the last act where, with the return of large public scenes on the battlefield and at court, national concerns supplant individual desires. Ms. Hodgdon's own focus is on both the visual look of the stage—whether twenty characters or only two help frame our perspective—and the more abstract ways in which Shakespeare, or a surrogate such as Richard, controls our vision no less than that of the characters within the "world" of the play.

I defined "nonverbal" earlier as all that either is below words or is left unsaid. Complementing its three predecessors, Robert Hapgood's essay on "Shakespeare's Choreography: Pace and Rhythm" raises an issue, the sense of timing in the play for both the characters and the audience who must pass judgments on them, which is literally beyond language. Investigating those who control or are controlled by time, who understand or fail to understand the importance of the natural temporal rhythms in our existence, Mr. Hapgood confesses that for the audience the kinetic appeals of characters "are hard to be positive and precise about since they make themselves felt beneath and between the lines.'' In his survey of winners or losers or simply comic dupes of time he treats those ''sequential values'' of the play equally important to characters and audience. For if characters experience the time-world of the play, its thematic reality as Murray Krieger would have it in his book on *Shakespeare Sonnets and Modern Poetics: Windows to Criticism*, we also experience the aesthetic reality of the stage's two hours' traffic.

The essays by Bernard Beckerman and Tommy Ruth Waldo cap those that precede since both writers survey many of the plays, Mr. Beckerman being concerned with the way the play ''looked'' to the Elizabethan audience and Ms. Waldo treating the theme of speechlessness, that state where words fail the characters, in eight Shakespearean plays, with a special focus on *Pericles*. In ''Shakespearean Playgoing Then and Now'' Mr. Beckerman moves from the radical ways, both physical and auditory, by which present-day directors try to revitalize Shakespeare, to a consideration of how Shakespeare's own company captured and then kept the attention of an often unruly, and surely festive public audience. Noting that eyewitnesses such as Thomas Platter most often confine their accounts to the appearance of the play, to the costumes and sets, or the sounds and movements of the production (particularly the dancing), Mr. Beckerman argues that an Elizabethan production maintained a balance between the visual and the auditory, and thus complemented the audience itself, who came to the Globe to see and be seen. After surveying Shakespeare's own references to sound and sight, he turns to three elements—mirth, wit, and passion—that were essential to any production hoping to sustain the attention of that large, heterogeneous audience.

Ms. Waldo treats Shakespeare's technique ''for conveying what is beyond words,'' emotions or states, particularly those of love and death, for which language proves inadequate. She looks at three young men (Benedick, Orlando, and Hamlet) who ''cannot compress their love into lines of verse or harness their feelings within verbal patterns,'' and then at Cressida's feigned speechlessness as contrasted with Hermione's silent acceptance of false accusations. In the last half of her essay she turns to the relationship between language and the emotions aroused by death's approach. Music takes over for words in the death scenes in *King John* and *Henry VIII*. And in *Pericles* Shakespeare can follow a young man from love to the very threshold of death. Pericles' own difficulty with language is Shakespeare's witness to the ''distance and paradoxically the connection between language and emotion.'' Like

John and Katherine, Pericles, "because of his increased receptivity," also goes beyond language to the far-off music of the spheres.

The final two essays try to gain a different perspective on Shakespeare's visual side by considering his plays in the context of the cinema, a medium that, most would agree, clearly elevates the visual over the verbal. In "The Visual Powers Denied and Coupled" the film scholar William Robinson challenges lovers of Shakespeare and his theater by arguing that both Hamlet and his play represent a dead end. Words chain Hamlet to the past, to a father's injunction to revenge, to a world view that clings to analysis, conceptualism, and to a deadly intellectualism working against man's natural and primal energy. That energy would lead us to "see" life rather than to speculate on it, to take pleasure in what is here and now, in the organic, fascinating, infinite alternatives of existence. Overwhelmed by his own words, Hamlet uses his eyes, the visual, only to justify his revenge, to restore authoritarianism rather than initiate a free new world for man. In an extraordinary comparison with the film *Fellini-Satyricon* Robinson contends that the movie hero, Encolpio, survives where Hamlet fails. Past-less, not chained to words and the stultifying society they both create and sustain, Fellini's hero encounters life with his eyes, his senses, taking pleasure in the physical, in the moment.

The greatness of *Hamlet*, Robinson holds, is that Shakespeare here comes to grips with the innate fallacy of the theater as a medium. For the tension Hamlet feels between the physical and the intellectual, between precepts and concepts, enervates the medium as well. Whereas the cinema, at the high level of a Fellini, *shows* us (rather than tells us) about the organic, tangible, endless possibilities in the real world, the theater falls under its own weight, caught as it is in a language that would remove us from reality, and torn as it is between its lively physical dimension and that linguistic abstractionism that, while pleasing to our philosophical nature, wars against what we are as creatures of flesh and blood.

Stated bluntly, Robinson's thesis is that *Hamlet* stands at the end of the line as Shakespeare's conscious valediction to his medium. The theater that follows either wallows in a verbal conceptualism for which there is no such creative tension, or degenerates to happenings or—to be specific—Mr. Beckett's recent miniplay, *Breath*, a piece without words, purely visual, but at best only a parody of the playwright and his theater. In line with the empiricism, the dynamic relativism of twentieth-century science, the cinema, in Robinson's view, takes over as the quintessential visual medium upon the death of the theater, that quintessential verbal medium.

If Robinson's article poses a challenge—perhaps an irritation—to scholars of the theater, even to those arguing, as in the present collection, for its physical and nonverbal dimensions, the final article is more properly a speculation. Here I trace Shakespeare's history in the movies and then consider a possible future for Shakespeare, for his words, words, words, in a primarily visual medium such as the cinema. After a survey of five arguments on the practicality of moving him from stage to screen, I argue that the stage is more physical than we often realize (since there is a creative, rather than an enervating tension between the philosophic implications of its language and the physical, temporal demands of the actors and the playing area). Conversely, the cinema is more abstract than cineasts would have us believe. If this is so, then perhaps the visual-verbal Shakespeare can, with adjustments, be taken from one public medium to the other.

I might point out that my collaborator here, Neil Feineman, adopted a position somewhat opposed to my own. From his own experience as a film director and a scholar of the cinema, he maintains that the translation is impossible since there is too great an aesthetic gap between the verbal theater and the visual cinema. As a result, his contribution, a stimulating one I believe, takes the form of a lengthy coda to my own speculations.

The movement in this collection, then, is from a proper scholarly performance on *Hamlet* by Mr. Charney, to three essays considering the nature of stage language and its oral-aural dimensions, then four essays on the visuality and timing of the plays, two essays surveying in the broadest terms the visual and nonverbal side of Shakespeare's canon (the first with reference to a reconstructed performance in the year 1600, the second with special emphasis on silence and music), and at length two pieces on the cinema as an aesthetic form illuminating Shakespeare's theater. The final essay, in its disagreement between the collaborators, will allow the reader to enter a personal opinion—on each essay and on the general focus of the collection.

And I believe the reader will do this since, apparently, spectators do it; they seem to insist that plays be something more than radio performances, that a production does not mean merely a concert reading, and that the delivery of the actor or the playwright's language, no matter how splendid, be complemented by the visual and nonverbal dimension inherent in the theatrical experience. I am reminded of this by the dilemma presented some years ago by the Broadway production of Peter Schaffer's *Black Comedy*. In the story itself the lights fail shortly after the start of a sophisticated New York cocktail party. For almost two hours the characters in the dark give vent to their true feelings, with the darkness here serving to remove inhibitions. Then, just minutes before the end of the party, and the play proper, the lights are restored and the guests return to the social posing and shallow cocktail dialogue of the opening. At first the director tried to play it straight, to be "realistic," by having the stage lights fail and then performing the majority of the play in darkness. An audience in their own darkness was to face an unlit stage and only hear the voices of the actors.

But audiences soon objected to this—they wanted to *see* the play, to distinguish between sounds and dialogue, to be alert to the rhythm and look of a production that, in Mr. Hawkes's words, is both oral and aural. The solution was simple and, I think, a testament to the conventions of the theater. A quick decision was made. The play now began with the stage totally dark (this symbolizing "lights on"), while the subsequent turning on of the stage lights stood for the failure of the lights within the world of the play. Realism here was not permitted to rob the spectator, the viewer, of his or her right to see and experience a live performance.

Gainesville, Florida   Sidney Homan

Note: I have regulated all Shakespeare quotations with the line numbering in *William Shakespeare: The Complete Works*, general editor Alfred Harbage, The Complete Pelican Shakespeare (Baltimore, Md.: Penguin Books, 1969). But I have retained spelling and punctuation from the texts originally chosen by the individual writers. My former graduate student Stephen Snyder has served as my assistant editor here, but such mistakes as remain, large or small, are entirely my own.

Acknowledgments

PUBLISHING ACKNOWLEDGMENTS ARE LISTED WITH THE INDIVIDUAL essays. I want to thank my friend, Maurice Charney, who suggested the idea of this collection, and Maureen Geruth, editor at Associated University Presses. My wife, Norma, went over the manuscript and page proofs with me, but she is perfection itself, and I am the sole Lord of Error.

I also wish to thank The English Association in London for permission to reprint ''That Shakespeherean Rag'' by Terence Hawkes from *Essays and Studies 1977* published by John Murray; The Johns Hopkins University Press for permission to reprint Maurice Charney's ''Hamlet without Words''; and Salisbury State College for permission to reprint Sidney Homan's essay that appeared earlier in *Literature/Film Quarterly*, © Salisbury State College.

Shakespeare's
More Than Words Can Witness

1

Hamlet without Words*

MAURICE CHARNEY

IT WOULD BE A PLEASANT FICTION TO SPECULATE ON THAT QUESTION
Martin Holmes has recently proposed for us: ''What sort of a play was
Hamlet in the eyes of its original spectators?'' [1] Or, to exercise us in an
even more demanding fiction, Jan Kott asks us to return to that moment
when the members of Shakespeare's company are seated around a table
for the first rehearsal of *Hamlet*.[2] They have the scenario in their hands,
but this is only the starting point of their play. They must still decide on
the appearance of the characters, their costumes, the gestures they will
use, and the music and sound effects that accompany the stage action.
They must draw up an accurate list of properties and arrange to have
them ready at the right cues. Many of these indications are already in the
text of the written play, and some have been noted in the margin by the
''bookkeeper.'' Some effects are so much a matter of accepted practice
that they hardly need be noted at all: for example, the trumpet fanfare to
announce the entrance of royalty, or the carrying off of corpses before a
new scene. There is a *Hamlet* of words that we all know almost by heart,
and there is a *Hamlet* without words that may be more unfamiliar to us,
but these two *Hamlets* cannot be separated in the play we see acted on the
stage.

It is worth pausing a moment to reflect on what is involved here. The
poetic play is a puzzling genre since so much in it is a matter of
presentation rather than words. What are we to make of the description
of the dumb show in *Hamlet*? This description does not exist in the play
we see in the theater. It is, literally, only a set of directions to actors, a
list of instructions on how to perform the pantomime. We honestly
regret losing that wonderful line that tells the Player Queen to make
''*passionate action*'' (3.2.138 s.d.)[3] when she finds the Player King

*Paper read in part at the Eleventh International Shakespeare Conference, Stratford-upon-Avon,
1964. Reprinted from *English Literary History* 32 (1965):457–77, by permission of the Johns
Hopkins University Press.

poisoned. Or that splendid description in *Timon of Athens* of how Apemantus is to enter the banquet of Timon: *"Then comes, dropping after all, Apemantus, discontentedly, like himself."* What sort of Janus-faced genre is this that has one form when read and another when seen? Which is really the play as Shakespeare wrote it and meant it?

I do not propose to answer these complex questions. Merely to formulate them suggests how difficult it is to speak about the style of a Shakespearean play. We are forced to think of the written text and its realization in performance at one and the same time. Sometimes a line in the written text is not complete without reference to the gesture that accompanies it. I am thinking of Polonius's triumphant assertion to the King of Hamlet's love melancholy: "Take this from this, if this be otherwise" (2.2.156). It is not a very significant line, yet it is unintelligible without the customary stage direction supplied by Theobald: *"Pointing to his head and shoulder."* The gesture is implicit in Shakespeare's text, yet in what sense can a gesture be said to exist in a literary work? Bartlett's *Concordance* solves the problem very simply and disastrously by omitting all stage directions. Or take the stage direction in Quarto 2 for the second appearance of the Ghost: *"It spreads his arms"* (1.1.127 s.d.).[4] If we consider only the words that the Ghost speaks in this scene, we cannot advance very far, since the Ghost does not speak at all, yet this gesture is intended as a reply to Horatio's bold line: "I'll cross it, though it blast me" (1.1.127). The Ghost answers by "crossing" Horatio and warning him off; it will not be trifled with. How are we, in our accepted literary categories, to deal with a nonverbal reply? Most studies of Shakespeare's style—for example, Spurgeon's book on Shakespeare's imagery—choose to ignore these uncategorizable details. This seems to me to distort the very nature of drama.

In the present study, I would like to go to the opposite extreme to see what can be said about "*Hamlet* without Words." So much has already been said about the words of the play that it might be interesting, as an experiment, to confine our attention to the play as Shakespeare intended it to be produced in the Globe theater. I don't for a moment believe that we can really recover Shakespeare's intentions, but the attempt might stimulate some fresh insight into *Hamlet*—if such a thing is still possible. We shall be concerned with the indications of sound effects, music, costumes, and stage properties in the text of the play itself, both in the spoken words and in the stage directions.

Let us begin with the sound effects of *Hamlet*. We are immediately struck by the fact that there is more cannonading in this play than in any other play of Shakespeare.[5] It is, in fact, a conspicuously noisy and active play. This cannonading is especially associated with Claudius and his "rouses," or drinking of healths. The whole sound effect consists of a roll on the kettledrums, followed by an elaborate trumpet fanfare, and concluded by the firing of the theater cannon or "chambers." These sounds are most explicitly described by the King just before the fencing match between Hamlet and Laertes:

> Give me the cups,
> And let the kettle to the trumpet speak,
> The trumpet to the cannoneer without,
> The cannons to the heavens, the heaven to earth,
> "Now the King drinks to Hamlet."
>
> (5.2.264–67)

This is as close as we ever come in the play to a feeling of "hubris," the insolent competition with the gods by mortal man, and Claudius's bravado leaves him vulnerable to the wrath of the gods. In a detailed description of the King's rouse, we are made to feel that Claudius is arrogating to himself the powers of Jove the Thunderer.

> No jocund health that Denmark drinks today,
> But the great cannon to the clouds shall tell,
> And the King's rouse the heaven shall bruit again,
> Respeaking earthly thunder.
>
> (1.2.125–28)

We remember the conventional associations of thunder with the anger of the gods.

It is a significant dramatic irony that we hear the King's rouse offstage just before the Ghost appears in act 1, scene 4. The Quarto 2 stage direction reads: "*A flourish of trumpets and two pieces goes off*" (1.4.6 s.d.), but there are also the kettledrums mentioned in Hamlet's description:

> The King doth wake tonight and takes his rouse,
> Keeps wassail, and the swagg'ring upspring reels,
> And as he drains his draughts of Rhenish down
> The kettledrum and trumpet thus bray out
> The triumph of his pledge.
>
> (1.4.8–12)

This drunken braying of the King prepares us for the confrontation with the Ghost: "So excellent a king, that was to this / Hyperion to a satyr" (1.2.139–40). The "wassail" and the reeling "upspring" of Claudius are literally a satyr's revel. We should also note that one of the "slight sullies" that Polonius will have Reynaldo put on Laertes is that he is "o'ertook in's rouse" (2.1.58). This is only one among many links between Laertes and Claudius.

In addition to the firing of chambers already mentioned, there are three examples in the final scene of the play. After Hamlet's first hit in the fencing match, the Quarto 2 stage direction reads: "*Drum, trumpets, and shot. Flourish; a piece goes off*" (5.2.282 s.d.). It is an ironic salute to one who is "Most generous, and free from all contriving" (4.7.134). The "warlike noise" and "volley" (5.2.338, 341) of Fortinbras's greeting to the English ambassadors are also ironic, since those ambassadors would not have the thanks they anticipated even if Claudius were alive. The "*March afar off, and shot*[6] *within*" of the Folio direction (5.2.337 s.d.) is almost the last sound that Hamlet hears, and it gives him assurance that his dying wish will be fulfilled: "I do prophesy th' election lights / On Fortinbras" (5.2.344–45).

At the very end of the play Hamlet is given a soldier's funeral by Fortinbras. His body is borne aloft by "four captains" to the probable accompaniment of a dead march (beat on muffled drums) and the trailing pikes of the soldiers. The very last line of the play is Fortinbras's order for another cannon salute: "Go, bid the soldiers shoot," followed by the Folio stage direction: "*Exeunt marching; after the which a peal of ordnance are shot off.*" In Joseph Papp's production of *Hamlet* in New York City's Central Park, those peals of ordnance at the end very effectively echoed and reechoed in the Gothic wildness of the park. There is a suggestion in 5.2.265 that the cannoneer is "without," that is, just outside the theater, and this suggestion makes good sense to me. To fire the chambers in the "huts" of the theater would seem to offer, at the least, a serious hazard to the plaster, if not to the theater building itself.[7] The burning down of the Globe during a performance of *Henry VIII* on 29 June 1613, could just as easily have been caused by cannon fire outside the theater as within.

Another important use of sound is for Laertes's rebellion in act 4, scene 5. In fact, that abortive uprising seems to me to be represented chiefly by the clamor, noise, and commotion of the unruly but successful mob that Laertes commands. The sounds of this "giantlike" rebellion are first heard in "*A noise within*" (4.5.96 s.d.), at which the Queen exclaims in fear: "Alack, what noise is this?" (4.5.96). A confused din of shouting and clashing of weapons could properly suggest the menace of a popular insurrection. Some of these shouted phrases are reported by a messenger just before the rabble batter in the doors to the King:

> They cry, "Choose we! Laertes shall be king!"
> Caps, hands, and tongues applaud it to the clouds,
> "Laertes shall be king! Laertes king!"
>
> (4.5.106–8)

We are back at the mob scenes following the murder of Caesar in *Julius Caesar*, and I suggest that the stage direction, "*A noise within*" (4.5.108[8] s.d.), includes those treasonous phrases. They are presumably what the Queen has just heard when she says:

> How cheerfully on the false trail they cry!
> O, this is counter, you false Danish dogs!
>
> (4.5.109–10)

I think, therefore, that there is good warrant for the Folio stage direction further in the scene announcing the entrance of the mad Ophelia: "*A noise within*: 'Let her come in.'" (4.5.152 s.d.).[9] This is Laertes's rabble again, restive at being excluded from the presence chamber and the promise of bloody action, making their wishes known in no uncertain terms. It is an unusual stage direction, yet it seems to me not essentially different from the previous directions for "noise within" at lines 96 and 108. They indicate not just miscellaneous noise, but a medley of shouted phrases. From my own limited experience as a supernumerary with the Metropolitan Opera, I can attest that the chorus always interprets a "confused murmur" as a collection of actual phrases spoken at random as the spirit moves.

There are two remarkable sounds associated with the appearance and disappearance of the Ghost that help to develop its portentousness for the audience. *Hamlet* begins, I believe, with the sound of the big bell in the theater tower being tolled twelve times.[10] "'Tis now struck twelve," says Barnardo, "Get thee to bed, Francisco" (1.1.7). This is the bell that also did duty for ringing alarums, and its solemn tolling here helps to mark the spiritual alarm of the soldiers. Some lines

further, the bell strikes one and the Ghost appears. On the second
appearance of the Ghost,

> It lifted up it head and did address
> Itself to motion like as it would speak,

(1.2.216–17)

but then, according to Quarto 2, *"The cock crows"* (1.1.138 s.d.), and
at the sound "it started, like a guilty thing / Upon a fearful summons"
(1.1.148–49). We learn from Marcellus that "It faded on the crowing of
the cock" (1.1.157), and later from Horatio that "at the sound it shrunk
in haste away" (1.2.219). The crowing of the cock was probably
imitated offstage by an experienced mimic; in the earliest extant
promptbook for *Hamlet* (about 1740), there is a direction at this point for
"One to Crow."[11] This is a tricky stage effect, which, if done badly,
will certainly provoke laughter, and that is perhaps why the direction is
omitted in the Folio. Horatio tells us that "the morning cock crew loud"
(1.3.218), which doesn't allow for any weakness in execution. It seems
appropriate that in an open-air, afternoon performance, the passage of
time should be marked by sound effects. This representation of time by
sound rather than by light (as on our modern stage) was one of the
received traditions of Elizabethan staging.

One other possible use of the tower bell is for the funeral of Ophelia.
Although it is not mentioned in the Quarto or Folio directions, her
"maimèd rites" do, nevertheless, include "the bringing home / Of bell
and burial" (5.1.220–21), and the tolling of the death bell would
make an expected and fitting entrance for her funeral procession.[12]
There is one other sound connected with Ophelia's death that has not
often been noticed. While the King is setting forth his plot to Laertes,
he is suddenly interrupted: "But stay, what noise?" (4.7.161). This
line occurs only in Quarto 2; the Folio has the colorless "How, sweet
queen," which editors emend to "How now, sweet queen?" But I
think that the sound the King hears is some sort of howl or shriek or
loud wail, possibly made by Gertrude herself, to mark the discovery of
the dead body of Ophelia. The staging is very similar to that terrifying
moment in *Macbeth* when we hear *"A cry within of women"* (5.5.7
s.d.), and we learn that Lady Macbeth is dead. These unearthly sounds
remind us in both plays of the presence of death and that ambiguous
spirit world "from whose bourn / No traveler returns" (3.1.79–80).

The music of *Hamlet* has been competently discussed by others,[13] so that we need only notice a few special examples. There is a good deal of expected trumpet play for the flourishes or fanfares announcing royal entries, but there is also an unexpected *"Flourish for the Players"* in the Folio (2.2.360 s.d.). Another unusual use is the *"Danish March,"* indicated in the Folio, to mark the royal entry to the play (3.2.86 s.d.). This was probably added after 1603 as a compliment to Queen Anne of Denmark, the wife of James I. It is remarkable how much singing of snatches of old ballads there is in *Hamlet*, not only by Ophelia, but also by Hamlet himself and the Clown Gravedigger. There are no songs at all that are called for and sung as set pieces, and we regret that Polonius was not given an aria to match the splendid performance of Pandarus in *Troilus and Cressida*.

Other notable instrumental effects are the illustrated recorder lesson that Hamlet gives to Rosencrantz and Guildenstern (act 3, sc. 2), and Ophelia's entry "playing on a lute" in her mad scene (Quarto 1, act 4, sc. 5). There was probably soft music offstage to introduce and to accompany the dumb show. The Folio direction, *"Hoboyes play. The dumb show enters.,"* replaces the less appropriate direction in Quarto 2: *"The trumpets sounds. Dumb show follows."* (3.2.129 s.d.). The intent here is to imitate the dumb show of an old play such as *Gorboduc* (1561), where, before the Fourth Act, we are told:

> First the musick of howboies began to plaie, during which there came from vnder the stage, as though out of hell, three Furies .... After that the Furies and these had passed about the stage thrise, they departed; and than the musicke ceased.[14]

There is a general Shakespearean association of oboes with the supernatural and the portentous, as in *Antony and Cleopatra* (act 4, sc. 3) and *Macbeth* (act 4, sc. 1).

The costumes of *Hamlet* may also help us understand that elusive *Hamlet* without words we are now pursuing. The costumes in a play are an obvious means of characterization, of translating into visual terms the character traits mentioned or implied in the text, for, as Polonius says, "the apparel oft proclaims the man" (1.3.72). The producer of a play is obviously trying to suggest very specific ideas of character in what he has his actors wear. One can see the special ironic point of modern-dress productions, which abandon the overworked conventions of historical period in favor of a more direct and more easily understood costume symbolism. Gertrude's mink coat in the

New York staging by Gielgud is an almost perfect expression of her complaisant vulgarity (although Claudius's blue blazer in the same production completely failed to convey any notion of a king). The reader of a play has thus a much wider range of character possibilities than the spectator who, in effect, sees certain character interpretations already presented to him through a combination of casting, acting, and costume.

Perhaps the most significant use of costume in *Hamlet* is for Hamlet himself. The changes in his outward appearance are used to mark changes in his role in the course of the play. He first appears in act 1, scene 2 in mourning. His "inky cloak" and "customary suits of solemn black" (1.2.77–78) are meant to offer the strongest possible contrast to the brilliant and lavish apparel of all the other members of the court. Everyone has come to celebrate the marriage and coronation of Claudius and Gertrude, but only Hamlet persists in "obstinate condolement" (1.2.93), an open affront to the new king. The staging of the scene is designed to isolate this peevish malcontent. He enters, according to the Quarto 2 direction, after all the others, and he refuses to participate in their gaiety. He does not speak until the bitter aside of line 65: "A little more than kin, and less than kind!" And his first substantial speech calls attention to his outward appearance as "but the trappings and the suits" (1.2.86) of his inner woe. He cannot be reconciled to this shallow court. It is interesting to note that in the passionate torrent of his first soliloquy, one of the most vivid images of disgust centers on Gertrude's shoes:

> A little month, or ere those shoes were old
> With which she followed my poor father's body
> Like Niobe, all tears . . . .

> (1.2.147–49)

We can imagine Hamlet brooding on those shoes during this long silence before the soliloquy, as his "vailèd lids" seek for his "noble father in the dust" (1.2.70–71).

Hamlet's next change of costume is for his "antic disposition," but I think we should not take too literally the figure Ophelia describes:

> My lord, as I was sewing in my closet,
> Lord Hamlet, with his doublet all unbraced,
> No hat upon his head, his stockings fouled,

Ungartered, and down-gyvèd to his ankle,
Pale as his shirt, his knees knocking each other,
And with a look so piteous in purport,
As if he had been loosèd out of hell
To speak of horrors—he comes before me.

(2.1.77–84)

This is a description of a scene that takes place offstage; there is no indication that Hamlet ever actually appears this way. It would seem to me very risky for a producer to have such a slovenly figure show himself to the audience. There must obviously be some disorder in Hamlet's dress to correspond with his feigned madness. The King himself reports that "nor the exterior nor the inward man / Resembles that it was" (2.2.6–7). More important, a contemporary minor poet, Anthony Scoloker, who saw *Hamlet* and was influenced by it, tells us in his *Daiphantus, or the Passions of Love* (1604) that his mad hero

Puts off his cloathes; his shirt he onely weares,
Much like mad-*Hamlet*; thus as Passion teares.[15]

To say, however, as J. Q. Adams does, that "Hamlet's 'madness,' as it impressed the audience of the Globe, was conspicuously a madness 'in clothes'"[16] seems to me to exaggerate the dramatic point. Everyone in the play knows that Hamlet's madness is chiefly a matter of words and wit. A little loosening and untrussing of his original costume or sagging of his stockings should serve amply well. Or we might choose to follow Scoloker and show Hamlet in his shirt, which, while not quite the equivalent of our modern undershirt, was still a notable offense against decorum.

There is a significant change in Hamlet's costume when he returns from his abortive voyage to England, and this change would help to point up a more general development or regeneration[17] in his character. I agree with William Poel and Granville-Barker that Hamlet should appear in the graveyard with his "seagown scarfed about"[18] him (5.2.13). There is a new resoluteness and informality about this costume that makes a visual link with the dress of the pirate sailors of act 4, scene 6. I imagine this "seagown" as a rough sort of cloak, appropriate for an outdoor scene such as act 5, scene 1, but inappropriate for the interior scene that follows. Since there is no time for a change of costume between act 5, scene 1 and act 5, scene 2, I assume that

Hamlet is wearing acceptable court attire beneath his seagown. He should have long since abandoned the black mourning suit of the earlier part of the play, since a considerable interval of time has elapsed—Shakespeare is at some pains to tell us that the formerly young Hamlet has now turned thirty. In sum, he needs here a comfortable costume suitable not only for a vigorous fencing match, but also for his military funeral at the very end of the play.

The costume of Laertes is in sharp contrast to that of Hamlet. We are presented with a very specific program for Laertes's dress in the precepts of his father:

> Costly thy habit as thy purse can buy,
> But not expressed in fancy; rich, not gaudy,
> For the apparel oft proclaims the man . . . .

(1.3.70–72)

I take this to mean that Laertes is to be fashionably dressed in what will immediately suggest expensive good taste; these precepts have some bearing on Polonius's costume, too. Laertes's close association with Paris, and his eager haste to return there, are signs of his pursuit of men's fashions, for Frenchmen "of the best rank and station" are "most select and generous" chiefly in their apparel (1.3.73–74).

It is important, however, not to make a fop out of Laertes. He is not intended to compete with Osric, who is rich *and* gaudy in his dress and has all the qualities of the dandified and effeminate courtier. Coming as he does just before the catastrophe, "this waterfly" is part of a bold experiment in comic relief. This is our last glimpse of the court before the triple plot of the King and Laertes is set into motion, a plot in which "young Osric" seems to be involved, since it is he who presents the foils (5.2.248). In the interchange with Hamlet, Osric's hat is the butt of an elaborate burlesque of politeness. It must be an absurdly ornate and long-plumed hat to draw so much attention to itself, but Osric is so intricately enmeshed in the web of words and ceremony that he is impervious to ridicule. He exits with the triumphant hat once again on his head, or, as Horatio puts it, "This lapwing runs away with the shell on his head" (5.2.178–79). Rosencrantz and Guildenstern probably belong in this Laertes-Osric courtier group, and something could surely be done to express their comic pairing in terms of what they wear. There is, however, a danger that one may do too much and make the symmetry too broad and expressionistic.

The costume for the Ghost in *Hamlet* is made very explicit in the play, so that there is no reason at all to believe him a vague sheeted presence hovering over the scene like a Ku Klux Klansman, or merely a disembodied voice. In Act 1 he appears in full armor, in fact, "the very armor he had on / When he the ambitious Norway combated . . ." (1.1.60–61). He is a "portentous figure" (1.1.109), "majestical" (1.1.143), and of "fair and warlike form" (1.1.47). We learn later that he was "Armèd at point exactly, cap-a-pe" (1.2.200), that "He wore his beaver up" (1.2.230), and that he walked with a stately tread, a "martial stalk" (1.1.66). He comes in armor and carries his marshal's truncheon in his hand because "Something is rotten in the state of Denmark" (1.4.90). He represents, as it were, an official emissary from Purgatory on a public mission of revenge. His armor was probably made of a supple, painted leather, the traditional "leathern pilch,"[19] which would give him much more flexibility than real armor in ascending and descending the traps.

In the closet scene the Ghost does not appear to Hamlet in armor (despite the notorious illustration in Rowe's 1709 edition of Shakespeare), but "in his habit as he lived" (3.4.136). This change in costume for the Ghost marks an important distinction between his public and private roles. Quarto 1 has the Ghost enter in his "nightgown," which makes very good sense if one remembers that the Elizabethan nightgown was a warm, lined garment, usually with a fur collar, worn both indoors and out and roughly equivalent to our dressing gown. Julius Caesar and Brutus both appear in nightgowns for drafty scenes in *Julius Caesar* (act 2, sc. 2 and act 4, sc. 3). The important thing to keep in mind is that act 3, scene 4 is a domestic scene in the Queen's "closet," or private room, where it would be inappropriate, as well as bad manners, for even her former husband to show himself in full armor. The Ghost does not now appear for reasons of state, but to whet Hamlet's "almost blunted purpose" (3.4.112) and to mollify his fierce attack on his mother: to "step between her and her fighting soul" (3.4.114).

By the way, the Elizabethan word "closet" means simply a private apartment, especially of a king or queen, which would distinguish it from the public rooms of the castle. It does not mean "bed chamber," and the ponderous marriage bed that usually dominates this scene is entirely out of place. No stage property is needed to reinforce Hamlet's blatantly sexual harangue.

Before we close this discussion of costume, it is worth noting that just about all the male characters in *Hamlet* are said to have beards. This is not precisely a matter of costume or makeup, since it is more than likely that the actors themselves wore beards. In his self-accusing soliloquy in act 2, scene 2, Hamlet asks:

> Who calls me villain? Breaks my pate across?
> Plucks off my beard and blows it in my face?
>
> (2.2.557–58)

And he notes of his "old friend," the First Player: "thy face is valanced since I saw thee last. Com'st thou to beard me in Denmark?" (2.2.413–14). Claudius assures Laertes:

> You must not think
> That we are made of stuff so flat and dull
> That we can let our beard be shook with danger,
> And think it pastime.
>
> (4.7.30–33)

Although there are no references to Laertes's beard, there are three to his father's. When Polonius protests that the Player's speech of Priam and Hecuba is too long, Hamlet mocks his literary judgment: "It shall to the barber's, with your beard" (2.2.487). Polonius is the butt of the "satirical rogue" who has written, in Hamlet's book, "that old men have gray beards" (2.2.196), and he is referred to obliquely in Ophelia's ballad: "His beard was as white as snow, /All flaxen was his poll" (4.5.193–94). Finally, the Ghost of Hamlet's father has a beard that is "grizzled," and Horatio attests: "It was as I have seen it in his life, / A sable silvered" (1.2.241–42). This is not a description of a vague and inchoate Ghost. It would be a perverse literalism to insist on a bearded production of *Hamlet*, yet I do think that the many references to beards give us some clue to how the characters looked on Shakespeare's stage.

I have left for the last the most obvious question of all: what properties are needed to produce *Hamlet*? In making a list of these properties, one is struck by the closeness with which they follow the symbolic concerns of the play. Since most discussions of Shakespeare's rhetoric ignore his nonverbal resources, it is necessary to insist that the properties are a "language" that work together with the words of the play to convey its full meaning. In this sense, *Hamlet* without words has its existence only in relation to *Hamlet* with words, and vice versa.

Let us begin with one of the most significant properties in the play, Hamlet's sword, and it is worth dwelling on this property for a moment if only to dispel those perfumed clouds that still hang about the "sweet prince." *Hamlet* is a much more military play than is generally thought, not only in the imagery, but also in the stage action. The play begins with a feverish military build up that "Does not divide the Sunday from the week" (1.1.76) and ends with "The soldiers' music and the rite of war" (5.2.388) for the dead Hamlet. In the fencing scene, Hamlet acquits himself so well with his weapon that he wins the first two bouts, ties the third, and is only touched by Laertes through foul play. After wresting the unbated and envenomed weapon from Laertes, he wins the fourth and final bout. He is an altogether formidable opponent, and one wonders why the King set a handicap of three bouts against Laertes— perhaps only to flatter his vanity. Hamlet shows himself a powerful combatant in act 1, scene 4, where he shakes off the grip of Horatio and Marcellus and threatens them with his sword: "By heaven, I'll make a ghost of him that lets me!" (1.4.85). He is in deadly earnest, and Horatio and Marcellus are forced to desist even though they fear the Ghost may be a devil. In the next scene Hamlet uses the hilt of his sword, which forms a cross, to administer the Ghost's oath of secrecy.

Notice how quickly and unthinkingly Hamlet draws his sword to kill Claudius in the prayer scene. He keeps it poised in his hand all during the debate with himself, and when he sheathes it (3.3.88), it is only to wait for "a more horrid hent," that is, a more damnation-provoking occasion to seize it again. This is not a pleasant scene, and Dr. Johnson had the right impression when he thought Hamlet's sentiments "too horrible to be read or to be uttered." [20] Hamlet is here speaking in the tone of the blackest stage revenger, whose lust for blood can only be glutted by killing the body and damning the soul at one blow. The upshot of this mood comes in the next scene, where Hamlet, on the first sound behind the arras, "Whips out his rapier" (4.1.10) and strikes without any hesitation or fear. He thinks it is the King, and he commemorates his death with the bravado of a professional swordsman: "How now? A rat? Dead for a ducat, dead! (3.4.25). We might almost be listening to Tybalt. It seems likely to me that Hamlet is wearing his sword through most of the play, except, of course, for those scenes after the murder of Polonius where the King has him under guard. I don't mean to exaggerate the significance of Hamlet's sword in and for itself, but it does rule out a whole set of romantic fallacies about the hero of the play.

Laertes's sword is a significant property for his rebellion in act 4, scene 5, although it is not mentioned in the text. This is a disorderly armed insurrection that has already put the King's "Switzers" to rout and broken through the doors. Gertrude's terror in this scene—and we may note how often she is frightened in the play—is based on the realities of the situation. The unarmed Claudius is directly menaced by Laertes, an angry young man intent on revenge, who has just burst into the room sword in hand. I don't see how this scene could be played without a sword or some other lethal weapon. There would be no terrors in a hand-to-hand wrestling match between Laertes and Claudius—and one would rather expect Claudius to be the winner.[21]

Another obvious class of properties is that connected with royalty. In the large court scenes, placed so symmetrically at the beginning (act 1, sc. 2), middle (act 3, sc. 2), and end (act 5, sc. 2) of the play, the King and Queen sit on the chair of state or throne, which was set on a dais with a few steps leading up to it. Presumably, only one large throne was used to accommodate both of them, as in _Macbeth_. In these formal court scenes, we must imagine that Claudius and Gertrude invoke all the ritual and pageantry at their command to display divine right: crowns, royal robes, scepter and golden ball, and elaborate ceremony. This ostentation has a special ironic purpose for

> A cutpurse of the empire and the rule,
> That from a shelf the precious diadem stole
> And put it in his pocket—
>
> $\qquad\qquad\qquad\qquad\qquad\qquad$ (3.4.100–2).

The royal accoutrements of "The Mousetrap" and its dumb show are meant to parody those of the Danish court and to create a symbolic confusion between the actors and the spectators. Who are really the Player King and the Player Queen? When the poisoner woos the Player Queen "with gifts," we think immediately of Claudius's winning of Gertrude,

> With witchcraft of his wits, with traitorous gifts—
> O wicked wit and gifts, that have the power
> So to seduce!
>
> $\qquad\qquad\qquad\qquad\qquad\qquad$ (1.5.43–45)

In their old-fashioned, exaggerated style, the players are miming the hidden realities of the main play. When the poisoner in the dumb show takes off the Player King's crown and kisses it[22] before pouring poison in his ears, we are meant to understand this as an enactment of the Ghost's description of its murder. This is the way "to catch the conscience of the king." It is noteworthy that the Ghost never appears in royal robes and crown—these properties have been tainted—but he does carry with him his marshal's "truncheon" as a sign of authority and command.

As we might expect, the properties of the graveyard scene (act 5, sc. 1) are all connected with death and burial. We have the gravedigger's spade and possibly a pickax (as in the song at line 87), as well as the earth, bones, and skulls that he throws up as he stands in the partially lowered stage-trap grave. The skull of Yorick that he hands Hamlet for closer inspection needs to be well preserved, since Hamlet refers to it so specifically: "Here hung those lips that I have kissed I know not how oft" (5.1.176-77). This certainly demands a skull with at least the lower jaw intact. The smell of Yorick's skull is, of course, only imaginary,[23] but to Hamlet it is vivid and disgusting: "And smelt so? Pah!" (5.1.188). One further funeral property is the open coffin needed for Ophelia (act 5, sc. 1). We would like to disavow the Quarto 1 stage direction that tells us that Hamlet leaps into Ophelia's grave after Laertes, but there is already so much rant and absurdity in the scene that this action only provides a context for the words. It is clear from "A Funeral Elegy on the Death of the Famous Actor, Richard Burbage" (1618) that this was one of Burbage's memorable exploits:

Oft have I seen him leap into the grave,
Suiting the person which he seemed to have
Of a sad lover, with so true an eye
That there I would have sworn he meant to die—.[24]

Flowers figure importantly in the "maimèd rites" of Ophelia's funeral. Besides the "bringing home / Of bell and burial," she is only allowed her "virgin crants," or garlands, and her "maiden strewments," or flowers thrown on her grave by the mourners (5.1.219–20). The Queen herself "strews" Ophelia's grave at line 230. Ophelia's flowers are, in fact, one of the most specifically developed character motifs in the play, and actresses of the part rarely allow themselves to be photographed without at least a nosegay or disordered wreath about their persons.[25]

Hamlet has a predictably large number of what we may call "aesthetic" properties: pictures, musical instruments, and writings of various sorts. The most controversial of these are the pictures of Hamlet's father and uncle that the son shows his mother in the closet scene.[26] That there

are two portraits on stage that can actually be seen seems to me absolutely clear from the words Hamlet uses:

> Look here upon this picture, and on this,
> The counterfeit presentment of two brothers.
>
> (3.4.54–55)

The word "this" is much too specific to exist merely in the mind's eye.
Or, again, note the transition from one portrait to another:

> This was your husband. Look you now what follows.
> Here is your husband, like a mildewed ear
> Blasting his wholesome brother. Have you eyes?
>
> (3.4.64–66)

It would be very simple to have two half-length portraits at the back of
the stage, such as those that appear in the illustration in Rowe's
edition—with the added convenience, as Lawrence suggests, of dust
curtains on rings. It is well to bear in mind that these portraits would
have to be extremely large to be visible to most of the audience. Where
would they hang? The "arras" behind which Polonius has just been
slain could not also serve for two heavy, framed pictures. It seems most
likely, then, that miniatures were used on the Elizabethan stage, the
pictures "in little" that Hamlet has spoken of (2.2.358). Hamlet would
then take from his pocket, or from a chain about his neck, a miniature of
his father, but he would seize the miniature of the detested Claudius
from a locket around his mother's neck.

Incidentally, to use Hamlet's frenzied imaginings in this scene as a
basis for the physical appearance of Claudius, as some critics have
done,[27] seems to me to completely distort the dramatic context. How
does this "bloat King" (3.4.183), this "paddock," this "bat," this
"gib" (3.4.191) happen to be such a formidable antagonist, and to be
acceptable to the Danish court? To see him as a monster destroys the
unctuous hypocrisy of the "smiling, damnèd villain" (1.5.106).

We cannot rightly consider the instruments of the stage musicians as
properties of the play, but the recorder does enter importantly into the
stage action in act 3, scene 2. After the excitement of the play-within-
the-play, in which Hamlet has indeed caught "the conscience of the
King," he proceeds to catch the consciences of Rosencrantz and
Guildenstern—if they are not mere moral ciphers—with the recorder.

Hamlet had called for a consort of recorders (that is, instruments of different range) immediately after the play. When the players enter with recorders (as in Quarto 2),[28] he takes one from them for his object lesson on the difference between men and things, and he shows a technical knowledge of how to play it: "Govern these ventages with your fingers and thumb, give it breath with your mouth, and it will discourse most eloquent music. Look you, these are the stops" (3.2.343–46). There is a stage tradition that Hamlet breaks the recorder in two at the end of this sequence, but I agree with the musicologist Christopher Welch in thinking that this is too cruel an act to be shown on stage.[29] There is, luckily, no indication for this destructive action in the text. For other musical instruments, there is only the interesting stage direction of Quarto 1 for Ophelia's mad scene (act 4, sc. 5): "*Enter Ophelia, playing on a lute, and her hair down, singing.*" If Quarto 1 as a reported text represents what was actually seen on stage, this touching direction is a very appropriate one. I don't think we need to insist on a reference in the play to lute lessons to believe that Ophelia could hold the instrument properly and strum a few distracted chords.

There is an unusual number of writings or literary properties in *Hamlet*. There is Hamlet's pocket notebook or "tables," which he carries about with him and in which he records one fixed truth in a whirling world: "That one may smile, and smile, and be a villain" (1.5.108). We have a nice symmetry between Hamlet "reading on a book" in act 2, scene 2, and Ophelia ordered to "Read on this book" in act 3, scene 1. But the one book, by the "satirical rogue," speaks the truth about old meddling fools, while the other, a devotional work or book of prayers, is merely a blind: "That show of such an exercise may color / Your loneliness" (3.1.45–46). There are quite a few letters in *Hamlet*: old Norway's to Claudius asking for "quiet pass" for Fortinbras (act 2, sc. 2), Hamlet's love letter to Ophelia with its trite little poem (act 2, sc. 2), Hamlet's letter to Horatio delivered by the pirate sailors (act 4, sc. 6), Hamlet's menacing letters to the King and Queen (act 4, sc. 7), and Polonius's notes for Laertes in Paris (act 2, sc. 1). One further document is the original royal commission that Hamlet "fingered" from the packet of Rosencrantz and Guildenstern, which he now gives Horatio to read "at more leisure" (5.2.26). Hamlet seems to have a research scholar's concern for the preservation of manuscripts.[30]

I am not sure that we have not strayed beyond the limits of our topic, "*Hamlet* without Words," if we insist on defining that topic in a narrow

and technical way. This essay is not intended to defend the promptbook
of the play as the only authentic document, or to champion the rights of
the audience over those who try to read the text carefully. My only
purpose is to see what can be said about *Hamlet* without speaking about
the language of the play, but I fear that I have had to violate the strict
letter of this purpose at almost every point.

I have tried to keep in mind an ideal *Hamlet* performed in the Globe
theater of the imagination before a particularly alert and exigent audience. For this end, I have deliberately limited the scope of our inquiry to
that pleasant fiction with which we began of *Hamlet* ''when new.''
Unfortunately, to accomplish this objective we have had to disregard the
fascinating temptations of theatrical history and to keep within the
possibilities of staging suggested in the Quarto 2 and Folio versions of
the play, with occasional glances at Quarto 1. From this perspective we
have tried to reconstruct a production of *Hamlet* ''possible'' in the early
seventeenth century.

Despite our avowed purpose, however, it may still be interesting to
look at one speech in the play through the eyes of the theater historian. It
occurs in the Queen's description of her terrified son, who has just been
speaking with the Ghost of his father:

> And as the sleeping soldiers in th' alarm
> Your bedded hair like life in excrements
> Start up and stand an end.
>
> (3.4.121–23)

This speech tells us as explicitly as we could wish that the actor of
Hamlet must make his hair ''stand an end.'' It is curious that the ghost
himself anticipates the same effect on Hamlet if he discloses his experiences in Purgatory; the recital will make

> Thy knotted and combinèd locks to part
> And each particular hair to stand an end
> Like quills upon the fretful porpentine.
>
> (1.5.18–20)

There is no equivocation here about the proper stage expression for
Hamlet's fright; it is simply a question of how this business could have
been performed. From what we know of the Elizabethan theater, there is
no indication that Burbage or any other actor then was able to carry out

these specific instructions in the text. But the great Garrick—so Arthur Colby Sprague informs us—was able to accomplish this effect with a mechanical wig.[31] O the charms of theatrical history!

NOTES

1. Martin Holmes, *The Guns of Elsinore* (London, 1964), p. 13.

2. Jan Kott, *Shakespeare Our Contemporary*, trans. Boleslaw Taborski (New York, 1964), chap. 2, "*Hamlet* of the Mid-Century."

3. Quarto 2 is especially useful for its stage directions.

4. This stage direction, omitted in the Folio, is emended in the Quarto of 1676 to "*He spreads his arms.*" Many editors assume that the gesture is made by Horatio.

5. Frances Ann Shirley, *Shakespeare's Use of Off-Stage Sounds* (Lincoln, Neb., 1963), p. 83.

6. The Folio reads "*shout*," which was emended to "*shot*" by Steevens. Most modern editors follow Steevens.

7. See Shirley, *Shakespeare's Use of Off-Stage Sounds*, pp. 30–31.

8. This stage direction, which occurs after line 108 in Quarto 2, appears after line 110 in the Folio. The Folio position changes the meaning of "*A noise within.*"

9. I disagree with Harold Jenkins's interesting suggestion that "Let her come in" should be part of the King's speech ("Two Readings in 'Hamlet,' " *Modern Language Review* 54 [1959]:391–95).

10. See William J. Lawrence, "Bells in the Elizabethan Drama," *Those Nut-Cracking Elizabethans* (London, 1935).

11. James G. McManaway, "The Two Earliest Prompt Books of *Hamlet*," *Papers of the Bibliographical Society of America* 43 (1949):311. See also William J. Lawrence, "Illusions of Sounds in the Elizabethan Theatre," in *Pre-Restoration Stage Studies* (Cambridge, Mass., 1927).

12. See Shirley, *Shakespeare's Use of Off-Stage Sounds*, pp. 162–65.

13. See, for example, F. W. Sternfeld, *Music in Shakespearean Tragedy* (London, 1963), especially chap. 10, which discusses the critical literature.

14. Quoted from Joseph Quincy Adams, ed., *Chief Pre-Shakespearean Dramas* (Boston, Mass., 1924), p. 521. The dumb show itself was at the height of its popularity at the time of *Hamlet*, but "The Mousetrap" is intended to be in an old-fashioned, antiquated style, and its dumb show also looks back to a more formal and symbolic manner. See B. R. Pearn, "Dumb-Show in Elizabethan Drama," *Review of English Studies* 11 (1935): 385–405.

15. John Munroe, *The Shakespeare Allusion Book*, rev. ed. (1909), reissued 1932 (Oxford), 1:133.

16. Joseph Quincy Adams's edition of *Hamlet* (Boston, Mass., 1929), p. 224.

17. See S. F. Johnson, "The Regeneration of Hamlet," *Shakespeare Quarterly* 3 (1952):187–207.

18. Harley Granville-Barker, *Prefaces to Shakespeare* (Princeton, N.J., 1946), 1:233. See also William Poel, *Shakespeare in the Theatre* (London, 1913), pp. 173–74 (first published in 1881).

19. See William J. Lawrence, " 'Hamlet' as Shakespeare Staged It," in *Pre-Restoration Stage Studies*, p. 109.

20. W. K. Wimsatt, Jr., ed., *Samuel Johnson on Shakespeare*, (New York, 1960), p. 111.

21. Other weapons used in the play are the partisans (or broad-headed, long-handled spears) with which Barnardo and Marcellus try to stop the Ghost (act 1, sc. 1). In the fencing scene (act 5, sc. 2) daggers are held in the left hand to ward off the opponent's rapier thrusts (Folio modernizes the foils and daggers of Quarto 2 to the newer fashion of foils and gauntlets; see John Dover Wilson's new Cambridge edition, 1957, pp. 250–52 and p. 309).

22. The action recalls Prince Henry's seizure of the crown in his dying father's bedchamber (*2 Henry IV*, act. 4, sc. 5).

23. The article by Richard D. Altick, *"Hamlet* and the Odor of Mortality," *Shakespeare Quarterly* 5 (1954):167–76, for all its excellent insights, comes dangerously close to insisting that the smells are physically present in the play.

24. Quoted in John Dover Wilson's new Cambridge edition of *Hamlet*, p. 308.

25. See the illustrations in Raymond Mander and Joe Mitchenson, *Hamlet Through the Ages*, 2d ed. (London, 1955), numbers 175, 177, 178, 180–82, 184, 185, 188, 191, and drawing on p. 122. See also the frontispiece to Arthur Colby Sprague, *The Stage Business in Shakespeare's Plays: A Postscript* (London, 1954). The flowers Ophelia names so aptly in her mad scene (act 4, sc. 5) may not be those she actually has in her hands. She is, after all, not a botanist like Friar Lawrence, but a young girl who is distracted in her wits. She may be distributing common wildflowers like the "crownet weeds" and "weedy trophies" (4.7.172, 174) that figure in her death by water, or like those "fantastic garlands" she has made out of "crowflowers, nettles, daisies, and long purples" (4.7.168–69).

26. See Hazleton Spencer, "How Shakespeare Staged his Plays . . .," *The Johns Hopkins Alumni Magazine* 20 (1932):205–21; Lawrence, " 'Hamlet' as Shakespeare Staged It," in *Pre-Restoration Stage Studies*, pp. 111–16; Arthur Colby Sprague, *Shakespeare and the Actors* (Cambridge, Mass., 1944), pp. 166–69, and Sprague, *The Stage Business in Shakespeare's Plays*, pp. 19–20; Fredson Bowers, "The Pictures in *Hamlet* act 3, sc. 4: A Possible Contemporary Reference," *Shakespeare Quarterly* 3 (1952):280–81; Holmes, *Guns of Elsinore*, pp. 47, 131, and photograph facing p. 128; and correspondence in *Times Literary Supplement*, August 30, 1928, p. 617; September 6, p. 632; September 20, p. 667.

27. See, for example, Weston Babcock, *Hamlet, A Tragedy of Errors* (Lafayette, Ind., 1961), p. 55.

28. Everything in the text of this scene indicates that we must follow the Quarto 2 direction: *"Enter the players with recorders,"* rather than the economizing direction in the Folio: *"Enter one with a recorder."*

29. Christopher Welch, *Six Lectures on the Recorder and Other Flutes in Relation to Literature* (Oxford, 1911), lecture 3: "Hamlet and the Recorder."

30. We may deal briefly with other miscellaneous properties. In order to make the dramatic point to the audience, the gifts the Poisoner uses to woo the Player Queen must obviously be rich and impressive ones; the same is true for the "remembrances" (3.1.93). Ophelia insists on returning to Hamlet. Claudius's "union" (5.2.261), or costly pearl, was probably one of those ingenious Italian poison-holders, at least big enough for one fatal chalice.

The seating arrangements in *Hamlet* may be quickly summarized. The most important chair in the play is the one in which Hamlet forces his mother to sit in the closet scene (3.4.19–21). Although not mentioned in the text, a faldstool (or prie-dieu) would be convenient for the praying of Ophelia (act 3, sc. 1) and Claudius (act 3, sc. 3). Stools are used for Horatio and Marcellus to sit on while listening to Barnardo's account of the Ghost. It will not do to have Barnardo sit down with them, since he is on guard duty. For the fencing scene in act 5, sc. 2, we have officers who enter to lay cushions on the seats of the spectators (cf. *Coriolanus* act 2, sc. 2 s.d.).

In this same scene we have also flagons and stoups of wine and the cups into which they are poured. There is also the "table prepared" (in Quarto 2) for these drinking vessels and the foils. In the play scene (act 3, sc. 2) Claudius's guard enter with torches, a conventional sign of night, and they are needed to light him out again. As a final note, we should not forget the "napkin" or handkerchief of Gertrude in the last scene of the play. She offers it to Hamlet during the fencing match to "rub" his "brows" (5.2.277), but he refuses it. Then she drinks the poisoned cup, and, in her ultimate act before she dies, she attends to her son: "Come, let me wipe thy face" (5.2.283).

31. Sprague, *Shakespeare and the Actors*, p. 382, n. 43.

2

Richard II to *Henry V*: Poem to Stage

JAMES L. CALDERWOOD

IN *RICHARD II* SHAKESPEARE FASHIONS NOT MERELY THE FALL OF A king but also the fall of kingly speech. On Richard's unexamined assumptions, language is bonded to nature and to the world order by virtue of God's certification of him as a Divine Right monarch. The original power of the divine Word—"Let there be..."—remains actively at work in the King's English, just as divine authority descending by way of primogeniture is immanent in Richard himself. But it is the business of *Richard II* to revoke these convenants between divinity and kingship and between language and nature. Richard's belief in the absolute identity of "King" and "Richard" shatters when he discovers that the name of "King" will as readily bear the meaning of "Henry IV" as that of "Richard II." An attendant belief—one more cherished by poets and playwrights than kingly divinity—falls too: Richard's faith in a sacramental, monistic language in which words are not proxies for things but the things themselves ("Is not the King's name twenty thousand names?").

Why should language fall with Richard? Kings have their proper involvements in language, to be sure, and yet in this play Shakespeare goes beyond a mere kingly concern for speech. Kings have died from time to time and worms have eaten them, but not for words. The mighty Caesar will fall, and the saintly Henry VI has already fallen, without our feeling that a world of words has toppled with them. What is Shakespeare's investment in Richard and his language? Surely he cannot pit Richard and his words against Bolingbroke and his armies, and expose the inefficacy of the former, without being reminded of the virtues and frailties of the very Shakespearean words in which their contest is couched. How much of his own verbal majesty—pitted against the armies of reality and the ears of his audience—is annulled by the demise of Richard's speech?

If we cannot believe that Shakespeare entertained Richard's naive faith in the absolute equation of word and thing, we may nevertheless discern in his own literary experience an analogy, an artistic version of Richard's faith to which Shakespeare was strongly attracted. As I have argued in *Shakespearean Metadrama* much of the tension in Shakespeare's early plays is generated by contrary impulses; on the one hand the poetic impulse toward the autonomy of the word, on the other hand the dramatic impulse toward vitalizing the word in the actional life of the theater. To oversimplify a complex process, the course of his dramatic development is one in which, after initial misgivings of the sort one finds in the early histories and *Titus Andronicus*, he gradually accepts the claims on poetry made by the theater. Accepting these claims inevitably entails a painful loss of the freedom conferred on the poet by the lyric or narrative modes.

For there is a distinctly monistic aspect to lyric/narrative poetry, to poetry itself as distinguished from drama. In his sonnets and in the two narrative poems Shakespeare's language creates and contains the world to which it refers. Though we make certain inferences about them on the evidence of their own speech, Venus, Adonis, and Lucrece *are* only as they are said to be—as the narrative voice describes them. How they look, how they act, how they feel, where they are situated—all these things are created in and by words alone, which possess the kind of arbitrary constitutive power vested in the divine Word at the Creation. Similarly, though the "you" of the sonnets presumably had an independent real-life existence as the mysterious "W. H.," his literary life as a second-person pronoun creates him afresh:

> And all in war with Time for love of you,
> As he takes from you, I engraft you new.

(sonnet 15)

Lacking a world independent of the one conjured up in our imaginations by the words of the poem, we have no grounds for denying the claims made by those words. Larks said to sing hymns at heaven's gate *do* sing hymns at heaven's gate. Morning light said to gild pale streams with heavenly alchemy *does* so gild the steams. Who can gainsay it? All lyric or narrative, all nondramatic poetry is possessed of this sophisticated version of primitive word-magic, the complete subjection of things to speech, and is granted in consequence an automatic truth.

Drama is another matter. What was a poem now metamorphoses into a script, and a script can never be wholly autonomous because its mode of being is contingent on actors, a stage, and an audience. If Venus and Adonis or the "you" of the sonnets were to appear on stage as dramatic characters, they no longer could be entirely as they are said to be; their verbal being is modified by their performed being. The Hamlet of words, the Hamlet we might imagine entirely from reading the play as though it were a poem, is not the dramatic Hamlet. The dramatic Hamlet can never get free of Olivier, Gielgud, Williamson, of whoever is playing him, and acquire a verbally-created life in our imaginations. We cannot tell the play from the players, the character from the actor. In drama the word, its poetic sovereignty lost, must now lead to, defer to, combine with action, since there is now an independent field of reference for the audience—the whole theatrical milieu that provides for the enactment of the word. And enactment notoriously has its limitations as the dramatic unities attest. The poet Homer may rely on verbal fiat alone to make Odysseus wander the seas for ten years, but the playwright Shakespeare pays a high price in nervous choral apologies merely to get Henry the Fifth's ragamuffins across the Channel and back. "Choral apologies"—that is to say, Shakespeare must revert to narrative to get done what dramatic enactment will not permit him.

If poetry then is a monistic language whose words contain its world—whose words do not need to collaborate with action because they are actions in themselves, creative edicts—drama is a dualistic language whose words must at least share their world with the visual dimension of the theater, the enactment. That Shakespeare has grown conscious of this seems evident throughout *Richard II*, but perhaps especially so in the opening scene. In the high-stomached dispute between Bolingbroke and Mowbray we are confronted with two narratives centering in the murder of the Duke of Gloucester. What is fascinating and troubling is that Shakespeare has scrupulously avoided stacking the deck of argument here. Knowing nothing about Gloucester's death except what we hear, we are totally incapable of judging what has happened or who is right. Each narrative is in effect a "poem" whose words create a past situation and assert their title to automatic truth. If they actually were poems there would be no problem. However contradictory they might be, each would retain an independent sovereignty within its fictional realm, like "L'Allegro" and "Il Penseroso." But once they are incorporated into drama they forfeit their rights to automatic truth and thus rest incomplete and unresolved. As

Shakespeare has set it up, what is required now is precisely what poetry does not supply, an outside standard, an authority, something by which the word may be tested. The poetic word need submit to nothing outside itself, but the dramatic word must submit—as Shakespeare now so pointedly underscores—to action. Mowbray puts it succinctly:

> 'Tis not the trial of a woman's war,
> The bitter clamour of two eager tongues,
> Can arbitrate this cause betwixt us twain.

$$(1.1.48–50)$$

And so we pass from the word alone, deprived of its final and total creative authority, to the test of drama: ordeal by combat.

The inability of the poetic word to survive in drama is further stressed when Richard, relying on his kingly word to "atone" the two antagonists, discovers that the act of reconciliation is not monistically embedded in his speech. "We were not born to sue, but to command," Richard says somewhat plaintively (1.1.196); but, as he learns, it is the nature of the word in drama not to command. Forced for the moment to adopt the mode of action demanded both by the disputants and by drama itself, Richard schedules the trial by combat, and then reneges. The king's "sentence" of exile forestalls and substitutes for action, and so truth is lost. Later, after his return from Ireland, Richard repeatedly ignores his captains' calls to action, preferring to "sit upon the ground / And tell sad stories of the death of kings" (3.2.155–56). That is, though repeatedly urged to act like a king by entering on actions that would assert his authority in England, Richard lapses instead into forms of lyric narcissism, creating sentimental verbal kingdoms that are gratifying because in them he holds uncontested sway. (In the deposition scene he reasserts his sovereignty over the kingdom of private feeling: "You may my glories and my state depose, / But not my griefs. Still am I king of those" (4.1.192–93). It is for these kinds of reasons that Richard can be called a poet.

Usually, however, when critics speak of Richard as a poet-king they mean that his preoccupation with words prevents him from being a man of action. If the present line of analysis is correct, though, Richard fails not only to become a man of action but through that failure fails to become a dramatist, which is the proper literary analogue to the role of king in political life. At the same time Richard's failure to act is not wrong but right—divinely right. A Divine Right king, duly anointed and all, Richard puts his faith in the conditions of his sovereignty. As

Bolingbroke's armies sweep over England and Richard dallies, doing the earth favors with his royal hands, the Bishop of Carlisle says "Fear not, my lord. That Power that made you king / Hath power to keep you king in spite of all" (3.2.27–28). But Carlisle tempers theory with tactics, quickly adding that kings must seize the means of defense heaven puts in their way. Richard is more absolute for Divine Right: "The breath of worldly men cannot depose / The deputy elected by the Lord" (3.2.56–57). Richard does not waver in this scene between action and inaction; he wavers between trust and distrust in the perfection of his title. To contest with Bolingbroke for his kingship, to claim title to his crown, would be precisely to call kingship and title into question. In the world of Richard's imagination God who gave kingship would defend it without the king's having to raise a scepter, much less a sword. But of course the angelic armies are slow to muster, and Richard takes his unassailable Divine Right logic with him to Pomfret Castle and to a grave.

What we have, then, is a parallel to the opening act of the play. It is clear that the "name" of king—the truth of the words "King Richard"—must be subjected to the test of action, just as the challenging words of Bolingbroke and Mowbray needed a truth-determining ordeal by combat earlier. But Richard refuses to submit to that test—no doubt half-sensing its outcome—just as he would not permit God to render judgment in the ordeal by combat earlier—no doubt half-sensing *that* outcome too. In relying on the monistic, magical claims of Divine Right—"monistic" in that they argue for an inseparable fusion of the words "King" and "Richard," of the man Richard and the name of king—and in therefore refusing to contest for his kingship through action, Richard metadramatically reflects Shakespeare's own resistance to the demands made on the sovereign poetic word by the theater.

The demands of the theater center in the word action, which may refer to the histrionics of the actor, to the decisive events of the plot, and to the overall staged performance of the play. These are the conditions of drama and the conditions that must be accepted by the dramatist. And it is Bolingbroke who conspicuously accepts, even embraces, such conditions. He can himself "act":

How he did seem to dive into their hearts
With humble and familiar courtesy,
What reverence he did throw away on slaves,
Wooing poor craftsmen with the craft of smiles
And patient underbearing of his fortune,

As 'twere to banish their affects with him.
Off goes his bonnet to an oyster wench;
A brace of draymen bid God speed him well
And had the tribute of his supple knee.

(1.4.25–33)

Unlike Richard, Bolingbroke also knows the virtue of decisive action, as the hapless Bushy and Green discover: "My Lord Northumberland, see them dispatched!" (3.1.35). And as for public enactments, Bolingbroke's dramatic shrewdness—his consciousness of the need for public ceremony, his sense of audience—is evident in his staging of Richard's deposition:

Fetch hither Richard, that in common view
He may surrender—so we shall proceed
Without suspicion.

(4.1.155–57)

And our final impression of Richard and Bolingbroke together is one in which their contrasting fortunes are expressed theatrically, with Bolingbroke easily dominant and Richard upstaged in an alien context:

As in a theatre the eyes of men
After a well-graced actor leaves the stage,
Are idly bent on him that enters next,
Thinking his prattle to be tedious,
Even so, or with much more contempt, men's eyes
Did scowl on gentle Richard.

(5.2.23–28)

I am not suggesting that by accepting the conditions of drama Bolingbroke has become for Shakespeare the dramatic model for language in action, that Shakespeare has symbolically killed off the poetic Richard in himself and replaced him with the dramatic Henry IV. No, Bolingbroke's attitudes toward the word must be repellant not merely to the poet but also to the dramatist in Shakespeare. But even so, Bolingbroke has done what Shakespeare must do and what Richard could never do; he has accepted the risks of action. Shakespeare too must submit to drama's ordeal by combat. In so doing, in committing himself to the mercies of action, he must leave behind the comforting securities of a poetic style and technique that offer free play to the narcissistic tendencies of the word. He must surrender the Divine Right verbal sovereignty that is guaranteed the poet—the elite seclusion of the park in Navarre, the lyric haven of the Capulets's orchard, the insular wealth and harmony of Belmont—and go into the wider world of dramatic affairs where his sovereignty must be earned anew with every play he writes. All of this he knows well enough because that is just what we see him doing. The scholars do abandon Academe, Romeo and Juliet are forced from their orchard, Portia does journey to Venice, and Richard does surrender to Bolingbroke.[1]

II

Bolingbroke succeeds Richard, to be sure, but it is hardly a happy succession politically, nor is it metadramatically. The poet whose words intrinsically contain their world has, as I've suggested, the equivalent of a Divine Right autonomy. But neither Bolingbroke the usurper nor Shakespeare the dramatist is so securely sovereign over his world. With no pretense to divine backing Bolingbroke relies entirely on natural selection to find his indirect way to the throne. His authority does not descend from on high but wells up through ranks of nobles from the commons; and its survival depends on the continuing fitness of his political skills to marshal popular support. Shakespeare's crown as dramatist rests no more securely than Bolingbroke's. The monistic autonomy of the poetic word having been deposed, he is left with the dualistic dependency of dramatic speech. No longer lyrically free, his words must answer to the actor's voice, the action of the play, and the audience.

I think it no accident that around this time (1595–97) in *Romeo and Juliet, A Midsummer Night's Dream,* and *2 Henry IV* we find Shakespeare directly acknowledging his audience for the first time in prologues and epilogues. And whereas in the sonnets he can speak with calm assurance of long readership—"So long as men can breathe or eyes can see, / So long lives this, and this gives life to thee" (sonnet 18); "My love shall in my verse ever live young" (sonnet 19)—to his dramatic audiences he addresses a strong concern for present pleasing. His sense of the element of risk involved in a commitment to drama is suggested by the metaphor for a play used in the prologue to *Romeo and Juliet*, "the two hours' traffic of our stage," and is made explicit in the epilogue to *2 Henry IV* where "traffic" becomes "venture." The hazards of the dramatic voyage are so great that the playwright, in the person of his dancer surrogate, must pray for a creditor-audience more inclined to mercy than Shylock:

> But to the purpose, and so to the venture. Be it known to you, as it is very well, I was lately here in the end of a displeasing play, to pray your patience for it and to promise you a better. I meant indeed to pay you with this, which, if like an ill venture it come unluckily home, I break, and you, my gentle creditors, lose. Here I promised you I would be, and here I commit my body to your mercies.

These metaphors of commerce, revolving around the equation of drama and the financial "venture," must give us pause. In the first place they seem curiously allusive. The venture reminds us of Antonio's argosies, which appeared about to but then did not "come unluckily home"; the "gentle creditors" suggests Shylock's puns on "gentile-gentle"; and the committing of one's body to a creditor's mercy, which seems corporeally gratuitous here, inevitably recalls Antonio's bond. Why should these allusions to *The Merchant of Venice* crop up in the epilogue to *2 Henry IV*? Possibly because, in writing *The Merchant of Venice*, as Sigurd Burckhardt claims, Shakespeare learned "that his work as a commissioned playwright need not be servile, money-grubbing prostitution of his talent . . . . There was dignity in his trade, truth and worth in the two hours' traffic of the stage."[2] That is quite true, but it was a hard-earned insight and one that Shakespeare could not always endorse.

Perhaps we need to take Shakespeare's metaphors more faithfully. That of the "venture" for instance ("Look in the history," as Bottom would say, "Find out venture!"). The most spectacular ventures of the sixteenth century were the voyages of discovery and trade, which were largely financed by a new economic entity, the joint stock company. These companies enabled anyone with capital and a speculative temper to gamble on the chance of high returns. The raids on Spanish America, for instance, were all conducted by joint stock companies—Drake's round the world voyage of 1577–80 yielding dividends of no less than 4,700 percent.[3] The relevance here of these independently engrossing facts is that Shakespeare's company, the Lord Chamberlain's Men, was itself a species of joint stock company.[4] Since at least 1594 when he, Kemp, and Burbage received payment from the Revels Office for a court performance, Shakespeare had been a "sharer" in the Lord Chamberlain's Men. It was by virtue of his income as sharer and actor, not as playwright, that he grew to prosperity.[5] Late in 1598 he added house-keeping to shareholding when he joined the younger Burbages and four other actors in financing the tearing down of the Theatre, the transporting of its timbers across town, and the building of the Globe. However, this scheme must have been proposed as a possibility much earlier, probably in late 1596 as soon as it became apparent that Giles Allen, owner of the Theatre land, did not intend to renew the company's lease when it expired in April of 1597. From this time until the Globe was completed—from the spring of 1597 until the fall of 1599—the Lord Chamberlain's Men were, as Bernard Beckerman so happily puts it, "adrift," playing part of the time at the Curtain, part of the time on the road.[6]

The point is that although drama had been a "venture" to the sharer Shakespeare since at least 1594, it must have seemed especially so during the period in which he was writing *The Merchant of Venice* and the Prince Hal plays, since he was now considering a financial and artistic commitment to the theater that would make it very unlikely that he could ever revert to poetry and patronage as a mode of living.[7] It is hardly the nature of such ventures to inspire unflagging conviction. If *The Merchant of Venice* reveals Shakespeare's acceptance of the com-mercialism of drama, the second tetralogy and especially the three Henry plays appear to reflect his ambivalence about setting forth on a dramatic enterprise so profoundly dependent on his own unaided tal-ents—"for what I have to say is of mine own making, and what indeed I should say will, I doubt, prove mine own marring" (Epilogue)—and on the unpredictable mercies of his creditor audience—"My fear is, your displeasure; my curtsy, my duty; and my speech, to beg your pardons."

III

Part of the riskiness of drama for the dramatist is that although so very much depends on him, he is by no means independent himself. If the poet Richard, independently autonomous by divine fiat, finds himself bereft of supporters, Bolingbroke is cursed as well as blessed with them. His "venture" for the crown is underwritten by Northumberland, Wil-loughby, Ross, Hotspur, and increasingly by the commons, a militant joint stock company whose goal is in various ways treasure—or a royal

treasury. Thus Bolingbroke, to his followers in the wilds of Warwick-
shire:

> All my treasury
> Is yet but unfelt thanks, which more enriched
> Shall be your love and labor's recompense . . . .
>
> Evermore thanks, the exchequer of the poor.
> Which, till my infant fortune comes to years,
> Stands for my bounty.
>
> *(Rich II*, 2.3.60–62, 65–67)

But once the venture has come luckily home and the king can lay hands
on more substantial currency than thanks, his creditors, as Richard
forsees when he rebukes Northumberland, may well expect inflationary
repayment:

> Thou shalt think
> Though he divide the realm and give thee half,
> It is too little, helping him to all.
>
> (5.1.59–61)

And so it indeed falls out in the opening act of *I Henry IV* as Hotspur,
thrust on by his father and uncle, duns the king for Mortimer's ransom
and gets a sharp reply:

> *Henry*:   Shall our coffers, then,
>   Be emptied to redeem a traitor home?
>   Shall we buy treason, and indent with fears,
>   What they have lost and forfeited themselves?
>
> (1.3.85–88)

Bolingbroke's reluctance to give adequate returns on their investments
in him makes his creditors suspect him of pondering alternative forms of
repayment. Hotspur thinks of him as—

> this proud king, who studies day and night
> To answer all the debt he owes to you
> Even with the bloody payment of your deaths.
>
> (1.3.184–86)

And Worcester concurs a bit later:

> The King will always think him in our debt,

And think we think ourselves unsatisfied
Till he hath found a way to pay us home.

(1.3.286–88)

With this attitude prevailing between royal debtor and noble creditors, counterventures are inevitable. Hotspur's life is a sustained venture for honor, but inflamed by Henry's slights he can venture for a "moiety" of England as well, and cavil on the ninth part of a hair about the distribution of shares (3.1.72–141). Because Northumberland, fallen "crafty-sick," and Glendower, "o'er-ruled by prophecies," refuse to venture anything at Shrewsbury, Hotspur loses all. Henry, meanwhile, is willing to put his money on Hal in single combat against Hotspur—"And, Prince of Wales, so dare we venture thee" (5.1.101)—but carefully hedges his own investments in kingship by populating the field with counterfeits. Not even this strategy can keep him beyond the reach of Douglas's sword, and so at the moment when Henry appears about to pay the ultimate price of usurping the crown, enter the Prince of Wales "Who never promiseth but he means to pay" (5.4.42) and who, by saving his father, "hast redeemed [his own] lost opinion" (5.4.47) as he said he would from the start (1.2.183–205).

Nevertheless, despite heavy losses, the rebels continue to reinvest in their enterprise, as Lord Bardolph assures Northumberland at the opening of *2 Henry IV*:

We all that are engaged to this loss
Knew that we ventured on such dangerous seas
That if we wrought out life 'twas ten to one;
And yet we ventured, for the gain proposed
Choked the respect of likely peril feared.
And since we are o'erset, venture again.
Come, we will all put forth, body and goods.

(1.1.180–86)

The remaining rebels "put forth" for Gaultree Forest where they are paid with Prince John's lies and sent on their final journey to the executioner's block. Shortly thereafter Henry reaches his destination also—the Jerusalem room at Westminister—an empty verbal substitute for the Holy Land that was the goal of the oft proposed, always postponed pilgrimage to atone for the murder of Richard: the redemptive pilgrimage abroad that was to pay the costs of the ambitious political venture at home.[8]

IV

The metaphor of the venture and of the debts incurred en route sums up the paradoxically dependent sovereignty of the usurper Bolingbroke, the man who, failing by inheritance to *be* a king, must *act* like one, so staging his plays of state that his impressed audience will sustain him in his role. In figuring drama as a venture also, Shakespeare reminds us, and no doubt himself, that as compared to the poet the kingly dramatist is something of a usurper too, and no less heavily indebted. Whereas the poet can wait for his audience and can have his poetic "title" automatically renewed by successive reprintings of his poem over the years (*Venus and Adonis* appeared ten times during Shakespeare's life, *The Rape of Lucrece* six times), the dramatist suffers from the ephemeral nature of his art. The songs on Keats's urn or in Yeats's Byzantium may be chiseled for eternity, but the speech breathed in the theater is less durable stuff. Better even than Ulysses, the playwright Shakespeare knows that neither the scraps in Time's wallet nor the scripts on his own desk can sate Oblivion. Good plays and good deeds alike

> are devoured
> As fast as they are made, forgot as soon
> As done.
>
> (*Troilus*, 3.3. 148–50)

Because of this the dramatist, like the self-invested king, has to return to the theater of action again and again to defend his title to his crown, or, figured differently, has to set forth again and again on new dramatic ventures in a futile effort to pay off theatrical debts that only increase with each payment.

If in this consuming sense the theater is a "great-sized monster of ingratitude," it is also the playwright's sustainer. No dramatist can fail to realize how much his title, as I am calling it, is dependent on his actors' ability to stir the words of his dead script into life and on his audience's ability to catch that vital spark and quicken it further in their imaginations.[9] Relying on the aid of actor and audience for the success of his enterprise, the playwright falls in their debt as well. The poet whose sovereignty is conferred upon him by the very nature of his literary mode has, if he like, only himself to please and pay. But writing plays is an education in humility. The dramatist must acknowledge his indebtedness to actor and audience not merely by an after-thanks; his debts to them must be discharged in advance if the dramatic venture is to pay off for all parties. His only negotiable currency, however, is the word. *His* word. In the beginning, at any rate, the word is his, and he will most likely resist the claims on it of actor and audience. Mistrusting his audience, unsure of his actors, he will appropriate to himself all dominion over meaning, instructing his audience how to interpret what they have just seen and what is yet to come, as Exeter does in *1 Henry VI* (e.g., 3.1.186–200); or verbally upstaging the actor by forcing him into a corner of self-description (e.g., Mortimer in *1 Henry VI*, 2.5.1–16); or keeping one actor in suspended animation while another supplies lofty commentary for the audience, as when Marcus dilates on classical parallels while the just raped and dismembered Lavinia stands attentively on stage trying to coagulate (*Titus Andronicus*, 2.4.11–57).[10]

In these and other ways the young playwright, especially the playwright come to the theater from poetry or prose fiction, will invest his language with powers of semantic confiscation. With the word absorbing all meaning to itself, the visual and actional dimensions of drama—Aristotle's "spectacle"—become largely superfluous. In *Titus* and the *Henry VI* plays, for instance, the word is largely a poetic cynosure of which the "spectacle"—the stagey warfare and ritualized court scenes—is merely a running illustration.[11] How the playwright *can* pay his debts to actor and audience is by shaping in his imagination a script instead of a poem, a drama that is not merely speakable but playable, a script that is not a set of laws governing the attitudes of actor and audience but an invitation to them to exercise an interpretive freedom of their own. In this sense the dramatist converts actor and audience from competitors into collaborators. That is at least one important choral refrain in *Henry V*: "Piece out our imperfections with your thoughts."

The choruses of *Henry V* are not yet part of the story. At our present stage we can observe that if the movement from Richard to Bolingbroke implies an abandonment of certain "poetic" tendencies of mind and style in light of recognized dramatic necessities, still as an emblem of artistic development Bolingbroke is sorely limited. His own successful venture into action gained him a crown but incurred debts he could never fully repay. Having seized upon Richard's crown and life— Bolingbroke, like Falstaff, being a taker of crowns who must afterwards fight off even more than eleven men in buckram—having made his way to the throne at the expense of Divine Right legitimacy, the King can no longer pose as God's spokesman. Indeed, in England the King is now a lie—or a counterfeit, indistinguishable among all the others who wear his coats at the battle of Shrewsbury Field—and therefore in the King's English the lie is King. Thus instead of the royal Word uniting all England in political community, we encounter in *2 Henry IV* the motley figure of Rumour binding the English together in lies. Thus we have Falstaff, the corporealized lie, playing "Sir John with all Europe" as the reputed killer of Hotspur—"If a lie will do thee grace," Hal said to the pseudoconquerer after Shrewsbury—and that other leaner John, the Machiavellian prince, parlaying an official lie into a bloodless triumph at Gaultree Forest and blandly crediting God with the accomplishment. And finally we have Henry IV himself dying in the "Jerusalem Room" and, in his moral obtuseness, rejoicing at having achieved this verbal counterfeit of his longpurposed pilgrimage to the Holy Land.

Moving from poet king to actor king, from the Divine Right sovereignty of poetry to an unstable theatrical realm in which the Word no longer holds automatic sway, Shakespeare find himself in a situation analogous to that facing Prince Hal. In the political theater Hal's problem is to transcend his father and a fallen kingship and achieve somehow a genuine sovereignty as Henry V—if not a Divine Right, which is no longer possible after Richard's death, then an earned human right. Similarly, in his theatrical kingdom Shakespeare must transcend Bolingbroke and a fallen language, a lost verbal authority, and achieve somehow a more authentic dramatic sovereignty. The details of this compound achievement by Hal and Shakespeare are beyond our present scope, but perhaps a glance at *Henry V* may suggest something of its nature.

Henry V is surely the most self-conscious, even the most apologetic, of Shakespeare's plays. By means of the Chorus he explores, exploits, and consistently laments the nature of dramatic presentation. How can this "cockpit hold / The vasty fields of France," or represent the passage of armies back and forth across the Channel, or telescope the historical accomplishments of decades into "an hourglass"? Such issues are of course visual, not verbal; they would not exist if Shakespeare were writing an epic poem instead of what is often called an epic drama. They do not surface in such word-dominated earlier histories as the *Henry VI* trilogy or even *Richard II*, where Shakespeare is concerned with the powers not of the stage but of speech.[12] But now, with the Word fallen into disrepute, Shakespeare addresses himself to the nonverbal dimensions of his art. If truth no longer resides automatically in language, to be conveyed through speech to the expectant ears of his audience, then it must be conveyed to their eyes, though, alas, by the implausible makeshifts of theater:

> Yet sit and see,
> Minding true things by what their mockeries be.
>
> (Prologue, Act 4)

Conveyed by such scapegrace means truth becomes something of an embarrassment. When Agincourt is represented by ''four or five most vile and ragged foils, / Right ill-disposed in brawl ridiculous,'' Shakespeare is not apt to boast about drama holding the mirror up to nature. What he does speak of again and again, and always apologetically, is the purely functional nature of theater. Visual enactment is not a mimetic illusion of historical realities but a practical means, a device devoid of truth in itself, rather shabby in comparison to the glories it depicts—indeed a mockery.

And yet the theater is not without a certain value and truth. These theatrical ''mockeries'' are analogous to the trappings of kingship that the troubled King Harry ponders the night before Agincourt. Under the head of Ceremony, the royal stage properties of balm, sceptre, ball, sword, mace, crown imperial, robes, and farced title may be ''thrice-gorgeous,'' but at bottom their value lies not in themselves but in their function of aggrandizing one man and ''creating awe and fear in other men'' (4.1.216–70). There is no inherent truth in the ceremonies of kingship. And yet at Agincourt King Harry makes his ''farced title'' a genuine title; by dressing in armor he earns the ''intertissued robe of gold and pearl'' worn by English kings. He does so in part by subordinating himself to the interests of England, by abandoning his individual identity as the roistering Prince Hal and acquiring a corporate identity as King Henry V. He achieves victory at Agincourt not by himself but as a member of a ''band of brothers.'' In contrast to Richard II, whose followers fell off while he awaited God's heavenly legions and played eloquently with words, King Harry employs the rhetoric of St. Crispian speeches to rally his soldiers around him in ferocious fellowship. Language in *Henry V* is no longer poetic, as it was for Richard II, but rhetorical, no longer an end but a means, a symbolic instrument whose value lies in its capacity to persuade, rouse, perhaps ennoble. In its most strident employment, in King Harry's pre-battle speeches, we have the

Word as adrenalin. "All things are ready," he says after delivering his St. Crispian speech, "if our minds be so." Rhetoric readies the mind, the mind readies the body, and a few unpromising English bodies, desperate with patriotism, go among the French like reapers. God, King Harry feels, has spoken—in English: "Take it, God, / For it is none but thine!" (4.8.106–7). Just as rhetoric, lacking the automatic sovereignty of poetry, earns its keep in action, by working upon its audience, so King Harry, lacking a Divine Right sovereignty, earns his title to kingship through an ordeal by combat at Agincourt.

I said earlier that the theater, as it is pictured in *Henry V*, is analogous to King Harry's Ceremony. Harry, rather like Falstaff in his famous speech on Honor, debunks Ceremony as so much tinsel designed to aggrandize kingship. To be sure, he does this only in private soliloquy; however, his behavior at Agincourt is consistent with his soliloquy. There he most truly earns his kingship, not by robing himself in Ceremony and so distancing himself from his awed followers, but by putting off Ceremony and addressing his soldiers as coequals in the martial enterprise: "For he that sheds his blood with me / Shall be my brother" (4.3.61–62). Thus it is not King Henry V who triumphs at Agincourt but "We few, we happy few, we band of brothers" (4.3.60).

Shakespeare achieves a similar freedom from hypocrisy by debunking as "mockeries" the enactments of his stage. Would it were otherwise:

> O for a Muse of fire, that would ascend
> The brightest heaven of invention,
> A kingdom for a stage, princes to act,
> And monarchs to behold the swelling scene!
> Then should the warlike Harry, like himself,
> Assume the port of Mars; and at his heels,
> Leashed in like hounds, should famine, sword, and fire
> Crouch for employment. But . . .
>
> (Prologue, Act 1)

It is, as Fluellen might say, an honest "but." Instead of attempting to foist theatrical illusions upon his audience in a sixteenth century forerunner of epic cinema ("on-site filming with a cast of ten thousand!"), Shakespeare honestly acknowledges the limitations of his medium—and the limitations of the playwright. God, the master dramatist whom Harry credits with bringing about the victorious *peripeteia* at Agincourt, may stage the epic of history unaided, managing by divine paradox somehow to plot and yet not plot the actions of men. And as the lines quoted above indicate, Shakespeare feels at least a passing temptation to compete with God's original enactments. But that way only madness lies. God may be a kind of dramatist, but the dramatist, despite Sidney's talk about poets creating a second nature, is not God. Better, in all modesty, to assume a kingly role. And therefore as the king in this play calls upon his followers to aid him as coequals at Agincourt, so the playwright Shakespeare calls upon his theatrical followers to aid him in recreating Agincourt. Indeed, in asking his audience to ''eke out our performance with your mind,'' he invites them to join him in coauthoring the play. The victory that follows is, like Agincourt, the result of a collaborative enterprise. The unity of English spirit on the battlefield is mirrored by the unity of English minds in the theater. This victory—so truly theatrical in being achieved by the collective imagination of playwright, actors, and audience—marks the distance Shakespeare has come from the self-containment, the purely individual sovereignty of the lyric-narrative poet.

One would like to stop on that note of dramatic triumph—but must, like Shakespeare, add an Epilogue. With the fall of a language of inherent truth and value, Shakespeare has passed (in the *Henry IV* plays) through a period in which language seems entirely corrupt, a multitudinous lie, to rhetorical speech, in which words acquire pragmatic value as instruments of action. The stress in *Henry V* is upon means, techniques, devices, uses—both in language as rhetoric and in the theater as performance. Thus we have the choruses that in themselves are a means of unifying an otherwise episodic play and that in their content emphasize the makeshift theatrical means by which the truths of English history are approached. The theater is not presented as the locus of truth and value but as an *agency* of them; it must act upon the imagination of the audience in such a way as to reach toward a truth of which it is in itself incapable. Shakespeare, as usual, seems aware of all this, and so reminds us in his Epilogue that all that King Harry achieved was soon lost, which suggests—if the parallel we have noted between King and dramatist remains in force—that his own dramatic achievements in *Henry V* are but temporary, a stopgap solution to theatrical enigmas of enduring complexity. But that, after all, is the fate of means—to serve the needs of the occasion and then, as occasions change, to fall out of fashion, having no intrinsic value of their own. Rhetoric inspires and, having inspired, dissolves with all the finality of a Shakespearean performance. It may be revived, like *Henry V*, whenever war is again in fashion and the hackles of the populace need raising. Shakespeare may settle for that for the moment, but only for the moment. To find truth and value by means of one's art is not the same as to find truth and value *in* one's art. And so the word serves its turn as rhetoric in *Henry V* and theater serves its turn as stimulus of the patriotic imagination, but the achievement is ephemeral, and we have not long to wait before *Hamlet* addresses itself obliquely to those familiar issues of theatrical illusion and poisoned speech.

NOTES

1. The fate of scholars, lovers, and Richard, if not of Portia, suggests the inability of their "style" to survive in the dramatic world. The scholars are offered a second chance, but "that's too long for a play," as Berowne says. Romeo's and Juliet's and Richard's deaths are invested with a poignancy that testifies to the regret with which Shakespeare acknowledges their limitations and girds himself to abandon the special poetic style that has characterized their dramatic lives. Portia is a different case. Unlike Romeo and Juliet with their secluded orchard, she voluntarily leaves Belmont to enter Venice; unlike Richard she accepts the risks of acting in the wider world. Unlike all the others, she adjusts her linguistic behavior to the rules, literally to the "law," of Shylock's Venice, accepting at least temporarily the necessity of "using" words, of reading liberating meanings into the language of the contract. Though this is no final solution, it is an important phase in Shakespeare's gradual realization of his own verbal debts to drama.

2. Sigurd Burckhardt, *Shakespearean Meanings* (Princeton, N.J., 1968), p. 227.

3. For an account of the rise of the joint stock company and its role in the voyages of discovery, privateering, and trade in the sixteenth century, see L. C. Knights's *Drama and Society in the Age of Jonson* (London, 1937), pp. 47–58.

4. Strictly speaking, Shakespeare's was a "regulated company" in that its shares, unlike those of a joint stock company, were restricted to specific persons—certain members of the company itself—instead of being made available to the general public. However, insofar as admission to the theater was open to the public, each audience constituted a gathering of investors whose one-performance shares got an immediate return in the currency of art.

5. According to Marchette Chute, "Ben Jonson once estimated that he had made less than £200 in his entire life from writing plays, and Shakespeare spent more than twice that sum on a single real estate investment" (*Shakespeare of London* [New York, 1950], p. 130).

6. Bernard Beckerman, *Shakespeare at the Globe* (New York, 1963), p. x.

7. This had been a distinct possibility in 1594 when he had completed two narrative poems that were to be enormously popular, when the influential and respected publisher John Harrison demonstrated confidence in his literary future by taking out the copyright on *Lucrece* and having the copyright to *Venus and Adonis* transferred to him, and when he had received impressive financial earnest of Southampton's interest in his career (as the dedication to *Lucrece* clearly implies). Marchette Chute, who has a well-grounded account of Shakespeare's literary situation at this time, claims that "it is no exaggeration to say that the spring of 1594 was the turning point of Shakespeare's life as a writer" since, given the facts above, the way of the private poet as opposed to that of the public actor and dramatist must have looked enticing. See *Shakespeare of London*, pp. 116–21.

8. The final testimony concerning Bolingbroke's monetary interests in kingship appears in his

deathbed speech on Hal's supposed greediness for the crown, a speech whose imagery of commerce, fortune hunting, and gold is instructive (*2 Henry IV*, 4.5.66–80).

9. The French director Jacques Copeau, emphasizing this vital contact between actors and audience, said "there will never be a new theatre until the day comes when the man in the audience murmurs in his heart and with his heart the same words spoken by the man on the stage" (quoted by Henri Gheon in his *The Art of the Theatre* [New York, 1961], p. 15). Richard Burton has an amusing story about Sir Winston Churchill's doing precisely that while Burton once played Hamlet; only Churchill, sitting in the front row, pronounced the words not in his heart but in his cups, accompanying Burton word for word throughout the performance in an unshakeable mutter while the harried actor ran in vain through his repertoire of evasive verbal maneuvers.

10. In "Some Dramatic Techniques in 'The Winter's Tale,'" *Shakespeare Survey* 22 (1969):93–107, William H. Matchett shrewdly analyzes some of the ways in which the later Shakespeare infuses meaning into his play through a complete acceptance of the stage and its resources. Matchett also gives some early examples of the poetic word rendering visual action and acting superfluous.

11. I should qualify this remark by adding that I am implicitly comparing the early Shakespeare with himself at a later date, not to other dramatists of the last 1580s and early 1590s. The fact that Shakespeare came to playwriting by way of the stage instead of the university (like Marlowe, Peele, Greene, and probably Chapman) endowed even his earliest work with a sense of theater often lacking in his contemporaries. Nevertheless, not even he sprang dramatically full blown from the forehead of Dionysus.

12. Thus *1 Henry VI* begins with Gloucester's heavy attempt to sum up the dead King Henry V's accomplishments, ending "What should I say? His deeds exceed all speech" (1.1.15), and the opening scene of *Richard II* features a long rhetorical harangue and ends with stress on the failure of Richard's royal word to "atone" the disputants.

3

That Shakespeherean Rag*

TERENCE HAWKES

"O, O, O, O"—NOT, YOU WILL BE PLEASED TO HEAR, THE TERMINAL hysteria of a cockney Santa Claus but, according to the Folio text, the last utterance of the Prince of Denmark. The rest there is not silence, but an expressive printer's signal, unanimously suppressed by editors as an "actor's interpolation": an odd verdict, it might be concluded, on what might well rank as a perceptive gloss on the part by its first, and very astute critic, Richard Burbage.

Hamlet's death, after all, is a particular case of a man who has struggled mightily to win back for language something of its natural human authority, after that has been debased and debilitated by the actions of his "mighty opposite" in the Danish court. That we should witness speech painfully and violently slain in him, hear his dying voice at last reduced to groaning, recognize in those O's how fearfully Claudius's poison denies him his just inheritance of silence, become revealing aspects of the play's statement. If this is interpolation, give us excess of it.

T. S. Eliot is not reckoned among the great Shakespearean critics. His failure with *Hamlet* has been seen as both notable and typical in that, as an American, he seems unable to grasp that play's links with a native, nonliterary *English* tradition.[1] The mind that had "never . . . seen a cogent refutation of Thomas Rymer's objections to *Othello*" finds *Hamlet* "most certainly an artistic failure" and " . . . full of some stuff that the writer could not drag to light, contemplate or manipulate into art." Moreover, he admits that this "feeling" is "very difficult to localize. You cannot point to it in the speeches." The essence of the play seems in fact to lie "beyond" the words that appear to embody it, in what he calls its "unmistakable tone."[2]

Recognition of "tone" as an illuminating adjunct to the words is, as

---

*Paper read at the annual meeting of the Modern Language Association, held in Chicago in 1973 and later published in *Essays and Studies*, published by John Murray, London, for the English Association, May 1977, pp. 22–38.

Christopher Ricks has argued, crucial to Eliot's own verse as it is to the whole Symbolist enterprise.[3] It is a quality, residing perhaps (to use G. L. Trager's term[4]) in the "paralinguistic" *voicing* of the words, over and above their overt meaning, that forms part of the oral dimension in which all plays deal. Constituting as it does a good deal of the ultimately achieved effect of Eliot's own verse, oral "tone" becomes the element he responds most sensitively to in Shakespeare's.

Of course, the word "tone" also has a melodic dimension, aptly suggestive of the power of nondiscursive musical sound to penetrate the heart and the brain. And the "tonal" combination of words and music in popular song, together with the capacity of that combination literally to invade, to "catch" our apprehensions and take them over, is intentionally hinted at in the title of this paper; a phrase that, however unlikely it may be to record the fact, nevertheless constitutes one of the most memorable links between two of the greatest poets in English: a wry "tonal" acknowledgement perhaps, from the heart of a modern masterpiece, toward one of its author's own masters.

It would be uncharacteristic if it were not also fairly acute. And when we turn again to *The Waste Land*, it is to discover that at least one of the levels of irony implicit in that acknowledgment inheres in its knowing use of the same symbol of language tonally, orally conceived, that we have already encountered: "O, O, O, O That Shakespeherean Rag."

It will come as no surprise to those with a taste for Eliotic humour to learn that there really was such a song, as B. R. McElderry has pointed out.[5] The work of the almost eponymous team of Gene Buck and Herman Ruby (words) and Dave Stamper (music), *That Shakespearean Rag*, with its chorus

That Shakespearean Rag
Most intelligent, very elegant,
That old classical drag,
Has the proper stuff, the line "Lay on Macduff"

was one of the hit numbers of 1912, a year that offered it considerable competition in the shape of *Everybody's Doin' It* and *Be My Little Baby Bumble Bee*. Interestingly enough, its success was positively identified, in the advertisements promoting the song, with its oral performance. In *Variety* for October 25 of that year, it was billed as "Roy Samuels' big hit in *Ziegfeld's Follies* of 1912," and the song's publishers, listing it fourth among ten titles in a *Variety* advertisement for July 19 of the same year, added "If you want a song that can be acted as well as sung send

for this big surprise hit." Eliot's "interpolation" of the extra syllable in
"Shakespeherean," together with the O's, confirms and reinforces an
oral dimension that obviously struck him as wholly appropriate (and
indeed has turned out to be efficacious: line 128 of *The Waste Land* has
preserved the song's banality far more effectively than the performance
of Mr. Samuels). The whole episode indicates a subtlety of ear, and a
degree of oral-aural acuity that is distinctive.

It was an ear that recognized its own capabilities in Shakespeare. In a
broadcast talk on John Dryden (published in *The Listener*, 22 April
1931, pp. 681–82) in which he compares parallel passages from *All For
Love* and *Antony and Cleopatra* Eliot had offered a precise instance. It
concerns the death of Charmian.

North's translation of Plutarch gives the following account of Charmian's last words:

> One of the soldiers seeing her, angrily sayd unto her: Is that well
> done, Charmion? Verie well sayd she againe, and meet for a Princes
> descended from the race of so many noble kings.[6]

Dryden's version of this is

> Yes, 'tis well done, and like a Queen, the last
> Of her great race: I follow her.
> > (*Sinks down and dies*)
> > (act 5, sc. 1)

Shakespeare's version is

> It is well done, and fitting for a princess,
> Descended of so many royal kings

—and then adds the two words

> Ah, soldier!
> > (5.2.325–27)

before she dies.

Eliot's comment on the difference between these versions indicates
his perception of Shakespeare's remarkable sense of oral "tone." You
cannot, he argues, "say that the two lines of Dryden are either less
poetic than Shakespeare's, or less dramatic." The difference lies in the
"remarkable addition" to the original text of North: the "two plain

words, 'Ah, soldier'.'' Eliot finds himself nonplussed by the inexplicable effect of these words, for

> there is nothing in them for the actress to express in action; she can at best enunciate them clearly. I could not myself put into words the difference I feel between the passage if these two words, "Ah, soldier", were omitted and with them. But I know there is a difference, and that only Shakespeare could have made it (p. 681).

The difference is the more remarkable perhaps because of the deliberation with which it has been manufactured. North's Plutarch is both explicit and emphatic in ending Charmian's words where Dryden leaves them, even adding

> She sayd no more; but fell down
> dead hard by the bed.

What Shakespeare adds, what Eliot discerns and finds himself inexplicably respondent to, are two words that signal a whole world of expressive bodily movement that must lie beyond the words themselves. It is nonsense, of course, to say that there is nothing in these words that can be expressed in action: nonsense because that denies the fundamental relationship of words to action that *Antony and Cleopatra* has been at pains fully to explore.

In fact, it may be argued that nobody just talks; that communication properly requires a complex and interdependent relationship between voice and body, sound and gesture.[7] *Antony and Cleopatra* is a play about two flawed worlds in which that necessary, humanizing interdependency has ceased to operate. Voice alone dominates the Roman world; body alone that of Egypt. Rome is a place of words, Egypt a place of actions. Rome is where love is talked of, Egypt where love is made.

Antony accordingly finds himself committed and limited—albeit willingly—to a way of life in which the body rules the voice. And his commitment finds itself unerringly signaled in the play's first scene, by an appropriately wordless gesture. "Kingdoms are clay," he pronounces,

> . . . the nobleness of life
> Is to do thus.
>
> (1.1.36–37)—

whereupon he turns and kisses Cleopatra.

The importance of this gesture to the play's theme can be judged from the risk it evidently takes of embarrassing or distracting an audience aware that women's parts are played by boy actors. Like most contemporary dramatists, Shakespeare rarely permits much physical contact on stage between men and "women" for this reason. The memorable reference on Cleopatra's part to the fact that her own greatness might be "boyed" in the Roman streets (5.2.220–21), together with other frequent reminders that "she" is a boy, serve to focus an "alienated" and so powerfully reiterated attention on this physical aspect of her relationship with Antony throughout the play.

In short, that moment when their bodies unite on the stage turns out to be paradigmatic. The word "thus," and its accompanying gesture, signals a totally physical way of life committed to communication primarily through and with the body. The beds in the east are soft. There, the intensest kind of wordless bodily communion prevails. Antony's blush (1.1.30) "speaks" volumes. Hands, not words, are "read." Close physical, tactile contact constitutes the mode of everyday existence, and in performance the spatial relationship between the actors' bodies must be a good deal closer in the Egyptian scenes than in those set in Rome. Cleopatra's own person proves word-defeating: it beggars all descriptions, and both she and her attendants tend to use language itself less as a vehicle for rational discourse than as a physically luxurious entity. Even a surprised messenger is likely to find himself urged alarmingly to

> Ram thou thy fruitful tidings in mine ears
> That long time have been barren.
>
> (2.5.24–25)

(An early instance of aural contraception?)

In this context, Antony's death presents itself in appropriately sensual, sexual terms: he resolves to be

> A bridegroom in my death, and run into't
> As to a lover's bed.
>
> (4.14.100–101)

And he ends in that vein by falling on his sword claiming, to the aptly named Eros, that

> ... To do thus
> I learned of thee.
>
> (102–3)

Of course there is an apt pun on "death" (in the sense of sexual climax) that the play exploits at length both here and throughout. In a world where the "nobleness of life" resides in "doing thus" with such frequency, Enobarbus's commentary on Cleopatra's "celerity in dying"—her response to the "mettle in death" (1.2.143ff.)—has a double edge. It is wholly appropriate, then, that at the play's end she should speak of "immortal longings" in her own body, discover that

> The stroke of death is as a lover's pinch
> Which hurts and is desired.
>
> (5.2.294–95)

and so generate the pun's final explicit irony. A life based on "doing thus" as its sole end finds nothing at its conclusion but a grimmer and more final version of the "death" it has punningly pursued all along. Cleopatra's physical death is the fitting "climax" of her many sexual "deaths." Induced by the fondled, phallic asp, it has, properly, an orgasmic dimension, overt, yet beyond the words:

> As sweet as balm, as soft as air, as gentle—
> O Antony! . . .
>
> (5.2.311–12)

And when Charmian dies, shortly afterward, that body-dominated world of "doing thus" finally dies—in every sense—with her. For her "Ah Soldier"—matching her mistress' "O Antony"—signals, indeed *is* its death knell, and it bespeaks an appropriate and orgasmic last gesture from the boy actor, fully suggestive of the pun on death, by whose means the uncomprehending Roman soldier, and the world of mere words he represents, is wordlessly mocked.

King Lear's reductive insistence upon explicit statement, and its analogue in the realm of knowledge, quantity and calculation, indicates by comparison a way of life utterly unable to cope with the wordless. It accordingly regards silence, and so, concomitantly, gesture, as uncommunicative. Cordelia's awareness that her love is more ponderous than her tongue, that she cannot "heave / My heart into my mouth," her resolve to "Love and be silent" in the face of her sisters' facile wordiness are thus fated to meet only incomprehension.

As Jill Levenson has pointed out, the play insists on the point.[8] Cordelia's silence is Shakespeare's own addition to the story. Its purpose is to demonstrate the limitations Lear imposes on language by his insistence on words alone as the carriers of meaning. And, in the division scene, we see him deceived by words alone; particularly by a sophistication of the word "love" itself, which, in its "punning" dimension of "assess the price or value of something," has a central subversive function.[9] Lear's simplistic misconception of that word's manifold dimensions finally draws from him the tragically reductive equation by whose lights his own punishment is ultimately calculated: "Nothing will come of nothing." Only a mind which links "something" inextricably with measurable verbal protestation could respond in such a limited fashion to the reality each of his daughters manifests *in propria persona.*

We have noted the central pun on "death" in *Antony and Cleopatra*, and the pun on "love" in *King Lear* has no less crucial a function. In fact, it would be salutary to remind ourselves at this point that it is only a highly literate society that judges the pun to be the lowest form of wit. In a community dependent upon the *sound* of the human voice and the physical presence of the body which, gesturally, can indicate the homonym, the pun enjoys considerable status. Because it draws upon the totality of communicative processes, and because, glorying in these, it literally is enabled to go "beyond" the simple word that generates it, the pun seems to embody almost the essence of the spoken language.

The potential Elizabethan pun on "nothing" seems to represent almost an affirmation of that society's orality because its homonym "noting" refers of course precisely to that perceptive act to which nonverbal communication—literally without words—appeals. In Lear's case, what is clearly at stake in the "nothing/noting" homonym is the question of looking beyond mere words to the "silence" that Cordelia indicates best expresses her love. Were Lear to "note" that, embodied as it is in her physical bearing, he would indeed "see better."

The body, after all, talks. And the nature of human communication requires, as I have said, that we "note" its language as adjunctive to and moderative of what the voice says. This, to use the modern term, "kinesic" dimension receives its clearest definition perhaps in that play of Shakespeare's whose title embodies this very pun.

In *Much Ado About Nothing* "noting" does indeed stand for the silent dimension of the speech-act: the "nothing" that must be added as a redeeming, validating agent to the "something" of verbal protestation. The inability to "note" beyond the level of mere words pervades the entire society of Messina. So, when Claudio falsely accuses Hero, only the Friar, who alone has "noted" her correctly, can save her from disgrace and death.[10] He breaks his own silence to make the point:

> Hear me a little;
> For I have only silent been so long,
> And given way unto this course of fortune
> By noting of the lady. I have marked
> A thousand blushing apparitions
> To start into her face, a thousand innocent shames
> In angel whiteness beat away those blushes;
> And in her eye there hath appeared a fire,
> To burn the errors that these Princes hold
> Against her maiden truth.
>
> (4.1.153–62)

When Lear enters, finally, with Cordlia dead in his arms, we find him very obviously having outrun the same limits of verbal protestation. As he throws back his head and howls, linguistic "something" offers no forms adequate for his situation:

> Howl, howl, howl, howl! O you are men of stones!
> Had I your tongues and eyes I'd use them so
> That heaven's vault should crack . . . .
>
> (5.3.258–60)

He looks beyond language, for breath to "mist or stain" a glass, for a feather to stir as evidence of life, not words. Indeed, the absence of words, and Cordelia's involvement with silence, her long-standing commitment to the nonverbal, is stressed; together with the newly urgent sense that her "nothing" now—as always—communicates:

> Cordelia, Cordelia, stay a little. Ha,
> What is't thou say'st? Her voice was ever soft,
> Gentle and low, an excellent thing in woman.
>
> (5.3.270–72)

Critics have differed about the import of Lear's last words, but their direction seems clear. It is toward "noting," away from "nothing."

The reference to the hanging of his "poor fool" (5.3.306) links the two thematically related functions performed by the body of the boy actor (who has perhaps also played both parts) and draws attention to that body lying now in his arms. The repeated "Never, never, never,

never, never'' (309) teeters on the edge of speech, virtually committing itself to a dimension of pure, nondiscursive sound (Eliot himself termed the line "sounding," meaning "musical"). And then, as music does, the play wordlessly draws from us the necessary final, completing response.

The body of the boy-actor is exhibited. "Pray you undo this button" (310) represents, surely, Lear's request for Edgar or Kent to undo a button on the boy-actor's costume. This done, after the phatic, "Thank you sir," there follows in the Pide Bull Quarto the wordless "O, O, O, O" that we have "noted" before. The boy-actor's head, perhaps because the button was restraining it, now lolls back, possibly revealing, also wordlessly, the damage to the larynx wrought by the hanging noose. And then Lear directs our attention with even greater intensity; "Do you see this? Look on her"—to the organs of speech themselves:

> Look, her lips,
> Look there, look there!
>
> (5.2.311–12)

Surely, Cordelia's mouth falls open. Perhaps the lips, in their deathly *rigor*, seem even to frame words. But the silence that comes from them weighs far more heavily than words ever could. In death, as in life, she speaks without words: says everything by saying—literally at last—"nothing." And Lear dies finally, tragically, "noting" the wordless eloquence in which her "nothing" consists.

He invites us to do the same, to "note" the oral, nondiscursive, *performed* dimensions of the play that lie beyond the words, animate, and ultimately transcend them. At the furthest reach of the pun on "noting" (*via* "notation") it is "tonal," it is "musical," it is "sound" advice.

The recent revival of interest in classical ragtime music has placed it in quite a different perspective from that encouraged by the word "ragtime" and its users in the years following the first world war, when an attempt was made to link it with the emergent, challenging music of black America in the form of the blues and jazz. In fact, ragtime represents a quite different, opposite mode. It is an essentially *written* music, to be played (the classical ragtime composers insist on this) *as written* on the piano. Its import is fundamentally opposed to that of the blues and of jazz, in that it represents a "writing down" of the *orality* that blues and jazz promote. Its whole bearing is the reverse of the black and the improvisatory. It constitutes a bid on the part of its early (and best) exponents for genteel, white, European respectability. Its aim is to be both "elegant" and "intelligent," and the monuments to this endeavour are the black ragtime composer Scott Joplin's (1868–1917) two ill-fated ragtime operas *A Guest of Honour* (1903) and *Treemonisha* (1911).

After Sedalia, Missouri, whose Maple Leaf Café is commemorated in Joplin's enormously popular *Maple Leaf Rag* (1899), the great formative center of ragtime was St. Louis. Joplin himself moved there in 1900; the lost *A Guest of Honour* achieved its single recorded performance there in 1903. And in 1904 the city was host to a National Ragtime Contest. Moreover, St. Louis was and is not unknown for its connection with the great native American art—ragtime's opposite—the Blues. Anyone with any connection with St. Louis in those years (and Eliot's was close enough for him to make an unwarranted, but clearly deeply felt and embarrassing reference in later years to his own oral relationship with the city; his "nigger drawl")[11] would have heard in the air—could hardly have avoided "noting"—the opposed polarities of native American music: on the one hand "written" ragtime, on the other the orality of blues and jazz that ragtime specifically denied.

On another level, such a polarization could be said to be of a fundamental order. It represents perhaps, in miniature, an unresolvable dichotomy that, experienced as indicative of a deeper rift, and raised to a higher symbolic power, might ultimately lay waste any culture: deny it, in terms of Eliot's later vision, the cohesion whose absence *The Waste Land* and much of his critical enterprise laments.

Ironically, the presumed embodiment of that presupposed cohesion, the plays of Shakespeare, have found themselves over the centuries forced into the service of the same cultural dichotomy. Beginning as the high peak of the English-speaking culture's *popular* art, they have over 400 years dwindled to become the exemplars of an exclusive high art. From their function as the demotic, oral externalization of the totality of their own culture, they have shrunk to be sacred written texts; their guardians, from Dr. Johnson on, ever eager to expunge from their pages the betraying signs of orality. "A dramatic exhibition," Johnson thunders in his *Preface to the Plays of William Shakespeare* (1765), "is a book recited with concomitants that increase or diminish its effect." If

"Familiar comedy is often more powerful on the theatre than in the page; imperial tragedy is always less . . . . A play read affects the mind like a play acted."

It is worth checking our risibility for the moment to reflect that the Johnsonian voice, ever ready to excise or "blot" from Shakespeare's "book" such "forced and unnatural metaphors" as may fail, *inter alia*, to match the requirements of *written* sense, still makes itself heard in the land. Terms as confident in their presuppositions as "intrusive matter," "actor's interpolations," "stage accretions" deriving from "corruption through performance" remain the common coin of one kind of Shakespearean criticism.[12]

But "intrusive" *into* what? "accretions" *onto* what? "corruptions" *of* what? There is no pristine manuscript of any of Shakespeare's plays. And if there were, on what basis would we grant it stronger authority, say, than the text of a promptbook that relates, with some immediacy, to an actual contemporary performance in which the author's acquiescence was not improbable?[13] Those who, seeking to make the plays "elegant" and "intelligent," speak slightingly of actors' "interpolations" in them should remember that Shakespeare himself was an actor.

We are dealing, after all, with constructs that are made out of and, as I have argued elsewhere, can be said to be substantially *about* speech.[14] And speech has, in drama as in life, a primarily oral-aural bearing. It thus appeals beyond the visual level of the imagination, to a level that Eliot himself described as "auditory":

> . . .the feeling for syllable and rhythm, penetrating far below the conscious levels of thought and feeling, invigorating every word; sinking to the most primitive and forgotten, returning to the origin and bringing something back, seeking the beginning and the end. It works through meanings, certainly, or not without meanings in the ordinary sense, and fuses the old and obliterated and the trite, the current, and the new and surprising, the most ancient and the most civilized mentality, (*The Use of Poetry and the Use of Criticism*, 1933).

It is a level where the Johnsonian *dicta* prove inadequate to the complexities generated by the multidimensional nature of Shakespeare's oral-aural art, with its sense of simultaneity effortlessly maintained between separately articulated levels of meaning.

Indeed, if we agree with Claude Lévi-Strauss that "impoverishment and mutilation" is the inevitable lot of orality reduced to the level of the written word, then the model of the play's own orality, of what (in the aptly named "Overture" to *The Raw and The Cooked*) he calls the "language which transcends the level of articulated language," must obviously and more precisely be located elsewhere.[15]

The link between drama and music lies of course in the element of performance. And no reader of Eliot can fail to feel at home with Lévi-Strauss's account of the process: "In listening to music—and while we are listening—we have achieved a kind of immortality . . . . The music lives out its life in me; I listen to myself through the music."[16] In Eliot's words (from the aptly named *Four Quartets*) this becomes

> . . .music heard so deeply
> That it is not heard at all, but you are the music
> While the music lasts.
>
> *(The Dry Salvages)*

The sense of "being" the performance is of course crucial to audiences of both music and drama. It is the response that validates and makes viable the act of "playing." Music works by literally involving itself with the "organic rhythms" of our bodies. Its rhythms connect with, invite a participatory response from, and finally invade and take over the rhythms of our cardiac and respiratory systems. This is how the performance of "popular" melodies "catches" us; it is how Eliot's own symbolist verse works, invading the mind, penetrating "below the conscious levels of thought and feeling."

And indeed, the essence of that native American musical tradition, ragtime's opposite, blues and jazz, lies in exactly this process: in its involving orality, the identity it insistently demands of audience and performance, and of performance and performer; a performance whose "interpolations" in and onto the original sequence of chords literally *constitute* the music, and make the player, what he plays, and his audience simultaneously part of the same momentary whole.

In an oral society, an actor's "playing" will involve the same process, invite the same implicating response. And in the form of qualities that cannot be "dragged to light," which you cannot "point to in the speeches," but which, as in "O, O, O, O" or "Ah Soldier," or Cordelia's mute body, exhibit an involving, identifying *musical* power *beyond* that of mere words, this is the fundamental "oral" feature that Eliot was perceptive enough to "note" as "unmistakable" in Shakespeare's plays. In fact, Eliot's continuing interest in popular and "performed" oral culture needs little demonstration. The typescript of the early draft of *The Waste Land* shows a distinctive oral bearing. It is full of voices (the first part of the poem in this version is entitled *He Do The Police In Different Voices*)—and these are memorably demotic.[17] It is also, as we have noted, strewn with snatches of popular songs. And it is hardly surprising that when Eliot transferred himself to England, this interest persisted in the form of his frequentation of Edwardian music halls.

He was, of course, not thinking specifically of Shakespeare when, writing of the "moral superiority" of the greatest British music hall star of her day, he pointed out, with little trace of distorting American presupposition, that

> The working man who went to the music hall and saw Marie Lloyd, and joined in the chorus, was himself performing part of the act; he was engaged in that collaboration of the audience with the artist which is necessary in all art and most obviously in dramatic art.[18]

But that creative "collaboration" clearly constitutes a good deal of what may be termed the genuine Shakespearean "music"—truly elegant, truly intelligent—demeaned by the exploitative vulgarity (and, incidentally, wholly mistaken musical assumptions) of Messrs. Buck's, Ruby's, and Stamper's *Shakespearean Rag*.

Perhaps only Coleridge has put it better. Speaking of Shakespeare he says "You feel him to be a poet inasmuch as for a time he has made you one—an active, creative being."[19] In short, like all oral art that is *genuinely* popular (as the blues was, as Marie Lloyd's was), Shakespeare's plays—the Shakesp*eh*erean rag—reach out to us (as it were, with that extra, paralinguistic syllable), invade us and invite us to make (with that "O, O, O, O") a sympathetic—an acoustic—act of "closure" with themselves. Properly "noted," as the groaning Burbage knew, they thereby turn us from spectators into participants.

One final point. An art committed to oral, involving performance is committed, by the same token, to ephemerality. Drama is permanent. But individual plays must be as ephemeral as individual performances of them.

Far from proving exceptions to this rule, Shakespeare's plays exemplify it. Events at any of our contemporary Stratfords unwittingly reveal far more about our own world's preoccupations than about Shakespeare's. Ephemerality will out.

Perhaps the full implication of *That Shakespearean Rag* lies in the fact that it is, quite simply, "dated." And "dating" bespeaks, literally, a commitment to immediacy, and so a release from posterity's crippling embrace. Who now frets to establish the "true text" of the *Ziegfeld Follies of 1912*? The presence of "interpolations" into (my own favorite) *Naughty Girls of 1947* wrings few withers. As clearly "dated" popular art, these inherit the ephemerality that their nature makes their right.

When Burbage died, a contemporary elegy claimed the same right in respect of *his* work:

No more young Hamlet, ould Heironymoe
Kind Leer, the greued Moore, and more beside,
That liued in him, haue now for ever dyde.[20]

Let his true monument then, and that of the parts that lived in him, be those poignant wordless wounds with which I began: O, O, O, O. They represent, orally, a language (as well as, visually, a theatre) that—beyond mere words—was able to generate the quintessence of drama. As Burbage himself, Shakespeare, and the American Eliot knew, that makes them *verba sapienti* every one.

NOTES

1. E.g. F. R. Leavis, *English Literature in Our Time and the University* (London, 1969), pp. 149–54.

2. T.S. Eliot, *Selected Essays* (London, 1951), pp. 141–46.

3. See the account of Christopher Ricks's unpublished lecture in *The Times Literary Supplement*, November 2, 1973, p. 1345. See also the subsequent correspondence, pp. 1372, 1404, 1476, 1540, and 1589.

4. G. L. Trager, "Paralanguage: a First Approximation," *Studies in Linguistics* 13 (1958): 1–2. See also Trager's essay in Dell Hymes, ed., *Language in Culture and Society* (New York, 1964), pp. 274–79.

5. B. R. McElderry, Jr., "Eliot's 'Shakespeherean Rag'," *American Quarterly* 9 (1957): 185–86.

6. C. F. Tucker Brooke, ed., *Shakespeare's Plutarch* (London, 1909), p. 193.

7. See my arguments in *Shakespeare's Talking Animals* (London, 1973), pp. 15–23 and 178–91.

8. Jill Levenson, "What the Silence Said: Still Points in *King Lear*" in Clifford Leech and J. M. R. Margeson, eds., *Shakespeare 1971: Proceedings of the World Shakespeare Congress* (Toronto, 1972), pp. 215–29.

9. See *Shakespeare's Talking Animals*, pp. 167–72.

10. This point is brilliantly made by David Horowitz in *Shakespeare, an Existential View* (London, 1965) pp. 19-21.

11. Quoted by Herbert Read in Allen Tate, ed., *T. S. Eliot: the Man and His Work* (London, 1967), p. 15.

12. See Harold Jenkins, "Playhouse Interpolations in the Folio Text of *Hamlet*," *Studies in Bibliography* 13 (1960): 31–47.

13. Cf. Jenkins, "An editor who thought so might have a pretty problem on his hands."

14. *Shakespeare's Talking Animals*, pp. 24–30.

15. Claude Lévi-Strauss, "Overture to *Le Cru et le Cuit*," trans. Joseph H. McMahon, in Jacques Ehrmann, ed., *Structuralism* (New York, 1970), pp. 31–55.

16. Strauss, "Overture."

17. Valerie Eliot, ed., *The Waste Land; A Facsimile and Transcript of the Original Draft* (London, 1971), pp. 4ff.

18. *Selected Essays*, p. 458.

19. Terence Hawkes, ed., *Coleridge on Shakespeare* (Harmondsworth, 1969), p. 65.

20. The elegy is ascribed to "Jo ffletcher." See C. C. Stopes, *Burbage and Shakespeare's Stage* (London, 1913).

4

Dramatic Personae in Shakespeare's Sonnets*

T. WALTER HERBERT

TO AN APPARENTLY SIMPLE QUESTION, "WHOM MAY WE PROFITABLY suppose we hear when we read a Shakespeare sonnet?"[1] this paper offers one answer: often we may hear a persona whom we understand well because we remember a character of a Shakespeare play caught in a similar predicament. Memories of the more extensively developed character provide illuminating implications for the sonnet's passions.

The question is unnecessary when a sonnet fits happily into the context of our own memories, as does "When to the sessions of sweet silent thought."[2] Recollection of old woes and lost friends is not peculiar to any grown person. I take the pronoun *I* for myself: the poem is not exclusively mine, but it is mine. It has educated my heart, giving manageable shape to my regret and my comfort. I includes me in a community of all those who, having encountered disappointment and loss, turn from loneliness to companionship. I now say to this sonnet, "Speak for me," and it obeys.

But many a sonnet demands contexts that the common experiences of men and women do not supply. A very particular person speaks in a distinctive situation. Responding to this demand, readers have tended to invoke a tradition, as ancient as Sappho or David the Psalmist,[3] that lyric poets in their own proper voices bestow poetic form upon their personal reactions to their worlds, to their friends, enemies, and lovers, and to their actual or personally imagined experiences. The very shape of a sonnet, proclaiming it a lyric, invites readers to adopt a frame of expectation like William Wordsworth's, who said, "With this key Shakespeare unlocked his heart." In their imaginations they have stood with the later poet on Westminster Bridge contemplating a quiet London

---

*A brief paper treating some of the materials in this essay was delivered at the 1965 meeting of the South Atlantic Modern Language Association.

at dawn, and they have looked into Milton's bright unseeing eyes when they have read a sonnet on his blindness. Similarly when they come to a sonnet whose speaker makes sport with this name, *Will*, or to a sonnet advising a young man to marry and beget children, they are apt to remember that Shakespeare's name was *Will* or remember that both the Earl to whom he dedicated two poems and the Earl who according to the Folio publishers befriended him worried their families by resisting wedded joys. Such readers may admit the possibility that an Earl's mother, wanting grandchildren, asked Shakespeare to help by phrasing her cause or that the person addressed in a *Will* sonnet owes his quality to the imagination that quickened Thersites and Cressida. But they often assume that all the sonnets are best read as Shakespeare speaking about situations and events he encountered in his own person.[4]

When they do they invite us to come to general agreement on a pathetic biography which, if we trust it, makes a substantial difference in our understanding of the sonnets as well as in our estimate of the man who wrote them. A high born youth, we are told, was Shakespeare's dear friend, but two vexations beclouded the friendship. The first involved a Dark Lady, with whom he is supposed to have had a passionate love affair and whom he lost when she found his friend a more appealing lover. The second troublemaker was, forsooth, a poet who flattered the young nobleman more skillfully than Shakespeare could.

The biographical assumption leads to inevitable questions: Who was the friend? Who was the Dark Lady? Who was the Rival Poet? People like A. L. Rowse still make confident identifications.[5]

Valid answers would go far toward justifying the questions. But we lack ordinary evidence that Shakespeare had the described relationship with any nobleman, or that he thought any poet his superior, his inferior, or his rival, or that any woman ever turned away from him. Indeed we lack evidence more compelling than a gossiped witticism that he linked himself personally with any woman other than members of his family.

If a number of central events in Shakespeare's authenticated life had found clear expression in the sonnets—as events in Wordsworth's life and Milton's surely did in theirs—we might be more strongly tempted to read all the sonnets biographically. But no such passion as grief over his son Hamnet's death nor exhilaration at his first sight of London provoked any extant sonnet.

When we distrust a biographical interpretation, either for lack of firm evidence or because the interpretation falsifies the Shakespeare whom we infer from the plays, we do not relegate to a featureless mist sonnets

that resist standing alone. Ever since the Book of Job, dramatic poets
have made their characters respond aloud to the fictional experiences
into which the poets have thrust them. Unlike the other great sonneteers,
even Milton, Shakespeare belongs with Aristophanes and Sophocles.
He was a supremely dramatic poet. When we quote a sonnet by Milton
we can simply report that "Milton said . . . ." When we quote lines from
Shakespeare's plays we do not with the same simplicity believe that
Shakespeare said them. We more properly quote his Falstaff or Viola or
Cordelia or Cleopatra. If he did not quit being a dramatic poet when he
wrote lyric passages for the plays, he may have remained a dramatic poet
when he wrote the sonnets. Particularly when a sonnet situation resembles a situation in a play, we may suppose that he conceived the speaking
persona with the same imagination that conceived Falstaff and Viola.

When persona and situation go beyond mere essential resemblance
and the sonnet rings true as an utterance by the dramatic character
himself, the whole play as we remember it makes the sonnet rich with its
overtones and resonances. We have, as it were, a new speech by a
known character, exploring a new aspect of a known situation.

The intellectual design of many sonnets lends some respectability to
our listening for the voices of personae whom Shakespeare created. In a
host of speeches throughout his career a character describes a situation
and makes a self-revealing comment. Thus Richard of Gloucester describes the peace that Yorkist triumph has brought to his family and
proclaims his own still wintry discontent (*Richard III* 1. 1. 1–31). Thus
Caliban describes the island noises and his delight in them (*The Tempest*, 3. 2. 135–43). Though of course the sonnet choruses of *Romeo and
Juliet* and the first dialogue between the star-crossed lovers (1. 5.
93–106) show other uses, most 1609 sonnets show how eminently
congenial with this intellectual design is the prosodic shape of quatrains
and couplet.

One Shakespeare sonnet has a suggestive history. William Jaggard
published it, in 1597 or earlier, in that strange collection of lyrics by
several hands called *The Passionate Pilgrim*. The speaker three times
confesses to a woman that he has broken an oath because of her, and he
repeatedly pleads that because she is, as he says, a goddess, he should
not be blamed.

Did not the heavenly rhetoric of thine eye,
'Gainst whom the world could not hold argument,
Persuade my heart to this false perjury?
Vows for thee broke deserve not punishment.

A woman I forswore; but I will prove,
Thou being a goddess, I forswore not thee:
My vow was earthly, thou a heavenly love;
Thy grace being gain'd cures all disgrace in me.
My vow was breath, and breath a vapor is,
Then thou, fair sun, that on this earth doth shine,
Exhal'st this vapor vow, in thee it is:
If broken, then it is no fault of mine.
    If by me broke, what fool is not so wise
    To break an oath, to win a paradise?

Like "Two loves I have of comfort and despair" which precedes it in
The Passionate Pilgrim, this sonnet demands a particular context. In
itself it does not indicate whom "A woman I forswore" refers to;
blaming a perjury on a "goddess" is not quite within the universal
experience of mankind; and Shakespeare's biography sheds no light.
But the plays contain several men each attributing his fickleness to the
influence of a woman whom he apotheosizes. In *Two Gentlemen of
Verona* Proteus forswears his love for Julia as soon as he sees the
all-commended Silvia. In *A Midsummer Night's Dream* Lysander,
bound by oaths to love Hermia, begins pursuing Helena; and Demetrius,
infatuated with the same Hermia, suddenly perceiving the same Helena
in a new light, blurts out, "O Helen, goddess, nymph, perfect, divine"
(3. 2. 137). Proteus, Lysander, and Demetrius are all foolish enough to
speak the same kind of twaddle that we find in our sonnet. But the fit of
situation to situation is not perfect, and (more to the point) these
dramatic contexts do nothing to lift the sonnet above amorous cliché.
    A better candidate appears in *Love's Labour's Lost*. The young King
of Navarre and some friendly lords swear to fast, sleep little, see no
woman, do nothing but study—a rash, sterile, if superficially high-
minded commitment. When a princess and her lovely ladies come to
Navarre, the men are embarrassed. The *Passionate Pilgrim* apology
might be spoken by any one of these as his logic-chopping effort to
persuade his chosen lady into his arms.
    Shakespeare thought so, and some years before Jaggard's publication
he wrote it for one of the young lords, Longaville, as his fashionable
sonnet declaring love (4. 3. 55-68).[6] Since an oath to study exclusively
is rarer than an oath to love exclusively, the tired hyperbole of praise
serves comic purposes as the frame of a fresh, beautifully absurd set
speech. We hear a youth who may yet learn what Jonathan Swift would

poetically emphasize, that the proper study of mankind is not goddesses but women. Rather than inviting us to invent an oath breaking episode for Shakespeare's personal life, the sonnet invites us to share the mood of Longaville's lady, who, capable of sorrow and forgiveness as well as laughter, has better wisdom than to capitulate immediately. Little as we may have duplicated the young lord's specific lunacy, we do not dismiss him from the humanity whose immature episodes we ourselves perhaps have not altogether escaped.

To illustrate the consequences of looking in the plays for contexts that may illuminate what is said by speakers of the 1609 sonnets, let us begin with three which are often attached to Fair Friend, Dark Lady, and Rival Poet, then read a sonnet often tied to public events contemporary with Shakespeare's mature years. In each instance let us consider briefly what the persona asks us to believe if we are looking for biographical evidence, then stir our memories and read the sonnet in a context that we can invoke because we know a dramatic character similarly situated.

If we take Sonnet 71 as Shakespeare's nondramatic admonition without imputing to him an adolescent gloom after he had grown up, we must picture him in dreadful plight. He was desperately ill, his reputation notoriously bad. A friend of times past now occupied an exalted position so precarious that in merely mourning the poet's death he would invite dangerous mockery.

No longer mourn for me when I am dead
Than you shall hear the surly sullen bell
Give warning to the world that I am fled
From this vile world with vildest worms to dwell;
Nay, if you read this line, remember not
The hand that writ it, for I love you so,
That I in your sweet thoughts would be forgot,
If thinking on me then should make you woe.
O, if (I say) you look upon this verse,
When I (perhaps) compounded am with clay,
Do not so much as my poor name rehearse,
But let your love even with my life decay;
   Lest the wise world should look into your moan,
   And mock you with me after I am gone.

No historical evidence suggests that any such moment ever belonged to William Shakespeare, but the Shakespeare who wrote the *Henry IV* plays and *Henry V* might well have composed the sonnet for the voice of banished Falstaff,[7] speaking, as it were, to the new, distant king.

As a wayward prince, Hal distresses his father. Instead of inventing military adventures like Hotspur of the north, and instead of attending judicial and administrative sessions to learn the ways of the court, he frolics with a clutch of tavern-haunting commoners whose highest ranking member is the old, fat, alcoholic, law-breaking, loose-living Sir John. The attractive quality of these disreputable people is a bubbling joy of living, and Falstaff's ready wit often graces a shabby episode with high laughter. But Falstaff regards himself as better than a jester. He thinks he has the friendship of the young prince, and Hal apparently encourages the thought.

When news comes that Hal's father has died, the fat knight sees a momentary vision of power. "The laws of England," he exults, "are at my commandement." Whereupon he rushes to Westminster, intercepts the coronation procession, and calls out gaily, "King Hal! my royal Hal!" But the new king says:

> I know thee not, old man, fall to thy prayers.
> How ill white hairs become a fool and jester!
> I have long dreamt of such a kind of man,
> So surfeit-swell'd, so old, and so profane;
> But being awak'd, I do despise my dream.

Forbidden to come within ten miles of the royal presence, Falstaff goes away, and after a while, forlorn, he dies unnoticed by King Hal.

Sonnet 71 fits Falstaff's state sometime between his rejection and his death, while, as we learn from *Henry V*, court politicians are still marvelling at the young king's abandonment of "companies unletter'd, rude, and shallow" (1.1.55), still calculating what profit they can derive from his reform.

Ill, his heart "fracted," (*H V*, 2. 1. 120) Falstaff hugs the colder and colder comfort of a wishful thought that he suffers only temporarily, because the king "must seem thus to the world" (*2 H IV*, 5. 5. 79). In order to put the sonnet fully into Falstaff's mouth we must believe that despite his appetites, his regard for the fifth Harry transcends greed, believe that the last words he has spoken to him tell a threefold truth: "My King, my Jove! I speak to thee, my heart!" (5. 5. 47). We must believe that Falstaff reverences Henry as his sovereign, worships him as a god, and loves him as a man.

If we do, we will not be astonished that he advises exactly what he knows the young king will do. His maudlin tone at the beginning tells of one far gone in sack, and the excessive palaver in the quatrains about bell, worms, clay, and the cessation of love tempts us to suppose that the old fraud is building up a case, making himself out some sort of martyr, still hoping for an invitation. But in the couplet with a shock we hear again the Falstaff whose knack for making an accurate estimate of a situation now and then locks him in our hearts at the very moment we are laughing at him for a hopeful con man. The beloved monarch addressed is not a Lear blinded by shrewd flatterers. He is a prince in whose mouth authority is sweeter than sack, who knows that he can be weakened more by plausible mockery than by the fact of his ingratitude.

If we imagine we hear Falstaff again in Sonnet 71, his message, never delivered to the mirror of all Christian Kings, may tell us that the old fat man is at last capable of an acquiescence in destiny that makes his payment of the debt he owed God almost tragic rather than merely pitiable.

Sonnet 42 has brought some embarrassment to commentators who profess the conventional sonnet story and yet would like to esteem Shakespeare a strong man. The story tells them that the noble friend and the Dark Lady have now entered into a liaison which leaves the poet to chilly nights. Shakespeare, they must infer, could actually console himself with remembering that the two would never have known one another had he not first loved them both, and with the notion that the woman loves the man *because* she loves Shakespeare. The consolation sounds like a weak grasp at a flimsy shred of self-respect.

That thou hast her, it is not all my grief,
And yet it may be said I lov'd her dearly;
That she hath thee is of my wailing chief,
A loss in love that touches me more nearly.
Loving offenders, thus I will excuse ye:
Thou dost love her because thou know'st I love her,
And for my sake even so doth she abuse me,
Suff'ring my friend for my sake to approve her.
If I lose thee, my loss is my love's gain,
And losing her, my friend hath found that loss;
Both find each other, and I lose both twain,
And both for my sake lay on me this cross.
   But here's the joy, my friend and I are one;
   Sweet flattery! then she loves but me alone.

If we had valid evidence that Shakespeare was ever in such a predicament and bragged about it, we should accept the sonnet as his consolation. While awaiting such evidence, we can look in the plays.

Thanks to the makers of stretch pants, ragged jeans, and elegant pants suits we are better situated than Shakespeare to find something exciting, joyous, and provocative about young women in clothes that emphasize how different they are from men. But he repeatedly conjures up the phenomenon, especially in witty comedies where some women take charge of their destinies. The Shakespeare who wrote *Twelfth Night* might possibly have composed a comic sonnet, full of wry, affectionate raillery, for the voice of a girl whose twin brother is about to wed an heiress undiscriminating enough to mistake the girl herself for an eligible bachelor.

The story begins with trouble. Viola, shipwrecked, alone in Illyria, her twin Sebastian lost and presumed dead, must now earn a living. She dresses herself as her brother dressed, gets a job in Duke Orsino's household and sets her cap, patiently, for the Duke himself. The Duke desires the beautiful Olivia, who will not see him. He sends Viola, whom he knows as the lad Cesario, to entreat her. Olivia likes the messenger's personality and proceeds to fall in love, as she supposes, with *him*. Viola, horrified, knows from her own instinct that for Olivia wit and manners in a husband, though desirable, are not enough.

Brother Sebastian, not dead, makes his way to Illyria. The Lady Olivia sees him in the street, believes him to be Cesario, and proposes an immediate binding betrothal. Sebastian is willing to take good fortune however madly arrived at, and perceiving in Olivia wealth, beauty, and skillful household government, agrees. A priest performs his office. When Sebastian learns how he owes wife and wealth to Viola, he quips to Olivia, "You are betroth'd both to a maid and man" (5. 1. 255).

The play demands that Viola, at length openly in her proper feminine role, give attention to acquiring a now accessible Orsino. But suppose she as well as Sebastian recognizes the wild metaphysical implications of the events wrought by her twinship. Suppose further that, as an aside not included in *Twelfth Night*, she addresses her brother in mock reproach. "Sebastian, my friend," she says, "Olivia has loved me, and now you have taken her from me. Moreover, she has taken you from me. Both thefts are flattering. Obviously it is for my sake that she loves you; obviously also, since you have barely met her"—here Viola perhaps flatters herself—"you love her because she is my friend. Well, fond of her, I am happy she has you, and fond of you, I am happy you have her.

But note this well, sibling: you suggested that Olivia is betrothed to what she likes in both of us. Since in her eyes you and I are spiritually identical, and since for this oh so spiritual lady love is a thing of the spirit, she really loves only me.'' I rather like my phrasing for Viola. Most people will prefer Shakespeare's Sonnet 42, whose ironic, complaining tone provides just the fillip that makes the lines appropriate to the outrageous situation in this witty play.

We have now looked at sonnets that are often understood to treat two of the three major characters in the sad sonnet-derived biography. No play gives us a poet painfully conscious of a glib rival, but in *King Lear* a daughter has similar trouble. Let us look at Sonnet 85.

My tongue-tied muse in manners holds her still,
While comments of your praise, richly compil'd,
Reverse[8] their character with golden quill
And precious phrase by all the Muses fil'd.
I think good thoughts whilst other write good words,
And like unletter'd clerk still cry ''Amen''
To every hymn that able spirit affords
In polish'd form of well-refined pen.
Hearing you prais'd, I say, '' 'Tis so, 'tis true,''
And to the most of praise add something more,
But that is in my thought, whose love to you
(Though words come hindmost) holds his rank before.
   Then others for the breath of words respect,
   Me for my dumb thoughts, speaking in effect.

Shakespeare's friends attested the extraordinary facility with which he turned thought and feeling into words. If he believed his pen less fluent than Chapman's or Marlowe's, he knew himself slenderly.

His plays, however, show that he understood the foolish and the weak as well as the shrewd and the mighty. Though Othello's polished apologia, containing the assertion that he is rude in his speech, is an eloquent statement, the Moor disastrously fails to master ''the soft phrase of peace'' (1. 3. 82). Shakespeare made Theseus of *A Midsummer Night's Dream* appreciate the dumb ''modesty of fearful duty'' as highly as ''the rattling tongue of saucy and audacious eloquence'' (5. 1. 102-3). He made Cordelia's tongue-tied moment the precipitating factor in her immense tragedy. Like every other Elizabethan, Shakespeare knew that flattery skillfully administered may like dark magic skew the judgment of monarchs, powerful nobles, businessmen, and desired women. It would be strange if the poet who gave life to Cordelia had failed to explore with the instruments of his trade the yearning of a loyal heart which, lacking diplomatic skill, cannot speak good words but knows that others can and deliberately will.

Cordelia is a princess and not a poet, and she speaks to her royal father, not to a patron, so that the accidentals of her situation differ sharply from those of the speaking persona in Sonnet 85. Yet essentially Cordelia's posture is the same: "My love has a valid claim, though imperilled because the great one whom I love is wooed with successful flattery." Just after her sisters, on demand, have richly described their adoration for Lear, her turn comes and she responds, uneloquently,

> Unhappy that I am, I cannot heave
> My heart into my mouth. I love your majesty
> According to my bond, no more nor less.
>
> (1. 1. 91–93)

Because we remember the whole play, Cordelia speaks to abundant memories. We know about her return to Britain, about her loving treatment of her tormented father, about her death. These memories modify our understanding of her curt answer. We love her and wish her well partly because she is not addicted to elaborate rhetoric.

Though we cannot impose the details of Cordelia's plight upon the speaking persona in Sonnet 85, we can transfer to him some of the sympathy we have learned from her career. When we read the sonnet much as we read a speech in the great tragedy, we do not hear Shakespeare sounding like an insecure petitioner. He sounds like the Shakespeare who makes us grieve over Cordelia beyond our grief over grave Cato's daughter and dazzling Cleopatra. This magnanimous Shakespeare invites us professionals in language and literature to imagine how it feels to be, as it were, a dumb freshman or a poor poet.

Let us look finally at Sonnet 107, which has brought a different kind of speculation from commentators.

> Not mine own fears, nor the prophetic soul
> Of the wide world, dreaming on things to come,
> Can yet the lease of my true love control,
> Suppos'd as forfeit to a confin'd doom.
> The mortal moon hath her eclipse endur'd,
> And the sad augurs mock their own presage,
> Incertainties now crown themselves assur'd,
> And peace proclaims olives of endless age.
> Now with the drops of this most balmy time
> My love looks fresh, and Death to me subscribes,

Since spite of him I'll live in this poor rhyme,
While he insults o'er dull and speechless tribes;
And thou in this shalt find thy monument,
When tyrants' crests and tombs of brass are spent.

This haunting sonnet implies a situation of vast political significance. Some have thought it refers to the destruction of the Spanish Armada, some to the tensions at the death of Queen Elizabeth and the accession of King James. No crisis in English life has quite seemed to fit the whole poem.

It is possible to imagine that here Shakespeare's Cleopatra expresses, just before her death, perceptions that the pace of tragedy gives her neither time nor occasion to articulate on stage. Cleopatra has so enchanted Antony that for her he has abandoned Roman wife, Roman duty, and Roman military initiative. Octavius, at last impatient, has decided to subdue this Antony and his Egypt to right Roman rule and carry Cleopatra, as a symbol of gaudy disorder tamed, back to Rome. In a swift campaign he has defeated Antony. Cleopatra has taken refuge in what she calls her monument. Antony, having botched a suicide, has been brought to her to die and now lies, still warm, at her feet.

This Cleopatra stirs the imagination that lets us understand pursuers of imperial power and personal danger, including the two heroic Romans whom she has fascinated. She has a wit unlike Viola's, quick with venom as well as laughter. No man would conjure her up for tender solace and peaceful evenings. Her discerning, resourceful mind is a weapon. From the vantage point of mistress to the first Caesar, she has improved her salad days observing the world and one world conqueror. She has put sharpened wits to effective if deplorable work on Antony. Though Shakespeare celebrates her as a most triumphant lady, he does not convert her into a Roman intellectual, any more than he makes her militarily competent. At her approach to death she speaks words of a sensual woman, attentive to clothing and to her passionate longings. She has had herself bitten by asps, thereby at once defying young Caesar and hastening to join Antony for some afterlife where kissing is still a pleasant business. Once the asps have done their kind, she makes explicit only her success in choosing a painless instrument of death. She entrusts the rest of her thought to a name:

As sweet as balm, as soft as air, as gentle—
O Antony!

(5. 2. 310–11)

Her soaring imagination has made Antony's a name for a magnitude wider than the ocean, past the size of dreaming, a name speaking now cosmic music and now thunder, betokening a bounty big as autumn.

If somebody suggested that in the next theatrical performance instead of saying "O Antony!" Cleopatra might rehearse the imperial Roman context of Antony's fall and hers, we might inquire acidly whether he thought he knew stagecraft better than Shakespeare. But we can dream that in addition to the great tragedy Shakespeare wrote a sonnet in the persona of his dying Cleopatra: an assertion of a love surviving eclipses past and outlasting attritions of the future until she is immortalized by a play in which she speaks with her own distinctive voice. There is more than an octave's worth of the past and present for this Cleopatra to recapitulate, more than a sestet's worth of the future for her to invoke.

If we imagine as we read the sonnet that it gives us Cleopatra's bittersweet, silent thought in the moment when the venom is quietly terminating her life, we may flesh out her allusions with details we remember from the play.

She knows that her own fears as well as the imperial Roman destiny have threatened to set controlling boundaries about her love for Antony. Yet she perceives that her love has proved stronger than these. She loves in defiance of all that Octavius and his sister, Antony's new wife, stand for, in defiance of the wide Roman world, dreaming of an end to the disturbing things she in her turn represents—the ungoverned Egyptian crown and excesses of couch, bed, and Egypt's grape.

She is aware that her vacillation, real as well as apparent, for a while validated an aspect of her epithet "moon," the changeable planet. She remembers that when Antony saw her treated with less than royal homage by Octavius's messenger—and thought she was choosing Octavius—he justifiably found the incident ominous. He said,

> Alack, our terrene moon
> Is now eclips'd, and it portends alone
> The fall of Antony!
>
> (3. 13. 153–55)

But she also remembers achieving constancy. In her latest moments she has said,

> Now the fleeting moon
> No planet is of mine.
>
> (5. 2. 240–41)

She is conscious of auguries. Some aururies have gone sour: a soothsayer half promised Antony supremacy if he would stay away from Octavius, but Octavius has followed Antony to Egypt. Some auguries have been neglected: swift Octavius, "too sure an augurer" (5. 2. 32) of Cleopatra's suicide, has moved but tardily to prevent it, so that Cleopatra has been able to say to the asp:

> Oh could'st thou speak,
> That I might hear thee call great Caesar ass
> Unpolicied.
>
> (5. 2. 305–7)

Some uncertain auguries no longer threaten the Romans: before Antony's last fight with Octavius the augurers said "they know not, they cannot tell" what the event will be (4. 12. 5). Now everybody knows.

Though Cleopatra has extolled Antony as "the garland of the war" and "the soldier's pole," she knows that Octavius, regarding a military campaign as a step towards achievements beyond booty and glory, has despised the same Antony as "ruffian" and "the word of War." In Octavius's eyes, Antony has used Roman armies to make Roman loyalties uncertain and to disrupt the empire. Even while fighting a battle, Octavius has thought of olives, symbol of peace. He has gloried in the prospect that

> The time of universal peace is near.
> Prove this a prosp'rous day, the three-nook'd world
> Shall bear the olive freely.
>
> (4. 6. 5–7)

He proclaims nothing less than the approaching Augustan age of Rome, a balmy time that Cleopatra, intractable to simplicity, proportion, and correct taste, must view with scorn even as she and Antony clear the way with their deaths.

Cleopatra's voice being appropriate to her infinite variety, we can hear an elaborate pun in "balmy." We hear much more than a sardonic comment on an orderly peace. For Cleopatra death is coming sweet as balm because it sooths as if with emolient fragrance and because it will bring an Antony healed of his wound and ready to kiss. If we imitate her sensual imagination we also hear an allusion to embalming (the Egyptian triumph over fleshly decay) as an image suggesting what she can call "immortal longings." But when she says that her love looks fresh she goes beyond eagerness for renewed posthumous sensuality: she invokes the eternal freshness and constancy of spiritual things and poetry.

She has dreaded the prospect that a Roman comedian might, as she says, "boy my greatness," but now, taking a great leap in time, she has a happier thought about the English play, "this poor rhyme," named for Antony and herself. In the tragedy Antony will find a monument less perishable than the imperial crests of the Roman emperors and more permanent than tombs of brass in the pyramids or anywhere else.

We may read Sonnet 107, then, not as a replacement for "O Antony!" nor as an allusion to some unknown crisis in Shakespeare's England but as a prophecy about Shakespeare's imaginative accomplishment from his Cleopatra's still "grape-moist lips."

If we accept an intimate complementing relationship between many a play and many a sonnet, we need not decide whether play or sonnet came earlier. Perhaps sometimes Shakespeare first rendered in a sonnet a passion he subsequently modified for the stage. Perhaps months after he had written a play he phrased in a sonnet implications he could not forget. Perhaps while composing a play he sometimes paused and wrote a sonnet to clear his mind of words clamoring (against his playwright's judgment) to be put into a character's mouth. He could not let Cordelia declare the full quality of her love without belying the trait that earned her banishment, nor was there a good theatrical opportunity to let Falstaff acknowledge certain attributes of his king and himself. In the sonnets we may hear Shakespeare commit to well-turned lines something that in his profession as playwright he committed to silence.

When we read the sonnets as lyrics written by a complete dramatist, we do not diminish our awareness of the personality that matters in William Shakespeare. Ben Jonson, who loved him, was referring mainly to the plays when he said that the offspring

Of Shakespeare's mind and manners brightly shines
   In his well turned and true filed lines.

The sonnets shine with the same mind, the same manners. When we call them companions to the plays we do not diminish our appreciation of the intensity with which he wrote. We may suppose that to him, as often to us, the predicaments of Falstaff and Cleopatra were as vivid as life.

Sir Philip Sidney claimed that he bit his pen and groped for an invention when he set about writing a sonnet. Only with difficulty could we believe that Shakespeare ever did such a thing. If he had been so at a loss, we might possibly read a really autobiographical sonnet concluding with the alexandrine, "Fool, said my muse to me, look in thy plays and write."

NOTES

1. The question implies profound and subtle problems, such as the nature of a poem's existence, of its statement, of "the poetical character," about which Keats spoke memorably in his famous letter to Richard Woodhouse, and of a reader's responsive experience. This paper, though it rests on a position in these deep matters, does not explicitly phrase it.

2. Quotations from Shakespeare, except for one noted departure, follow the text of *The Riverside Shakespeare*, ed. G. Blakemore Evans and others, (Boston, Mass., 1974.) See footnotes 6 and 8.

3. Some who have disputed the biographical contexts of the sonnets give what appears excessive weight to the influence of Wordsworth and the other Romantics. The personal lyric is old: David's "Against Thee, Thee only have I sinned" refers directly to his behavior with Bathsheba and Uriah the Hittite.

4. James Winney, in *The Master-Mistress: A Study of Shakespeare's Sonnets* (New York, 1968), pp. 1–25, provides a succinct review of opinion about "the extent of Shakespeare's personal involvement in the story of the sonnets." A larger sample of opinions is in *A New Variorum Shakespeare: The Sonnets*, ed. H. E. Rollins, 2 vols. (Philadelphia, Pa., 1944).

5. A. L. Rowse, *William Shakespeare, A Biography* (New York, 1963), and *Shakespeare the Man* (New York, 1973).

6. *Love's Labour's Lost* shows substantially the same wording. In the *Riverside* texts it has these variants: line 2 *cannot* for *could not*; line 9 *Vows are but breath* for *My vows was breath*; line 10 *my earth dost* for *earth doth*; line 14 *lose* for *break*.

7. William Empson, in *Some Versions of Pastoral* (London, 1935), pp. 89–115, suggests a connection between Falstaff and certain other sonnets. For still another fancied connection between Falstaff and Shakespeare see T. Walter Herbert, "The Naming of Falstaff," *The Emory University Quarterly* 10 (1954): 61–69.

8. I have ventured to emend the received reading *reserve*. *Reserve* gives a strained meaning, while *reverse*, its anagram, produces a characteristically Shakespearean multiple pun. *Character* may allude to manuscript lettering as well as to essential disposition, so that *reverse their character* implies *decorate with fancy flourishes* as well as *turn their essential disposition upside down* and so falsify it. *Character* has generated so many metaphors in our lexical stock that other senses of the phrase suggest themselves. The emendation was suggested by an oddity that I came across while observing the not astonishing phenomenon that, as in other instances of the kind we are noticing, certain key words in the sonnet are the same as words in the neighborhood of Cordelia's embarrassment in *King Lear*. Responding to Lear's words of banishment, Kent remonstrates in a speech much the same in Folio and First Quarto except for one sentence: In Folio Kent says, "Reserve they state," and in Quarto he says, "Reverse thy doom." I do not attempt a bibliographical accounting for the variant.

5

Shakespeare's Patterns for the Viewer's Eye:
Dramaturgy for the Open Stage*

ALAN C. DESSEN

OVER THE LAST TWO DECADES, THE CAREFUL WORK OF THEATRICAL historians has cleared away much of the debris that had accumulated around the Elizabethan stage. Not long ago we talked of elaborate sets, spacious upper stages, and a roomy acting area in an inner stage; now we recognize only an unlocalized platform, a limited "above," and a discovery space. We may never fully understand the Swan drawing; we may never know what an audience looking at the empty Globe stage would have seen. But thanks to the healthy iconoclasm of recent scholarship, we are closer to the true Elizabethan stage than at any time since the seventeenth century.[1]

But, to borrow a question from our students, what difference does it all make? For those of us not vitally interested in the history of theatrical architecture, why bother with such sifting of evidence? Or, to be more specific, does our hard-won knowledge about the Globe in any way advance our understanding of Shakespeare's plays?

The answers to such questions will vary widely according to the assumptions brought to the plays by the reader. On the simplest level, information about Elizabethan stages and staging can correct the false assumptions of the beginning student who has been nurtured on realism and the fourth wall convention. Thus, without an awareness of the bare platform, we cannot really understand the Prologue to *Henry V* where Shakespeare's spokesman first apologizes for the physical limitations of his stage but then asks the audience to "piece out our imperfections with your thoughts"—to supply, through "imaginary forces," what stage

*Based in part on a paper read at the annual meeting of the Modern Language Association, held in Chicago in 1973.

and players cannot specifically provide. Clearly this "open stage" (as Richard Southern aptly describes it) does demand a greater imaginative participation from the viewer than would be required in a more realistic presentation and does make certain effects possible, others difficult or impossible. For example, scholars have pointed to the fluid, unimpeded movement of the action possible on a stage unencumbered by curtains or fixed scenery, a kind of effect easily spotted in the exits and entrances of any battlefield sequence and best summed up in the many varied scenes of *Antony and Cleopatra*.[2]

Yet in spite of such general insights, discussions of the physical stage in the age of Shakespeare often do seem divorced from the plays themselves. Meanwhile, claims about Shakespeare's dramaturgy often do not seem to draw upon our knowledge of the Elizabethan theater. In short, there has been no marriage of true minds between critics and theatrical historians.

Such a consummation (although "devoutly to be wished") is too ambitious a goal for this essay. Rather, my more modest aim is to call attention to some possible links between the Elizabethan stage and Elizabethan dramaturgy. Consider, as a point of departure, the basic acting area for Shakespeare's company—a large bare platform with no formal sets, no artificial lighting (except for the occasional torch), no extensive stage properties. Not only Nature abhors a vacuum; so, modern readers and directors with critical reflexes conditioned by realism immediately start to *fill* this bare platform with personnel, properties, thrones, arbors, hangings, and more. But for a moment let us (in our imaginations) leave this stage bare and then carefully, as in a controlled experiment, introduce *one* sword or *one* crown or *one* kneeling figure. In the theater of our minds we can recognize that what to the modern reader might seem a liability could indeed be an asset. Indeed, on such an unadorned, uncluttered stage, the introduction of *one* significant property or *one* distinctive figure can have a particularly strong impact upon an audience because that property or figure is not competing with many other details on stage and is not absorbed into a rich "busy" set. Similarly, the stage business or gestures provided by the actors would receive greater emphasis given fewer distractions for the viewer's eye. Whether we are talking about stage properties or gestures or groupings or some combination of the three, the obvious limitations of the open stage (as acknowledged by the Prologue to *Henry V*) could prove to be an asset, especially if particular details or moments are singled out for an audience's attention. In Southern's terms, such moments can be free "from the fetters of the trivial, the factual and the irrelevant, which exist in natural surroundings."[3]

Several corollaries follow from the distinctive nature of the open stage. First, since so little evidence about properties or gestures or stage business has survived in stage directions and dialogue, any extant details should be granted special attention, particularly those details that initially seem puzzling or extraneous or inappropriate (often because they defy our sense of decorum or realism). If the modern reader is truly interested in the logic or strategy behind a Shakespearean scene or character, what better place to start than a theatrical moment, highly visible on the Elizabethan open stage, that defies our expectations?

Consider a striking example—the blinding of Gloucester in *King Lear*. This savage moment often evokes bizarre renditions in modern productions; thus, at Stratford, Ontario in 1972, the scene was drawn out interminably while Cornwall stripped down to a leather tunic and then chose his gouging tool from a large rack of gleaming instruments that had been wheeled onto the stage. To gain on stage a direct physical extension of the human animality of Cornwall and Regan, most actors and directors resort instinctively to hands (or thumbs or nails) for the blinding. But the text directs otherwise, at least for Gloucester's first eye, for Cornwall instructs his servants: "Fellows, hold the chair, / Upon these eyes of thine I'll set my foot" (3.7.67–68). Since Shakespeare does not specify how a foot is to put out an eye, modern actors and directors often try to sidestep this line, finding the implicit action awkward and "unrealistic" (although Peter Brook gave his Cornwall golden spurs). But if we are willing to apply a different logic (in order to understand the original effect rather than translate it into our terms), Shakespeare's clear signal could set up a striking, unforgettable stage picture, one that can be particularly rich in significance for this tragedy. For if Gloucester, bound to a chair, is lowered to the stage floor so that his head is under Cornwall's foot, the audience will witness a powerful symbolic tableau that epitomizes not only injustice and oppression but, given the associations with the head throughout this play, also acts out the failure of reason and "cause" to deal with the world of the storm. This visual image is linked to other moments in the play (for example, Tom "throwing his head" in the previous scene or Lear beating upon his head in 1.4.262–63), and, as with the blindness / sight motif, can generate meanings and associations that inform the entire tragedy. To recognize that the logic of this blinding is symbolic rather than physiological is to recognize the presence of a kind of theatrical *italics* that transcends our sense of verisimilitude to yield a larger, richer effect, especially on the open stage.

For another example, consider the practical joke that Prince Hal plays upon Francis the drawer in *1 Henry IV*. Critics usually argue that through his test of the drawer's bond to his master Hal is expressing his own awareness of bonds, debts, and truancy, but such discussions rarely include the obvious and striking stage business. Thus, on one side the prince keeps drawing Francis back to him by offering various rewards, while Poins, off stage, uses the drawer's name to elicit a mechanistic response: verbally—"Anon, sir"; physically—a movement towards the speaker. Poins never grasps the purpose of the action (2.4.86–88); rather, it is the audience who sees Francis act out his limitations, jerked back and forth like a puppet on two strings until: *"Here they both call him. The Drawer stands amazed, not knowing which way to go"* (76 s.d.). This frenetic, puppet-like behavior sets up for the viewer a lively demonstration of a figure controlled by others, unable to cope with the strings that manipulate him, while establishing the prince as a controller or puppet-master rather than one of the controlled. The more extreme and unrealistic the staging, the more effective will be the symbolic point. To present the scene in a restrained, subdued fashion may satisfy our sense of realism or propriety, especially if we are concerned about Hal's heartlessness or bad taste, but such a choice by critic or director can easily undermine or obscure the larger point. Again, action implicit in a stage direction or dialogue sets up a strong theatrical signal that points us toward the major themes of the play.

Symbolic staging, of course, need not be limited to the Elizabethan open stage, but, in my opinion, such an arena is more conducive to theatrical italics than later stages (or cinema or television). Other effects, however, may be linked more closely to the bare stage uncluttered by the trappings of realism. If properties or gestures or costumes do receive greater distinction for the viewer's eye, then two equivalent moments in different parts of a play might more readily be linked together as a visual analogy by the watching audience. On the open stage, with less competition for the viewer's attention, I find a greater likelihood that such links would be recognized and would become an essential part of the viewing experience.

From this corollary follows a significant and often overlooked part of Shakespeare's dramaturgy: his use of visual analogues to link various moments in his dramatic continuum for the eyes of his audience, a device especially suited to the "uncluttered" Elizabethan stage. The general principle behind such linkages has long been recognized and has already received considerable attention. Thus, many astute critics have dealt with double plots and analogous situations in Shakespeare's plays[4]; Madeleine Doran has reminded us of "multiple unity" as an aesthetic principle for the Elizabethans[5]; more recently, Richard Levin has provided a full length study of the multiple plot in the age of Shakespeare.[6] But to establish such links (or "spatial" relationships), critics must often resort to very subtle reasoning, a kind of mental gymnastics that would be difficult to demand of an audience watching a play for the first (or even second) time. I am not, I hasten to add, challenging the assumptions of such critics or even quarreling with their conclusions; such relationships are there and can be quite revealing. But would not a dramatist of Shakespeare's caliber have been able in some way to call the attention of his audience in the theater to such links? The visual analogue, especially suited to the open stage, could readily have served as one such signal.

Let me start with a classic example. By now surely every reader is aware that the Gadshill robbery in Act 2 of *1 Henry IV* bears some relation to the rebellion in the main plot that climaxes at Shrewsbury. But does such a relationship exist solely on an abstract or spatial plane, available only to a kind of retrospective reasoning process? Or can this link be established or realized for an attentive audience watching a performance? Consider first the robbery scene. After the merchants have been robbed by four figures (Falstaff, Gadshill, Peto, and Bardolph), the stage direction reads: *"As they are sharing, the prince and Poins set upon them"* (2.2.93); when interrupted by Hal and Poins, the four thieves are somehow sharing or dividing the spoils, probably grouped around their loot that is laid out in front of them. A few scenes later (act 3, sc. 1) Shakespeare again brings on stage four figures, this time Hotspur, Glendower, Worcester, and Mortimer, and again has the four grouped around an object of common interest (this time a map of England) and again has them dividing the spoils (this time England itself). With no strain a director could block these two scenes so that the analogy would be emphatically clear. The result would be a link for the viewer's eye between two seemingly disparate actions that, we soon realize, are not as disparate as they first appear. There is, of course, much more to the analogy; thus, the rerobbing at Gadshill by Prince Hal anticipates his equivalent role in putting down Hotspur, spelled out in the latter's dying comment—"O Harry, thou hast robbed me of my youth!'' (5.4.76). But my primary concern here is with the visual analogy between the scenes in Acts 2 and 3, a linkage for the eye that could call the attention of a viewer to a relationship far less obvious to the reader faced with the printed page. Such an analogy, moreover, would be more readily perceived in a production on an uncluttered open stage than in a typical modern performance.

Unfortunately, most visual analogues are far less accessible than this one. The lack of stage directions, indeed the lack of evidence in general, makes analysis difficult; we have no videotapes of the original productions, no photographs, no extensive reviews, few if any detailed accounts. Nonetheless, when the potential for such an effect is recognized, many details fall into place. Thus, there are numerous examples of what I call the short-term analogue whereby a link is established within a brief span of dramatic time to make a point quickly and deftly. For example, at the outset of act 2, scene 2 of *The Tempest* the stage direction reads: *"Enter Caliban with a burden of wood"*; at the beginning of the next scene the stage direction tells us: *"Enter Ferdinand, bearing a log."* Although critics may disagree in interpreting this relationship, quickly (within less than two hundred lines) a link has been established for our eyes, an analogue that could help to structure our experience of the play, especially if Caliban and Ferdinand are viewed as contrasting figures taking different routes that lead to quite different rewards.

More significant but harder to substantiate are the longer term analogues that range over a broader expanse of dramatic time. As demonstrated by the Gadshill robbery, such a visual analogy can link two different plots or integrate comic and more serious actions or foreshadow later events. A particularly striking example is set up by the First Player's description of Pyrrhus and Priam at the end of Act 2 of *Hamlet*. Pyrrhus is here characterized as the archetypal dire revenger—"hellish," "roasted in wrath and fire," covered "with coagulate gore," "horridly tricked / With blood of father, mothers, daughters, sons"; eventually, we are told, he makes "malicious sport" by mincing Priam's limbs (2.2.444–52, 501–2). But how is the Player to deliver the central part of his speech? Is it only a rhetorical presentation, a declamation, or is there some stage business to accompany it?

The text, it seems to me, definitely calls for at least one bit of business. Thus, when Pyrrhus first sees Priam, we are told:

> For lo! his sword,
> Which was declining on the milky head

Of reverend Priam, seemed i' th' air to stick.
So as a painted tyrant Pyrrhus stood,
And like a neutral to his will and matter
Did nothing.

(465–70)

This verbal picture of the revenger with his sword poised in the air is sustained for over ten lines until:

after Pyrrhus' pause,
Aroused vengeance sets him new awork,
And never did the Cyclops' hammers fall
On Mars' armor, forg'd for proof eterne,
With less remorse than Pyrrhus' bleeding sword
Now falls on Priam.

(475–80)

There is no difficulty here for the reader; certainly the picture is clear, even overdone. But for an actor or director, the key words are "for lo!" and "now" (465, 480), terms that cry out for physical action with a sword. By introducing only this one prop, a director could take his audience beyond the words alone to a picture of the revenger in action and, more specifically, a picture of the revenger first pausing with his sword in the air and then following through to commit a ghastly murder.

Once this stage image is established, the analogue can be vividly displayed in the prayer scene. This time Hamlet, not Pyrrhus, stands over Claudius, not Priam; but visually the parallel could be quite clear, especially if the actors and director perceive the analogy and use similar blocking and gestures to heighten it (for example, by having one of the players in the earlier scene portray the kneeling Priam). Again, the text firmly supports the parallel. So, Hamlet's reaction to the sight of the kneeling, oblivious king has all the trappings of purposeful revenge: "Now might I do it pat, now 'a is a-praying, / And now I'll do't" (3.3.73–74). But then follows his version of Pyrrhus's pause: "That would be scann'd" (75). For reasons that have horrified many readers, the hero concludes: "Up sword, and know thou a more horrid hent"; a moment for revenge must be chosen "that has no relish of salvation in't" (88, 92). Like Pyrrhus, Hamlet has raised his sword over his enemy and then paused with that sword in mid air. To be sure, the hero does either sheathe that sword or carry it off stage in his hand, thereby (for the moment) differentiating himself from the bloody revenger of

Act 2. But for many readers and viewers, Hamlet's stated reason for putting up his sword (his desire for the damnation as well as the death of his enemy) seems as black and as hellish as Pyrrhus's rationale. Any distinction between the two may be short-lived, moreover, because in the next scene Hamlet *does* use the sword, making his pass through the arras to kill Polonius.

The many implications of this important analogue for this complex and perplexing tragedy lie beyond the scope of this essay. I am primarily concerned here with the device itself, the linking analogue directed at the viewer's eye that sets up a suggestive relationship between two figures, a relationship that should give *us* pause. Such a device could call attention to the similarity between Hamlet and Pyrrhus or, indeed, could heighten the contrast. Either way, Shakespeare has set up a constant (Pyrrhus) in an earlier movement of the play and then played off his protagonist against that constant through this emphatic theatrical technique. Such a device, to repeat, could be particularly effective upon the Elizabethan open stage where an audience would be watching actors in costume performing on a bare, uncluttered platform without elaborate sets or properties, without any "placing" of the action. The few props that *are* used (here, the sword) and the emphatic gestures or stage business (here, the raised sword, the pause, and the subsequent follow through or putting up) can become even more striking or memorable because there is so little competition for the eye to draw our attention away from this sequence of potent visual images.[7]

Given this potential for linking analogues on the open stage, consider the implications for the modern critic, director, and editor. Growing emphasis upon the theatrical dimension of Shakespeare's plays has yielded new insights and spawned new problems; at the least, scholars have recently been devoting more attention to the evidence provided by stage directions and signals in the dialogue. But any treatment of staging and dramatic meaning must take into account the possibility that the logic or rationale behind a given moment may be based upon Elizabethan assumptions not fully consistent with modern expectations drawn from Ibsen, Freud, Henry James, and Stanislavski. Thus, as demonstrated by the Gadshill robbery or the First Player's speech, an event in an Elizabethan play, especially an event with distinctive appeal for the eye on the open stage, need not be considered solely as an end in itself, an expression of "character" or "theme" for that moment, but could equally well realize its logic and full significance as part of a larger pattern that transcends the individual scene. The full meaning or effect would then only be available when an analogous moment or a strong visual echo follows or when a series of such moments provides an accretion of meaning (a situation familiar to readers adept at tracing patterns of verbal imagery). Behind many apparently puzzling moments in Shakespeare's plays may lie a logic based upon patterning or analogy.

Modern spectacles, however, can prevent the director or editor or critic from seeing such moments clearly. Thus, in modern productions the Elizabethan penchant for analogy or multiple unity often collides with a director's sense of dramatic economy or psychological realism, with the obvious result being a truncated acting script. Let me cite two examples from the Oregon Shakespearean Festival of 1976. First, in his rendition of *King Lear*, director Pat Patton (to conserve dramatic time and keep the focus upon Lear and Cordelia) did not bring on stage the dead bodies of Goneril and Regan. This concern with heightening the effect of the final moments, however, diminished the full resonance of Edmund's "the wheel is come full circle" (5.3.175), especially the potentially meaningful visual echo of the opening scene, the last time the audience had seen the old king on stage with all three of his daughters. Shakespeare's informing pattern, a final turning of his dramatic wheel, was sacrificed to a modest gain in narrative pace. Again, in his heavily cut acting script for *2 Henry VI* (an episodic play that gains its coherence from diverse yet analogous moments), director Jerry Turner omitted from act 3, scene 2 the appearance on stage of the recently murdered Humphrey of Gloucester in his bed and, in the next scene, had the Cardinal die not in bed but kneeling on the upper stage, grasping the railing. Since bed scenes were not that common on the Elizabethan stage, to present two figures on their deathbeds in consecutive scenes is to set up an obvious and striking relationship that, among other things, may help to explain the logic behind the Cardinal's death (indeed, the actor who played the Cardinal was overheard complaining that no one could tell him from what ailment he was supposed to be dying). But the director's search for economy and faster tempo eliminated the logic of the original pairing, however interpreted, as well as the highly theatrical signal Shakespeare had provided for his audience. In neither case would such patterning have resolved all the problems of the two plays; nonetheless, lost for the viewer was a significant link built into the original design.

For various reasons, the logic of analogy will remain alien to the actor and director. Rather, the actor seeking "his" Hamlet will be more concerned with the emotional logic of the prayer scene than with any potential link to Pyrrhus and will usually resist strenuously any parallel blocking imposed upon him. For most actors and directors, to present identical staging of two such moments cuts against the modern theatrical grain. But if our concern is with *Hamlet* rather than with Hamlet, we will only realize the full richness of such a moment when we place it in Shakespeare's carefully orchestrated continuum (that may include Laertes waving a sword in act 4, sc. 5). The actor or director's "feel" for the scene should not obscure the patterned logic woven into the fabric of the tragedy by the original craftsman. "Good theater" is not incompatible with a larger, coherent view of the diverse events in a Shakespearean play.

The critic too can be highly selective when dealing with such situations, although his omissions or changes in emphasis are often less obvious than those of the director. Still, the same problems and dangers pertain, especially when strong theatrical signals are ignored or misinterpreted. Consider one curious, intrusive detail—the Duke of York's boots in *Richard II*. Thus, after discovering the plot against Henry IV that includes his son, Aumerle, York quickly makes his decision:

> YORK.
> Bring me my boots! I will unto the king.
> *His Man enters with his boots*.
> DUCHESS.
> Strike him, Aumerle. Poor boy, thou art amazed.—
> [*To York's Man*]
> Hence, villain! Never more come in my sight.
> YORK.
> Give me my boots, I say!
> [*Servant does so and exit.*]   (5.2.84–87)

Since there is no equivalent stage direction elsewhere in Shakespeare's plays, the verbal and visual heightening of York's boots is unusual and puzzling. Editors usually add their own stage directions (like the bracketed insertions above) to make more sense out of the two lines of the Duchess, but few editors or critics treat the logic of the scene or the curious insistence upon the boots. One exception is Sheldon P. Zitner who finds here "harsh geriatric slapstick." "Drawing on a pair of Renaissance riding boots," he argues, "could not have been among the more graceful endeavours of the age. Drawing them on in a rage would add to the difficulty, as would a shouting wife—whether one leaned unsteadily on a servant or sprawled in a chair while the unruly woman stood above one."[8] The possibility of a tug-of-war over the boots is enhanced by York's exit line ("Make way, unruly woman!") and his earlier "away, fond woman" (110, 101). Still, an interpretation based solely upon the potential comic effect treats a highly italicized theatrical moment in terms that isolate its significance from the rest of the play.

But an Elizabethan stage convention for the viewer's eye may be relevant here, a convention associated with the theater rather than with the learned tradition in treatises or the visual arts (the usual hunting ground for iconic or emblematic details). Thus, in stage directions from a wide range of plays, boots (and other parts of the riding costume) are used as a dramatic shorthand to denote on the open stage a journey recently completed, often with the associations of haste and anticipation. In *Friar Bacon and Friar Bungay*, Greene directs: "*Enter* Lacy, Warren, Ermsby, *booted and spurred*," while later in the scene Lacy announces: "We have hied / And posted all this night to Fressingfield";[9] similarly, in *James IV*, Greene directs: "*Enter* Sir Bartram, with Eustace *and others, booted*."[10] In *The History of King Leir*, the suitors to Goneril and Regan are first seen hastening to their brides: "*Enter the King of Cornwall and his man booted and spurd, a riding wand, and a letter in his hand*," and a few lines later: "*Enter the King of Cambria booted and spurd, and his man with a wand and a letter*."[11] The convention was probably widespread, even though extant texts often omit specific details or stage directions; for example, only the 1597 "bad" quarto of *Romeo and Juliet* indicates that at 5.1.11 Romeo's man, Balthasar, should enter "*booted*." The potential associations attached to such stage boots are clearest in Act 5 of *2 Henry IV*. First, Justice Shallow urges Falstaff not to depart with the injunction: "Come, come, come, off with your boots" (5.1.48). Falstaff's reaction to the news of Henry IV's death then includes "get on thy boots. We'll ride all night" and "Boot, boot, Master Shallow. I know the young king is sick for me. Let us take any man's horses" (5.3.128, 131–32). While awaiting the coronation procession in the final scene, Falstaff argues that his zeal, devotion, and "earnestness of affection" will be evident in his willingness "to ride day and night" and "not to have patience to shift me" but rather "to stand stained with travel, and sweating with desire to see him" (5.5.13–27). The boots and travel– stained costume are thereby interpreted by the wearer as an index to his commitment— "as if there were nothing else to be done but to see him" (26–27).

Falstaff's lines provide a useful transition back to *Richard II*. Thus, at the end of act 2, scene 1, Northumberland reveals Bolingbroke's imminent return to two disaffected lords; when he asks them if they wish to join him "in post to Ravenspurgh" or "stay and be secret," Ross responds: "To horse, to horse! Urge doubts to them that fear" and Willoughby: "Hold out my horse, and I will first be there" (2.1.296–300). Two scenes later, after first Northumberland and then Harry Percy have offered their services to the returning Bolingbroke, Northumberland introduces the two nobles with: "Here comes the Lords of Ross and Willoughby, / Bloody with spurring, fiery red with haste" (2.3.57–58). The allusion to "spurring" may or may not imply actual spurs or boots; nonetheless, Ross and Willoughby are here acting out their choice of Bolingbroke over Richard II and, like Falstaff, have expressed that choice through their haste that, according to stage convention, could readily be conveyed summarily through their riding costume. Shakespeare, it should be noted here, does not follow Holinshed, who had Ross and Willoughby join Bolingbroke earlier at Ravenspurgh (as suggested by Northumberland at the end of act 2, sc. 1), a change that sets up this highly visible entrance of two figures newly committed to the duke. If Ross and Willoughby were booted in the original production, their choice to follow the comet of Bolingbroke rather than the sinking star of Richard is associated visually with riding costume and haste. In addition, if the bringers of bad tidings to Richard in act 3, scene 2 (Salisbury and Scroop) are unbooted and different in demeanor from these two lords, the contrast between the newly-fired commitment to Henry and the failing allegiances to the reigning king could be further enhanced.

York's calling for his boots and his exit in act 5, scene 2 would then correspond to the departure of the two lords in act 2, scene 1, while his arrival, booted, to the king in act 5, scene 3 would parallel the arrival of Ross and Willoughby "bloody with spurring, fiery red with haste" to Bolingbroke in act 2, scene 3. Moreover, both key scenes, act 2, scene 3 and act 5, scene 3, are about divided allegiances. In the earlier scene, York, the symbol of Richard II's power in England as his Lord Governor, had provided limited resistance to the returning Bolingbroke before announcing that he would "remain as neuter" (159); in the later sequence, however, it is York himself (rather than Ross and Willoughby) who, through his haste, acts out a spirited commitment to Henry, now the *de facto* king. The figures who burst in upon Henry in act 5, scene 3 again act out divided loyalties in England (especially if York is booted

while Aumerle and the Duchess are not), with the switch in York's role
(as opposed to act 2, sc. 3) telling us a great deal about new allegiances
under the new king (reflected also in York's account to his Duchess at
the beginning of act 5, sc. 2 of the crowd reactions to Richard and
Henry). The one stage direction from act 5, scene 2 and the hints in the
dialogue would then be the only surviving evidence of a visual pattern
used to single out and link together figures who choose the new king
over old allegiances, whether political or familial.

But to stop here is to miss the third and potentially most interesting
part of the series. For immediately after the departure of the king and the
York family in act 5, scene 3, the Folio reads *"Enter Exton and
Seruants"* and the Quarto reads *"Manet sir Pierce Exton, &c."* After
recounting the king's words (*"Have I no friend will rid me of this living
fear?"*), Exton proceeds:

> And speaking it, he wishtly looked on me,
> As who should say, 'I would thou wert the man
> That would divorce this terror from my heart!'
> Meaning the king at Pomfret. Come, let's go.
> I am the king's friend, and will rid his foe.

(5.4.7–11)

Exton's purposeful departure at this point could readily parallel the
exits at the end of act 2, scene 1 and York's exit in act 5, scene 2.[12]
Again a figure has chosen Henry over Richard, but this choice leads not
to a pledge of service or to a series of kneelings but to the murder of the
deposed king. Moreover, in the major scene that follows, as in act 2,
scene 3, act 3, scene 2, act 5, scene 3, and act 5, scene 6, the kingly
figure on stage faces a series of entrants—the groom, the keeper, and
finally Exton and his men (eight in Holinshed, an unspecified number in
Shakespeare). I can offer no proof that the entering Exton would have
been booted, but the Quarto stage direction (*"The murderers rush in"*)
certainly is consistent with the entrances of Ross and Willoughby in act
2, scene 3 or York in act 5, scene 3. In the final scene, the king (in
contrast to Richard in act 3, sc. 2) is greeted with good news about
various rebels from first Northumberland, then Fitzwater, and then
Hotspur, only to be confronted finally with: *"Enter Exton, with the
coffin."* Exton has made the same choice as Willoughby, Ross, and
York, but the former associations boots/haste/commitment now must
include blood/guilt/conscience/Cain (*"Lords, I protest my soul is full of
woe / That blood should sprinkle me to make me grow"*—5.6.45–46).

I certainly cannot prove conclusively that, in a performance of *Richard II* in the 1590s, Willoughby, Ross, and Exton would have been booted. But the text does provide theatrical italics for York's boots in act 5, scene 2; careful consideration of this highly visible accessory then does lead the modern reader to analogous situations under Richard II and Henry IV that heighten major themes and links. The final appearance of Exton with the coffin, moreover, reinforces such patterned thinking. As often noted, this play starts just after the political murder of Gloucester, so, in the final moments, Exton takes Mowbray's place while Henry, like Richard, has on his hands a kinsman's blood, a taint that will haunt him and his reign. Such links and emphases, to be sure, can survive without recourse to boots. But in performance before an audience, then or now, the analogous situations involving booted figures in haste acting out their commitments to Bolingbroke could be obvious and theatrically meaningful, especially on the unencumbered open stage. The stage direction and stage business from *Richard II*, act 5, scene 2 can thereby lead the modern critic, editor, or director not only to a new insight but to a distinctive way of making the structure and meaning of this play visually accessible to any audience.

Given the limited evidence, the skeptic may well doubt that my suggested stagings would have been carried out under Shakespeare's direction. Nonetheless, I do not feel that I have distorted such scenes or even gone against prevailing interpretations. Rather, by adding very little I have sought to heighten points or relationships already noted by careful readers working in their studies but points that could be far more obvious in performance, especially on the Elizabethan open stage. Although modern readers praise Shakespeare's craftsmanship and even his expertise in theatrical (as opposed to poetic or literary) matters, they have not confronted the full implications of that craftsmanship. Thus, if we take for granted iterative verbal or imagistic patterns woven through the fabric of the plays, can we afford to ignore the same principle at work for the eye (as opposed to the ear) of the viewer? Are we ready to conclude that the dramatic poet who took such obvious care in developing iterative verbal imagery was unwilling or unable to use patterns for the eye to reinforce his effects for audiences in the theater? Most critics, to be sure, prefer working with a text, not a play in performance or a play in potentia; similarly, most directors prefer streamlined acting versions that often omit moments like the Player's speech. But the words alone are only part of the total effect; modern audiences, moreover, nurtured by the cinema, would not be surprised by a patterned structure based upon analogues and visual repetition with the links perhaps clearer on an uncluttered open stage than on film. In other words, if we do assume that Shakespeare knew his craft and act on that assumption, we may indeed discover such language for the eye as an integral part of his best plays.

In conclusion, let me emphasize some simple yet basic principles for that modern reader who wishes to do justice to the visual dimension of Shakespeare's plays. First, any firm evidence about theatrical details, whether York's boots or Gloucester's eyes or Pyrrhus's sword, should be prized and given the careful scrutiny usually reserved for major speeches or verbal images. Second, the modern critic or director or editor should assume, until proven otherwise, that Shakespeare knew what he was doing and should therefore seek strenuously the logic or purpose behind the clear theatrical signals that do survive. And finally, that logic should not be limited to easy, modern assumptions about comedy or psychology or stage realism or to arguments confined to an individual scene but should encompass other possibilities, especially those linked to that larger sense of analogy or pattern demonstrably there throughout Elizabethan drama. In the sixteenth century, "to give one the boots" meant "to make game of" or "to make foolish."[13] I doubt the relevance of this proverb to the stage direction in *Richard II*, but it could apply to that modern reader unwilling or unable to appreciate the richness and complexity of Shakespeare's dramaturgy for the open stage.

NOTES

1. For a helpful summary of our present knowledge, see Richard Hosley, "The Playhouses and the Stage," in *A New Companion to Shakespeare Studies*, ed. Kenneth Muir and S. Schoenbaum (Cambridge, England, 1971), pp. 15–34. See also T. J. King, "The Stage in the Time of Shakespeare: A Survey of Major Scholarship," *Renaissance Drama* 4 (1971): 199–235.

2. See the chapters on dramaturgy and staging in Bernard Beckerman, *Shakespeare at the Globe 1599–1609* (New York, 1962).

3. Richard Southern, *The Open Stage* (London, 1953), p. 73.

4. See, for example, H. T. Price, "Mirror-Scenes in Shakespeare," in *Joseph Quincy Adams Memorial Studies*, ed. J. McManaway *et al.* (Washington, D.C., 1948), pp. 101–13 and Paul Aldus, "Analogical Probability in Shakespeare's Plays," *Shakespeare Quarterly* 6 (1955): 397–414.

5. Madeleine Doran, *Endeavors of Art* (Madison, Wis., 1954), p. 6 and passim.

6. Richard Levin, *The Multiple Plot in English Renaissance Drama* (Chicago and London, 1971).

7. For a fuller discussion of linking analogues, including examples from many non-Shakespearean plays, see the third chapter of my book, *Elizabethan Drama and the Viewer's Eye* (Chapel Hill, N.C., 1977).

8. "Aumerle's Conspiracy" *Studies in English Literature* 14 (1974): 247–48.

9. Daniel Seltzer, ed., *Regents Renaissance Drama* (Lincoln, Neb., 1963), 14.38.s.d., pp. 105–6.

10. Norman Sanders, ed., *Revels Plays* (London, 1970), 1.3.O.s.d.

11. Ed. W. W. Greg and R. Warwick Bond for the Malone Society (Oxford, 1907), lines 398–99, 408–9. In *When You See Me, You Know Me*, Will Sommers enters "*booted and spurred, blowing a horne*" (ed. F. P. Wilson and John Crow for the Malone Society, Oxford, 1952, lines 198–99). The opening stage direction of *Look About You* has two figures enter "*with ryding wandes in theyr handes, as if they had beene new lighted*" (ed. W. W. Greg for the Malone Society, Oxford, 1913).

12. A link between York and Exton could have been suggested or reinforced by a verbal link in Holinshed. Thus, York, having discovered the plot, "in a great rage caused his horsses to be sadled out of hand, and spitefullie reproouing his sonne of treason . . . he *incontinentlie* mounted on horssebacke to ride towards Windsore to the king, to declare vnto him the malicious intent of his complices." A few pages later, Holinshed writes that Exton, after overhearing the king's comment, "*incontinentlie* departed from the court, with eight strong persons in his companie, and came to Pomfret" (my italics). See *Holinshed's Chronicles of England, Scotland, and Ireland* (London, 1808), 3: 10, 14. "Incontinentlie" on the page could have been translated into boots, haste, and travel stains on stage.

13. See Morris Palmer Tilley, *A Dictionary of the Proverbs in England in the Sixteenth and Seventeenth Centuries* (Ann Arbor, Mich., 1966), B 537, p. 59. See *The Two Gentlemen of Verona*, 1.1.27.

6

Choral Juxtaposition in Shakespeare*

ALFRED HARBAGE

CHARLES LAMB REMARKS IN ONE OF HIS LETTERS THAT IT IS THE "SUM total" of Shakespeare that affects us: the separate parts even of his princely pieces looks beggarly and bald when divorced from "connection and circumstance." "Everything," says Lamb, "in heaven and earth, in man and in story, in books and in fancy, acts by confederacy, by juxtaposition, by circumstance and place." The conviction thus expressed may explain why Lamb, whom Bradley considered the best critic of the nineteenth century, produced so little formal criticism. He was aware of the enormous difficulties and risks. Criticism even at its best is bound to distort and diminish. Since it cannot encompass the "sum total," it must always be something other and something less than the work of art itself.

Nevertheless we cannot, or at least will not, cease writing criticism. The practical question is, how best we can reduce the risks by recognizing the difficulties? In drama the initial difficulty is that the "sum total" of the work that descends to us from a former age must be hypothesized. No play of Shakespeare exists as a fixed object that we can contemplate in common, as, let us say, could an original audience at the Globe. What we habitually speak of as the play is the script of the play. It supplies the verbal component and indications of the action, but it is not the whole work. We may scrutinize some portion of the script, yet fail to see the corresponding portion of the play. As literary persons, our natural concentration upon words may even divert our attention from total effects.

Acting upon the suggestion of Lamb's word "juxtaposition," I shall try to illustrate what I mean. The mere entrance of a given character at a given moment may serve as silent commentary, apart from anything the

*Paper read at the annual meeting of The Modern Language Association of America, held in Philadelphia in 1960.

character says or does. An early scene in *Macbeth* provides an instance. A dialogue upon the execution of the treacherous Thane of Cawdor is thus concluded by King Duncan:

> There's no art
> To find the mind's construction in the face.
> He was a gentleman on whom I built
> An absolute trust. *Enter Macbeth, Banquo, Ross, and Angus.*
> O worthiest cousin....
>
> (1.4.11–14)

This entrance of Macbeth, present Thane of Cawdor, upon such a pronouncement about the past Thane of Cawdor lends the words the quality of a conjuration. Past Thane of Cawdor—present Thane of Cawdor—again false face may hide "what the false heart doth know" (1.7.82). The original Cawdor, a character mysteriously compounded of good and evil, whom we have never seen but of whom we have constantly heard, functions in these early scenes as a prefiguration of Macbeth himself. Who can deny the calculation involved in this particular entrance at this particular moment, the silent prompting, canceling our right to say, as Bridges once said, that the dramatist obscures his design in the early scenes of this tragedy? Here the critic caught the dialogue but missed the play, despite the intimations of the script. He missed it because there is nothing poetic or striking about the words, "Enter Macbeth, Banquo, Ross, and Angus," and because Macbeth's name is but one of four. But Duncan's particularizing greeting, "O worthiest cousin...," and Macbeth's precedence in order of entrance focuses attention upon him—another "gentleman" upon whom Duncan builds "an absolute trust."

Some famous passages in Shakespeare strike a sympathetic chord in the modern mind because of their reductive quality. We do not want them too wholeheartedly received as Shakespearean gospel, but in coping with the young cynics in our classes, we might profitably point out the technique of silent commentary through juxtaposition instead of relying upon earnest expression of our own idealism. Falstaff's speech dishonoring honor precedes the stage direction, "Enter Worcester and Sir Richard Vernon" (act 5, sc. 2) and is forthwith chorally qualified. In the preceding scenes Hotspur has been shown not, as Shaw fancied, as the barbarian aristocrat in love with death as refuge from his big-brawned emptiness, but as a brave and frightened man. He learns that the odds against him are decisive, and as one after another piece of frosty news is dinned into his ears, he repeatedly quails, then recovers:

> A perilous gash, a very limb lopped off.
> And yet, in faith, it is not!

> (4.1.43–44)

or again,

> No more, no more! Worse than the sun in March
> This praise doth nourish agues. Let them come.
> (4.1.111–12)

There is nothing suicidal in this. He is meeting the first obligation of the military leader, containing his fear lest his followers lose heart. He behaves on the eve of Shrewsbury as Henry V behaves on the eve of Agincourt, and as Richard II fails to behave at Harlech. And we are shown that we will accept honorable compensation if it is offered. The last words we hear in his camp are these:

> BLUNT. I would you would accept of grace and love.
> HOTSPUR. And may be so we shall.
> BLUNT.	Pray God you do.

> (4.3.112–13)

And now, after Falstaff's speech dispraising honor, appear Worcester and Vernon. They have been entrusted with the King's offer to Hotspur of "grace and love," but to save their own skins they withhold it. Vernon's whispered words at Hotspur's entrance have the ring of Pilate's, "Deliver what you will, I'll say 'tis so" (5.2.26). The method of scene division in sophisticated texts, from the first folio onwards, may obscure the fact, but Falstaff's famous speech, in actual performance, is the prologue to this action. There is no division in the quartos—just Falstaff's "practical" devaluation of honor, his exit, and then "Enter Worcester and Sir Richard Vernon" to engage in the one thoroughly base action protrayed in the serious scenes of this play. In consequence the honorable Hotspur perishes, but so also do the dishonorable Worcester and Vernon. Who has dishonor? They that die o' Thursday. Falstaff's speech is funny, and also fairly sensible, but it is less conclusive than it seems to be when isolated from the juxtaposed action of the play.

Jaques's speech on the seven ages of man, each age emptier than the last, is followed by the direction, "Enter Orlando, with Adam" (2.7.166). A character bearing another in his arms is an emblem of value in these plays—Bedford with his son, Lear with his daughter—Shakespeare does not use it casually. Jaques has supplied a commentary on the woeful pageant of life, inspired by the case of Orlando and Adam itself. Now they appear, their appearance a commentary upon the commentary, silently juxtaposed. What Jaques has said is, within its limits, true; indeed Orlando will soon be writing poor sonnets upon his mistress' eyebrow, while Adam will hereafter be assigned to "mere oblivion" in the play itself. But Adam is not the purse-hugging pantaloon of Jaques's sixth age of man, and Orlando's ludicrous postures as romantic lover are somewhat dignified by this prior proof of his capacity for love of a different kind. With the binding attachments of old to young, young to old, of generation to generation, the conclusion of the single life may not be quite "sans everything" (2.7.166). The suspicion of sentimentality inevitably attending the direct affirmation of such a truth may explain why Shakespeare elects to state it silently, but he does state it. Jaques's speech meets the structural need of filling an interval while Orlando goes to fetch Adam, but great artists are great economists, their means serving multiple ends. "Enter Orlando with Adam"—the words on the page are colorless, but to take Jaques's speech without recognizing their implication is to take its sentiments raw.

Again, Edmund's celebrated speech, "This is the excellent foppery of the world" (1.2.115), which Hazlitt deemed "worth a million," is offered at a discount. Here an entrance is cued in an oddly suggestive way. At Edmund's word "Edgar," the latter makes his appearance, and Edmund breaks off with "—and pat he comes, like the catastrophe of the old comedy." The "old comedy"? This could not mean the "old comedy" of Aristophanes, nor the "new comedy" of Menander with its Roman and Renaissance progeny. All English comedy, as we think of comedy, was "new" when *King Lear* was written. By "old comedy" Shakespeare surely intends the moral interludes, where the denoument, the "catastrophe," is usually personified, as in the case of Mercy in the *Morality of Mankind*. Edmund is saying in effect, "Enter Good to me, Evil." Although proud of this little footnote, I must concede its dispensability. Edgar may not yet be identified as Good, but Edmund is already identified as Evil, and it is with the speech of Edmund as so identified that we are concerned:

This is the excellent foppery of the world, that / when we are sick in fortune, often the surfeits of our own / behavior, we make guilty of our disasters the sun, the / moon, and stars; as if we were villains on necessity; fools / by heavenly compulsion; knaves, thieves, and treachers / by spherical predominance; drunkards, liars, and adul-/ terers by an enforced obedience of planetary influence; / and all that we are evil in, by a divine thrusting on. An / admirable evasion of whoremaster man, to lay his goatish / disposition on the charge of a star . . .

(1.2.115–24)

"Worth a million," said the stalwart Hazlitt, and perhaps it is, but the question is not what the speech is worth when excerpted for use in the open ethical market, but what it is worth in the play, or rather what it *is* in the play. When Iago makes an almost identical speech, it is addressed to one of his dupes, and of course the devil can quote scripture for his purpose. But Edmund is alone, and what shall we say if the devil quotes scripture when alone? That he is not *really* devil? Or that this is not *really* scripture? Both views have been strongly defended, but the indispensable gloss upon the speech is Lamb's dictum that everything "acts by confederacy, by juxtaposition, by circumstance and place." A speaker's own character, as cumulatively established, supplies a silent commentary upon everything a character says. Alone or with others Edmund is evil, and scripture ceases to be scripture in Edmund's mouth. The entrance of Edgar "like the catastrophe of the old comedy" here only underscores the obvious. A declaration of virtuous self-responsibility is transformed into a declaration of vicious self-sufficiency when spoken by an Edmund. An ever-meaningful juxaposition in Shakespeare is the word and the mouth that utters it.

One reason that there has been some distrust of criticism based upon iterative imagery is that the method has not been used cautiously. There is nothing wrong with the method itself: imagery truly does underscore themes and act as a unifying agent. But like everything else an image is affected "by circumstance and place." The risk is that the critic's groupings will slight immediate context and become a rival construct, substituting the critic's juxtapositions for the playwright's juxtapositions. In drama there is constant cross-commentary of images produced by auditory and those produced by visual means. This is the defining characteristic of drama as an art form: words chorus what the eye sees, and sights chorus what the ear hears in constant juxtaposition. As literary persons we are naturally interested in the images produced by words, but they are not the only ones. Like forms in the plastic arts, the mere presence, appearance, and groupings of actors on a stage form images, a product of the poet's imagination and part of his total vision. They can be so powerful as to modify everything we hear.

Upon his return from Ireland, Richard descants beautifully upon the miseries of kings. His words would coerce our sympathies utterly, as they did those of William Butler Yeats, were they not juxtaposed with the living image of Richard himself and the followers grouped about him. The king we see as well as hear prostrates himself upon the ground in a way that makes his followers wince. Their survival depends upon his fortitude. We must see these followers and what they see, as well as hear what Yeats hears. The Bishop of Carlell tells him in effect to stand up. In *King Lear* the concluding visual image is simply overwhelming—a pieta emblemizing all the heartaches of mankind. Words, of course, are spoken, unforgettable words, but it is impossible to abstract from them any judicial opinion on what we see. The surviving characters, the symbols flanking this central symbol, pass no judgment. They speak what they feel, not what they ought to say.

Words and images, associated with each other instead of with particular circumstance and place in the play where they appear, may not illuminate its art but only suggest an impoverishing homogeneity. Of course they need not be so exclusively associated, and the method of verbal linkage, and of isolating image clusters, need be no more distorting than other critical strategies. I have been speaking of "choral juxtaposition," and in our technological age the term may have an enticingly technological sound, but if elevated to the rank of a critical approach, it could produce another kind of myopia, an overvaluing of mere proximity, and discovery of relevances where none exist. The danger is devotion to method instead of to the material to which method is applied. It has certainly not been my intention to italicize the cliché that we must see Shakespeare's plays as plays, especially if it is taken to mean that they must be seen in the theatre to be understood.

I shall end as I began, with an allusion to Lamb. He was unable to see *King Lear* until he had ceased looking at performance of it. These were travesties in the theatre he knew, and Shakespearean performances can be travesties in any age, including our own. Staging a play does not automatically insure the functional relationship of its visual and auditory imagery. A play must be staged in the mind, with intelligent, imaginative, and respectful attention to the script before it can be staged in a theatre. In other words, those who stage plays and those who write about them toe the same starting line. Great plays beseech the intercession of good minds, if not great ones, and to assume that good minds are the exclusive possession of members of one's own profession is to offer living proof of the contrary.

7

Shakespeare's Directorial Eye: A Look at the Early History Plays

BARBARA HODGDON

I

SHAKESPEARE CONTROLS NOT ONLY WHAT WE HEAR BUT WHAT WE see, either at a live performance of one of his plays or at the performances we stage in our imaginations. Although the stage directions are often sparse or ambiguous, Shakespeare's heightened concern with the contextual and sequential values of his stage images and with the manipulation of his spectators' awarenesses and responses[1] through changes in dramatic focus[2] show that he approaches playwrighting with a directorial eye. To be sure, Shakespeare's texts, as they come to us, are not clear prompt copies; but we can discover enough about the directorial techniques that govern his presentational intentions to appreciate the ways in which he directs the director who chooses to work with his plays. As an effort in this direction, I should like to examine Shakespeare's syntax of stage pictures[3] and his use of dramatic focus in the early history plays—*1, 2,* and *3 Henry VI* and *Richard III*—touching on some of the comprehensive and specific effects of the plays as performed without limiting my investigation to the imagined realization of these effects in the Elizabethan theater, through Elizabethan stagecraft. Assuming, as most scholars now do, that Shakespeare authored all three *Henry VI* plays and that these plays and *Richard III* were composed in chronological order, it is possible to outline Shakespeare's general stylistic trend as a movement away from strict patterns (except where they remain a useful formalism) and the exterior narrative emphasis toward structures that commingle action with reaction, carrying the thrust of the drama through narrative movement that emphasizes interior thought and feeling.

Early Shakespeare is not "as you like it." In the *Henry VI* plays and in *Richard III*, Shakespeare's directorial techniques are unusually specific; he exercises rather strict controls over dramatic focus. Consequently, audience response is often directly channeled or limited in a particular moment, scene, or scenic sequence by what Shakespeare chooses to show and by how these dramatic facts and impressions are presented. Further, Shakespeare experiments with techniques that give each play an individualized vision—a particular look that reflects his dramatic and thematic concerns.

The plays are drawn together by strong external similarities—their common sources in English history, their use of political and social ideas and ideals that vividly inform Shakespeare's dramatic conception. There are also internal similarities to the look of the plays, the most obvious of which is Shakespeare's consistent use of large court scenes as an organizing feature. But the plays also differ from one another in their overall visual perspectives, and here the polar contrast is between *1 Henry VI*—Shakespeare's first experiment in broadly conceived historical drama—and *Richard III*, his first use of a single central character.

This contrast is immediately obvious in the opening stage pictures of the two plays. Compare the full sight and show of *1 Henry VI* act 1, scene 1:

> Dead March. Enter the Funeral of King Henry the Fifth, attended on by the Duke of Bedford, Regent of France; the Duke of Gloucester, Protector; the Duke of Exeter, the Earl of Warwick, the Bishop of Winchester, Heralds, &c.

with the first moments of *Richard III*:

> Enter Richard, Duke of Gloucester, solus.

One play requires our visual attention to relax, spreading objectively over a number of figures, presented as in a formal narrative frieze: we see the overall picture and patterning until movement or language signals a narrowed perspective on a particular figure or group of figures. The other shows us a subjective portrait that demands close attention. The opening of *1 Henry VI* contributes to our understanding of the social relevance of the action by showing us exterior, public perspectives, initiating one context of future actions. At the other extreme, Shakespeare shows us Richard alone, beginning his play with an interior, private point of view that he will continue throughout the stage action, focusing audience awareness of Richard's primary visibility, energy, and control over the play world. In each play, Shakespeare relies upon an extreme of dramatic focus to give us a reference point in stage space that controls or balances other ways of seeing. The procedure is swift and precise, and it is a hallmark of Shakespeare's directorial style in the early histories.

In all three *Henry VI* plays, Shakespeare depends upon heavily patterned, panoramic opening stage images to bring his audience into the play, giving us immediate sight of and insight into the world at court. Each image is organic, urgent, and direct, theatrically viable as spectacle alone. Here, there is a clear relationship between Shakespeare's visual vocabulary and the dramatic heritage of his predecessors and contemporaries—the pageantry of the mystery plays and of court ceremonies, triumphs, royal progresses, and processionals. The plays rely, in varying degrees, upon this inherited "vocabulary of motif"[4] that indicates at once the broad scope of the historical action and the social significance of that action through easily recognizable, visually engrossing pictorial images. The images that recur in the *Henry VI* plays, their variations blending into an overall, primarily visual impression, show a king surrounded by groups of nobles; panoramic views of the court; messengers entering with news, good or bad; battles, either individualized or presented as mass action; and the dead or dying, with the stillness that ensues. These large, simple effects, repeated for their gathering power, form a strong unifying and ordering device and establish a syntax of expressively concrete dramatic images that channel and direct men's responses.

II

On one level, gestures and stage pictures alone tell the story—what Brecht called the "gest of showing"[5]—and *1 Henry VI*, the most pictorial of the plays, illustrates Shakespeare's ability, at the beginning of his career, to shape the broad visual elements of his drama to some form beyond the incidental. What we see is of primary importance; and physical presentation often carries the entire weight of the drama, for Shakespeare seldom calls upon the imaginative vision of either the characters or the spectators of this play to enrich the expansive qualities of the narrative. The most comprehensive effects of the play derive from spatial change—from broad, outward, public action. And the look of the play reflects this breadth and scope: the continuing movement from

England to France and back again, the outdoor perspectives, the feelings of space—even if it is only linear space—evoked by the massed groupings of nobles.

Shakespeare conceives the dissension, faction, and controversy of his sources, the chronicles of Hall and Holinshed, within a fixed iconography based upon recurrent patterns of court pageantry, battles, funerals, and death. Pictures of conflict and opposition pervade the play: eighteen of the twenty-seven scenes indicated by most modern editors (1.2, 1.3, 1.4, 1.5, and 1.6; 2.1, 2.2, and 2.4; 3.1, 3.2, 3.3, and 3.4; 4.1, 4.2, 4.3, 4.4, and 4.6; and 5.2) focus on battle, either on the fields of France or in the courtrooms of England. Seven scenes (1.1, 2.4, 3.1, and 3.4, 4.1, 5.1 and 5.5) show some pageantry or court occasion; and seven scenes (1.1 and 1.4, 2.1 and 2.5, 3.2, 4.7, and 5.4) focus on death or on a funeral. Shakespeare interrupts or abbreviates both kinds of moments either by introducing enmity into the generalizing, stabilizing ceremonial pattern, as in act 4, scene 2 when Henry's coronation is marred by Sir John Fastolfe's cowardice and by the Vernon–Basset quarrel, or by cutting short the development of possible sympathetic feeling and its consequent narrowing focus (although he allows it, briefly, for the deaths of Talbot and Joan) through continuing narrative drive, thus fulfilling audience expectations of seeing the larger gestures of history.

Most scenes have an active, anticipatory movement that strengthens narrative progression. All but one (act 2, sc. 3: Talbot with the Countess of Auvergne) end in a forward reference, pointing toward the future either in terms of language—"I will do" or "I prophesy"—or more broadly, through using a scene (e.g., act 5, sc. 1, which introduces Henry's possible marriage; or act 5, sc. 2, which shows the French about to enter Paris) as an information bridge or as a way to place either past or future events in some controlled perspective. The broad narrative rhythms of the play attempt to convey the form and pressure of wide dramatic issues—the English succession, the reconciliation of the nobles, and the outcome of the war—rather than to explore individual relationships and responses. Shakespeare's primary sequential technique is an alternating focus, best seen in the battle between England and France (act 1, sc. 4–act 2, sc. 2), where the spectators' attention is held by the rapid succession of a number of snapshots through the total action. These represent Talbot surprised and Salisbury killed (act 1, sc. 4), Talbot and Joan in single combat (act 1, sc. 5), the victorious French (act 1, sc. 6), the French surprised and Talbot winning (act 2, sc. 1), and then, Talbot with Salisbury's body after the battle (act 2, sc. 2). Although Shakespeare's choice of Talbot and Joan as personages who reveal history has an effect of urgency and confirmation not given by the chronicles, the overall focus on both stresses their active roles, not their private moments; and their later deaths are conceived as structural markers of the total action of war rather than being seen only as personal crises.

Looking at *1 Henry VI* much as though it were a dumb show both broadens our perceptions of some of the meanings Shakespeare achieves simply through a repeated syntax of stage pictures and makes us aware that the language of the play offers rather limited opportunities for looking further into the play world, for seeing "in the mind's eye," with insight. Overall, the language draws attention, often self-consciously, to an event, as in the heavily patterned exchanges among the nobles in act 1, scene 1 or in act 2, scene 4, when Warwick remarks, in a retrospective overview, on the significance of the quarrel in the Temple Garden (2.4. 124–27). Rhetorical stasis, as in Mortimer's set speeches in act 2, scene 5 and in Talbot's psalms of war and death (act 4, sc. 6 and 7), provides some moments of pause in an otherwise busy surface impression, channeling audience understanding of a particular moment by framing a single point of view; but Shakespeare's major emphasis rests on a comprehensive, primarily active conception of history. Acts 4 and 5 bring a closer scrutiny of character, seen particularly in Talbot's final moments with his son (act 4, sc. 5), in Margaret's and Suffolk's "love duet" (act 5, sc. 3), and in Joan's encounter with her captors (act 5, sc. 4); but Shakespeare's growing interest in the range of effects made possible by an intimate focus on individual responses remains subordinate to the moments of pageantry, pomp, and battle that ask only for limited, easily evoked responses.

III

In *2 Henry VI*, although many stage images—public councils, ceremonies, battles, death—repeat the situations of *1 Henry VI*, there is more flexibility to the look of the play: both actors and audience are freed, through increasingly expressive language and through a strengthened scenic articulation that reconciles broad iconographic presentation with moments of private discourse, to see more aspects of both action and reaction in a greater variety of ways. The well-observed court scenes still stand as devices that focus attention on large issues and on cosmic grouping, but the increased insights into character and motivation offered by the privately conceived scenes qualify the meanings of both the previous court scenes and of the ones to come. This is, in part, a play about vision. Much depends upon what or how much the characters see of themselves and of the others, and upon how these contending points of view are revealed to the audience. The most striking changes of vision occur either as focus narrows quickly, stressing the separateness of an individual or a group; or as focus expands from a concentrated look at one or several persons to the released intensity of a broader perspective. In Acts 1–3, Shakespeare alternates between these extremes of wide and narrow focus in order to increase audience awareness of the discrepancies between public, cosmetic "shows" of love and duty and private, truthful thoughts, feelings, and reactions. In Acts 4 and 5, Shakespeare's juxtaposition of public and private views reveals the differences between Cade's forthrightness and the actions of the King and nobles. Overall, the shifting focus stresses the correlation between the designing political nature of the characters and the controlling political themes of the play, a relationship best seen (although it does not by any means articulate all the complexities of the play) by tracing Shakespeare's varying presentation of York and his dramatic surrogate, Jack Cade.

In act 1, scene 1, as attention moves away from the occasion of Margaret's welcome and the ratification of the articles of peace, York breaks through the others' speeches with a sustained outline of his desire, continuing and tightening the tones and tensions of the action thus far. The private quality of act 1, scene 2, where Gloucester chides Eleanor's ambition, has been prepared for by the narrowed focus on York; we will see their behavior through the shadow of York's decision to "make a show of love to proud Duke Humphrey" and, eventually, to claim the crown. When we next see York (act 1, sc. 3), it is within a public, generally accusatory atmosphere: his regency of France is questioned, his anger erupts against Suffolk, and he is accused as a traitor. These impressions yield to another public view of York acting now as the King's officer, arresting the Duchess of Gloucester for witchcraft (act 1, sc. 4). The ending of this scene hints toward a future private meeting with Salisbury and Warwick, where York asks for, and receives, support for his claim to the title (act 2, sc. 2). In the following scene, York is again in public, vindicated by the Horner–Peter combat; later (act 3, sc. 1) he is a relatively silent, though acquiescent, party to Gloucester's arrest and to the developing plot against his life. Called to Ireland, he again reveals his thoughts in private (3.1.331–83) and introduces Jack Cade, who takes up his role as actor-spectator-commentator throughout Act 4.

Up to the end of Act 3, Shakespeare has allowed audience attention to linger over the plotting and the detailed private behavior of certain characters, acknowledging visual and verbal comparisons of both incidental behavior and the larger event. But as soon as Cade takes the stage in act 2, scene 2, demanding urgency from all actions and response, Shakespeare's presentation of his comic behavior and his vigorous prose ensures that we will see him with some detachment. His extraordinary vitality—actions uncannily fused to speech—controls our perceptions of his practical single-mindedness, which is stressed visually by his stage presence. What we see literally depends upon what he does and says: he seems to body forth his "infinite numbers" alone. Thematically, Shakespeare uses the Cade material to give us a perspective on the limitations of a world where justice operates in black and white contrasts, where if a man writes, he is arrested (act 4, sc. 3) and if a man pleads for his life, he dies (act 4, sc. 7). The angle of vision is very foreign to Gloucester's paradigm for justice, but not so far removed from the ways of the plotters. Shakespeare measures, in these scenes, our vision of all that has gone before by placing it in Cade's exaggerated frame: "in order we are most out of order." Theatrically, the broad active scope of Act 4 contrasts with and seems to result from the earlier, more intense focus on the intrigues of the court, building a sense of comprehensive focus that prepares us for Act 5, where the Cade disorders and the earlier dissension are made complete and are reformalized by York's battle at St. Albans.

In these final moves, there are now only brief echoes of the internal formalities and secrecy of the scenes at court. York now acknowledges his private desires in public as he claims the crown (act 5, sc. 1); and the stage crackles with faction, brought, for the first time among these men, from the interior private rooms and places of power onto the open field. At last, as though repeating and clarifying the rhythms of the opening of the play, the rigid sidings of the battle show love and duty on trial in several perspectives—in the realm, among the nobles, in the family.

The ending brings little sense of a new and forthright patterning; but, insecure as it is, it does suggest a comprehensive focus that assesses our overall experience of *2 Henry VI* in terms of the political consequences following earlier intrigues and factions. In itself, this is a trenchant comment upon the facts, effects, and impressions Shakespeare has brought before our mind's eye. In *1 Henry VI*, he is fascinated by the spectacle of history; here, he directs his vision to men and their motives. Paradoxically, the narrowed viewpoint expands his drama: history has become his frame for evoking and communicating the designs he sees in the behavior of men.

IV

Shakespeare relies heavily upon three major directorial techniques to give structural integrity to *3 Henry VI* and to dramatize the disintegrative struggles of the Lancaster-York civil war. The overall conception depends upon ironic intensification within the design; and Shakespeare achieves this by consciously promoting ironic contrasts within sequences of stage images, by characterizing his persons so that they help to define the development of irony, and by controlling an iterative image theme of blood through elaborate repetition in all elements of the stagecraft, particularly in the presentational imagery of the play.

As a primary means of reinforcing this ironic vision, Shakespeare repeatedly shows his audience an event and then follows that event with a moment that points the discrepancy of awarenesses between characters and spectators. The play begins by setting up a central irony: both York and Henry seem to believe that York's takeover can be bloodless; but this is immediately qualified by Margaret's decision to defend her son's birthright (1.1.147–56; 215–56) and by York's broken oath and move toward battle (act 1, sc. 2). From here on, the blindness multiplies[6]: York is unaware of Rutland's murder; his murderers use it to mock him at his own death (act 1, sc. 4). Edward and Richard, ignorant of their father's death, are confident of victory until the news, coupled with Warwick's defeat, comes to spoil their success (act 2, sc. 1). Several brief battle scenes preface King Henry's meditative view of the father and son unaware that each has killed his kin (act 2, sc. 5). Warwick believes Clifford dead, and Edward asks that the groaning man "be gently us'd": both are unaware of Clifford's death beside them (act 2, sc. 6). In France, Margaret imagines Henry still in Scotland and is unaware of his capture; both she and Warwick are ignorant of Edward's marriage until messengers arrive with the news (act 3, sc. 1). Throughout Act 4, the reversals of fortune come fast: Edward lacks knowledge of Warwick's changed allegiance and of his alliance with Margaret (act 4, sc. 1 and 3). In a moment of liberty, Henry is unaware that Edward has been freed (act 4, sc. 6); later he praises his own rule just before he is captured by the Yorkists (act 4, sc. 8). In the next scene, Warwick is ignorant of Clarence's intent to desert him; and Edward is given a hero's sense of success just before this switch of allegiance. Warwick dies, lacking the knowledge that Margaret's forces are near by (act 5, sc. 2). A bit later, Edward marks the end of the battle (act 5, sc. 5); but the murder of Prince Edward follows in minutes, with Henry's murder after it. And finally, Edward proclaims a new reign of peace and joy in the face of Richard's hypocritical kiss (act 5, sc. 7).

Shakespeare's conception of his characters magnifies the effects of these ironies. As A. S. Cairncross puts it:

> . . .They are almost Morality types—the lustful Edward, perjured Clarence, the unscrupulously ambitious Richard, holy Henry, the revengeful Clifford, the she-wolf Margaret . . . . The very narrowness of their aims—revenge, ambition, pleasure—lends itself to the pervading irony. They are so many fragments in the chaos, heedless of the general course of events . . . .[7]

Because of the restrictions of vision imposed upon the characters, the dramatic effectiveness of Shakespeare's ironic conception depends, in large part, upon retrospection—upon remembering who killed whom and who said what under which circumstances to whom. To support and enhance this retrospection, Shakespeare makes a directorial choice in favor of a strong visual presentation of these ironies: the play has a very fast, active surface, punctuated by a heightened presentational imagery of blood and bloody deeds.

The rituals of bloodshed replace the court scenes of *1* and *2 Henry VI* as stage images that gather our perceptions of the action around single events, channeling and redirecting dramatic intentions and character relationships toward both the past and the future. Making ready for war, and the blood-letting, revenge, and retribution that follow, are the major "festivities" of *3 Henry VI*; Shakespeare patterns the physical gestures of blood so that they echo the broader rise-fall pattern of the ascending and descending blood lines of York and Lancaster. Thus the visual facts of violence form a structural network that directs audience awareness to the general reversals surrounding the broader thematic issues—the succession, kinship, kingship—and to these ironies as they are revealed for (and within) each character.

The presentational imagery of blood, displayed in the opening scene only in brief, shocking gestures (the bloody swords of Edward and Montague; Richard's show of Somerset's head), is forcefully taken up by the murders of Rutland and York (act 1, sc. 3 and 4), marking the height of the Lancastrians' victory. Shakespeare keeps the impression left by the Yorkist deaths alive by narrative reports (act 2, sc. 1 and 2) and by mechanical vows toward new revenge (act 2, sc. 3 and 4) before permitting the stage picture to generalize the particular horrors of the earlier violence in act 2, scene 5. Since narrative progression stops here in order to allow for Henry's meditation upon the ironies of war, the irony essential to the play—that bloodshed, separation, and death secure reconciliation is sharply defined and isolated. Shakespeare places this deliberately theatrical, extraordinarily resonant scene at a point in the total action where it can become a cross-reference, uniting both earlier and later acts of remembrance and revenge.

As the look at violence continues, we see, in the death of "bloody Clifford" and the Yorkists' mockery of his corpse (act 2, sc. 6), a recollective parallel to York's ritual slaughter. Revenge "measure for measure must be answered"; and the mechanistic chain seems complete with the suggested substitution of Clifford's head for York's on the city gates. Accordingly, Acts 3 and 4 show no physical violence; here, Shakespeare traces a long middle development, where blood ties in relation to the crown and quick reversals of allegiance and kingship asume more dramatic importance than blood revenge, before drawing the first two Acts and the last together by introducing further bloodshed. Now we see Warwick's death (act 5, sc. 2), and this is followed by attempts at balance and ordering before the final battle (act 5, sc. 3 and 4); but Shakespeare thwarts any expectation of ordering perspectives by showing two final deaths, ironically marking the fall of Lancaster by explicit echoes of the paired deaths of Rutland and York. These final presentational images of blood—the triple stabbing of Prince Edward (act 5, sc. 5) and Richard's murder of King Henry (act 5, sc. 6)—are more closely observed than the others, seen as private rather than public executions, foreshadowing Shakespeare's treatment of politic death in *Richard III*.

The end of the play shows Richard at the peak of his development. Henry's dying prophecy (5.6.35–56) and Richard's final soliloquy (5.6.61–93) obviously anticipate *Richard III*; and Tillyard's view that Shakespeare, impatient with his broad chronicle creations, shows more interest in Richard as a central character than in his historical themes, stresses this anticipation.[8] Yet Shakespeare does not concentrate exclusively on Richard's personal metamorphosis; there are many moments in *3 Henry VI* when others—Henry, York, Edward, Warwick, and Margaret—demand and receive equal or more compelling attention than Richard does. In fact, we could easily complain that *3 Henry VI* is not more of a "Richard play"—if it were, Acts 3 and 4 might focus on his growing power. Yet Shakespeare chooses to trace Edward's rise and the ironic reversals of the crown: these more objective concerns take precedence over the narrowed point of view that central character development imposes. Here, Richard is not the whole play: Shakespeare reconceives and exaggerates his character in *Richard III* to achieve that impression. In *3 Henry VI*, Richard's development reflects and concentrates the prevailing vision of the play. His brutality and mockery exceed that of the others; his opportunism is the most self-seeking; his final rejections of love and brotherhood are the most telling comment on the struggle for peace.

V

Although *Richard III* retains some of the developmental and structural virtues of the *Henry VI* plays, Shakespeare exaggerates many of his earlier directorial techniques by building the play around a single, self-dramatizing character who directs the course of the drama himself by copying or adapting Shakespeare's previous directorial techniques when they suit his purposes and by inventing improvisational techniques of his own.

From the beginning, the situation is Richard himself, and Shakespeare permits him to take the play in his own hands and to show his shaping imagination immediately. His character is first defined by his onstage presence and by his incisive self-conscious soliloquizing, and both announce his difference. Because Richard observes himself closely, so does the audience; and this first glimpse is so sharp and complete that its further use is a known element. Richard becomes the convention of the play; and the close-up focus dictates the unconventional look of the play, a method that effectively eliminates space and allows Richard's presence to substitute for the ordinary processional narrative framework. This permits further exaggerations, not the least of which is the freedom for Richard's audience to enjoy his luxuries of pure style.

Richard's exaggerations of style derive from Shakespeare's stress on his actorly abilities, particularly his dissembling; and the first Act quickly outlines the range of his control over the play. Each scene is an anecdotal, magnified character portrait that silhouettes Richard's talent as a virtuoso performer against a background of personages who cannot compete with his improvisational talents. Anne wavers and gives in to him (act 1, sc. 2); Elizabeth and her kinsmen, by stopping their protests against his accusations, yield unwittingly; and Margaret's curses and warnings, though noted, are momentarily ignored (act 1, sc. 3). Clarence's dream and subsequent murder climax these illustrations of Richard's violence and the society's ineffectiveness against it. Even though Richard does not appear in act 1, scene 4, our knowledge that he has arranged Clarence's murder as well as Clarence's references to him within his dream and the murderers' imitation of his vocal postures, place him behind the scenes, suggesting that he has, like Margaret, a supernatural presence. Overall, Richard's visual and verbal bustling opposes the others' rhetoric and stasis, so that the struggle between Richard and the society is defined and further exaggerated by presenting its polar attitudes through sharp contrasts in both language and action.

Richard's own language, and that of the others, is a primary focusing device within the play. His usual manner is a colloquially brilliant, witty, bitter-comic, proverbial style, yielding in soliloquy and in those moments when he admires or criticizes his own performance (1.2.227–63; 1.3.324–38) to near-lyrical self-praise. His may be the voice of the event, as in act 1, sc. 1, where his speech reflects his sense of opportunism; or he may choose to conform his own language patterns to those of the others (for his own convenience, and often out-doing them, as in act 1, sc. 2 with Anne, in act 2, sc. 1 with Edward, and in act 3, sc. 7, when he "accepts" the crown) or to transform the conventional, balanced rhetoric of the others to his own conversational smoothness (again, act 1. sc. 2, with Anne). Both methods highlight his hypocrisy, illustrate his manipulative use of language, and show his own eloquence and the others' dependence upon him.

Although Richard's particular style is unique, the rhetoric of curse and lament also calls attention to itself, balancing, in elaborate counterpoint, Richard's informality and defiance of dramatic conventions with pictures of the others' helplessness (see particularly act 1, sc. 3; act 2, sc. 1; act 4, sc. 4). Shakespeare makes no attempt to weld the extremes of theatrical effect and tone: his recognition of and emphasis on their contrast both heightens and stabilizes Richard's monumental conception. Each extreme asks for a different kind of attention; and for the greater part of the play (Acts 1–4; the stylized speeches of the Ghosts in 5.3.118–75), excesses of language are the only recourse against Richard. The balanced tones create a paradox: they widen and distance focus away from Richard, but they also increase audience delight in Richard's language.

Shakespeare misses no opportunity to balance Richard's extravagances with other exaggerations that either complement or offset them. Several characters other than Richard receive special kinds of emphasis. Among them, Buckingham echoes and supports Richard's theatricalizing—he rehearses a scene with him in 3.5.1–11; he directs Richard's motivation and blocks his movements in 3.7.45–51—until he falls away from the king Richard becomes in act 4, scene 2. The others are drawn with varying degrees of contrast. Margaret, for example, is a strongly theatrical force coming from the past to comment upon and to influence the present. Like Richard in that she judges her fellows, exploits her own suffering, and prompts the deliberate ordering of the stage picture, she is also a studied antithesis to Richard's possible success who enriches audience awareness of the broad themes of retribution and revenge. Clarence's reflective dream vision (act 1, sc. 4) echoes and extends this awareness in another key. Although Richard tells his audience about most events before they happen, he does not anticipate this dream. The sudden rush of images surprises the audience with one of the few moments of unexpected vision that looks beyond the play. Two significant themes—dream and conscience, and their linking together within a framework of violent death—lift the episode into the wider design of the play; but this comes clear only in retrospect, by comparison with Richard's later dream (act 5, sc. 3) and his death.

Shakespeare uses scene-by-scene revelation to present Hastings, who is defined by his qualities—openness, credulousness, hearty well-being—as a direct contrast to Richard. Hastings's speedy demise demonstrates Richard's efficient removal of obstacles; and because this goal is achieved through theatrical exaggerations—the morality play of act 3, scene 2; Richard's carefully choreographed performance in act 3, scene 4—we sense that Richard himself is controlling the dramatic method.

In Acts 2, 4, and 5, Shakespeare subdues Richard's actorly preoccupation by showing the effects of and reactions to Richard's plots (which have become, in a sense, the plot of the play), and he deliberately pulls close focus away from Richard in order to do so. Tightly controlled and balanced stage groupings—especially act 2, scene 1, which adapts and abbreviates the show of love familiar from *2 Henry VI*; act 4, scene 4, the mourning queens; and act 5, scene 3 with its simultaneous staging and alternate focus on Richard and Richmond—indicate an extremely cautious stagecraft. Language assumes increasingly formalized postures, and there are several moments, including the final scene, which comment upon the action (act 2, sc. 3 and 4; act 4, sc. 1, 3 and 5; act 5, sc. 1, 2, and 5). Once Richard gains the throne in act 4, scene 2, he no longer dissembles to his onstage audience, and the play widens to confirm a more distanced perspective on the man Richmond finally tells us to see as "the bloody dog." But audience response may not necessarily take up Richmond's last look at the future. Rather, the tensions beneath the formal onstage poses further reveal Richard Gloucester. The most comprehensive effects of the conclusion are carried by the uneasy focus of this final stage picture: Richmond's presence and his pat, conciliatory words beside Richard's corpse, an eloquent reminder of his versatile dominance over his audiences. The moments can awaken a response that reinvokes Richard's presence, and this is not limited by Richmond's conclusion.

What results from the theatricalities and exaggerations of *Richard III*? It seems to me that they offer, by example, some very specific commentary on the directorial techniques of Shakespeare's predecessors and contemporaries, especially Marlowe, and on his own earlier methods as well.

In *Richard III*, Shakespeare puts the most theatricalizing conventions of what he might call "the old drama"—a morality play, stylized and simultaneous staging, Senecan ghosts and revenge, heavily rhetorical language patterns—into a structure that makes them part of a new convention, his own—unique to this play. He demonstrates his ability to use these conventions as techniques only, not as the structural mechanics of the whole play. By doing this, he not only pays tribute to their usefulness but also qualifies their effectiveness as controls over an entire play. Each of the old conventions is used to distort Shakespeare's subject—Richard—even further; and this distortion makes an explicit comment on Marlowe's creation—the outrageous central character who exhibits himself in a variety of episodes. Like Tamburlaine and Faustus, Richard is an overreacher, but Richard is not simply a magnificent puppet, as they are. Although his centrality approaches Marlovian proportions, Shakespeare presents Richard's overreaching as far richer hyperbole: he is an entertainer-actor-playwright who shapes a variety of episodes for his own delight. Here, Shakespeare surpasses Marlowe at his own game; but here, too, Shakespeare finds the limits of the self-dramatizing character and of narrow, close-up focus.

The experimentation leads Shakespeare to reject or modify some of his earlier directorial techniques and to discover new forms in which focus shifts easily between action and reaction in patterns more inconsistent and less apparent than those of a play. In this trend, Shakespeare as a director is like Richard as a director. Because of Shakespeare's emphasis on Richard's manipulative abilities, there is a strong sense throughout *Richard III* that Richard is evaluating, interrupting, and modifying what might have been an otherwise utilitarian (though always carefully constructed) scene, enlivening it by his presence and directions. What this implies is that Shakespeare exaggerates, in Richard's person, the necessity for a play to remain, ultimately, in the hands of the actors. And while this is something Shakespeare realized from the beginning in many of his directorial techniques, *Richard III* does seem to comment upon his rediscovery of its significance.

NOTES

1. The idea of Shakespeare's manipulation of spectators' awareness and response is taken from Bertrand Evans, *Shakespeare's Comedies* (Oxford, 1967).

2. My approach to dramatic focus depends upon the work of John Russell Brown in *Shakespeare's Plays in Performance* (Baltimore, Md., 1969).

3. The phrase "syntax of stage pictures" derives from Arthur Gerstner-Hirzel's concept of a "syntax of gestures" in each Shakespearean play. *The Economy of Action and Word in Shakespeare's Plays* (Bern, 1957), pp. 56–57.

4. E. H. Gombrich, *Art and Illusion* (New York, 1960), p. 90.

5. John Willett, ed. and trans. *Brecht on Theatre* (New York, 1964), p. 203.

6. I have adapted and extended this list from *3 Henry VI*, ed. Andrew S. Cairncross (London, 1964), pp. lvii–lviii.

7. Cairncross, ed., *3 Henry VI*, p. lviii.

8. E. M. W. Tillyard, *Shakespeare's History Plays* (New York, 1946), pp. 188–96.

Shakespeare's Choreography: Pace and Rhythm

ROBERT HAPGOOD

THE PACE AND RHYTHM WITH WHICH SHAKESPEARE'S LEADING characters live their lives has not received much comment.[1] Yet it rewards attention. Their sense of timing has much to do with who loses and who wins. It also has much to do with who they are: each is unique in the workings and interworkings of his or her mind, heart, will, tongue, hand. These are very fundamental matters. For how a character thinks is at least as basic as what he thinks. The mercurialness of Mercutio's thought and action is no less important to an understanding of his nature than is his attitude toward love and honor. To be sure, kinetic appeals are hard to be positive and precise about since they make themselves felt beneath and between the lines. But if we are to see Shakespeare whole they cannot be neglected. Indeed, they can bring us very close to the heart of drama, drama being in origin and essence a "thing done" and the dramatist a "maker of actions."

Shakespeare's plays presuppose a feeling for the normal rhythms of life—the cycles of day and night, birth and death, youth and age; the seasons; the revolutions of the heavens; the inheritance through generations of custom, property, and status. The Elizabethan world-order governed succession as well as hierarchy. But his leading characters are constantly violating these rhythms. Like his blank verse, the flow of the action gets its vitality from the interplay between the regular beat that we expect and the distinctive variations and inversions that individuals play upon it. For every character who feels with Sir Andrew that "to be up late is to be up late," there are dozens who, like Sir Toby, would have things their own way: "Not to be a-bed after midnight is to be up betimes" (*Twelfth Night*, 2. 3. 1–5). Macbeth's murder of Duncan actually disrupts the coming of day; Ross observes: "By th' clock 'tis day, /And yet dark night strangles the travelling lamp" (2. 4. 6–7). Because of the dissension between Oberon and Titania:

The spring, the summer,
The childing autumn, angry winter, change
Their wonted liveries; and the mazed world,
By their increase, now knows not which is which.
                    (*A Midsummer Night's Dream*, 2. 1. 111–14)

When Richard II seizes Herford's inheritance from Gaunt, York warns:

Take Herford's rights away, and take from Time
His charters and his customary rights;
Let not to-morrow then ensue to-day;
Be not thyself; for how art thou a king
But by fair sequence and succession?
                                        (2. 1. 195–99)

Since such violations demand resolution, they add impetus to the momentum of their plays. Sometimes Shakespeare creates further urgency by throwing a special time-frame around the action. Egeon's life depends upon the clearing up of the comedy of errors in a single day. Oberon and Puck must insure that "all things shall be peace" before the midsummer night is over. Puck reminds Oberon that "this must be done with haste, / For Night's swift dragons cut the clouds full fast" (3. 2. 378–79); Oberon's sense of the time allowed him is precise: "till the eastern gate, all fiery red, / Opening on Neptune with fair blessed beams, / Turns into yellow gold his salt green streams" (3. 2. 391–92). Prospero frequently reminds himself of the need to complete his projects within the destined time.

These rhythms are rather abstract and in the background, told more than shown. The rhythms that have most immediacy come from the actual actions that characters perform, the way they determine their purposes and seek to carry them out. Here again Shakespeare presupposes a norm governing the pace and rhythm with which sane and responsible actions should be conceived, decided, planned, initiated, carried through obstacles, and at last completed. Again this norm is chiefly defined through its violation. Characters may tell one another when their acts or words are too fast or too slow, as when Northumberland tries to restrain his "wasp-stung" son (*1 Henry IV*, 1.3.235) or the ghost of King Hamlet returns to whet his son's almost blunted purpose (act 3, sc. 4). Or they may remark on their own pace; Juliet feels her contract with Romeo "too unadvis'd too sudden, / Too like the lightning" (2.2. 118–19). It is not easy to name leading characters who honor this norm in the observance, although we may feel that in ordinary circumstances the pulse of many of them would as temperately keep time as anyone's. That is because Shakespeare was not interested in ordinary circumstances; his times are almost always out of joint. To achieve their purposes, his characters must perform heroic improvisations.

Successful people in Shakespeare know not only what needs doing but when to do it. They know how to seize the moment; Prospero explains to Miranda:

> my zenith doth depend upon
> A most auspicious star, whose influence
> If now I court not, but omit, my fortunes
> Will ever after droop.
>
> > (*Tempest*, 1. 2. 181–84)

They know that if they allow themselves to be distracted events can get out of hand, as when Albany is preoccupied and thus fails to save the lives of Lear and Cordelia: "Great thing of us forgot!" Prospero comes close to such a lapse when in his absorption with the wedding masque he forgets the plot of Caliban and his co-conspirators; but he catches himself when "The minute of their plot / Is almost come" (4. 1. 141–42) and is fully in charge once more. Shakespeare's masters of timing also know when to wait and let nature take its course, as Viola waits, like Patience on a monument, for events to fulfill her love for Orsino. It takes sixteen years before "'Tis time" for Hermione to be stone no more.

More commonly, such characters impose their own timing on the course of events. So masterful can they be that it sometimes seems that, as Kate acknowledges to Petruchio, "the moon changes even as your mind" (*Taming of the Shrew*, 4. 5. 20). Helena's promise of a prompt cure for the King has the sound and effect of an incantation:

> Ere twice the horses of the sun shall bring
> Their fiery torcher his diurnal ring,
> Ere twice in murk and occidental damp
> Moist Hesperus hath quench'd her sleepy lamp,
> Or four and twenty times the pilot's glass
> Hath told the thievish minutes how they pass,
> What is infirm from your sound parts shall fly,
> Health shall live free, and sickness freely die.
>
> > (*All's Well That Ends Well*, 2. 1. 161–68)

Strong-willed as these masterful characters are, however, there is nothing inflexible about their timing. Rigidity is a sure path to folly in Shakespeare, particularly when it is dictated by a memory of the past or a dream of the future, whether Olivia is prolonging her mourning for her dead brother or Malvolio is anticipating his elevation to Count. The scholars of Navarre are foolish on two scores: their doctrinaire disregard of their immediate physical urgencies is foolish in itself, and they compound their folly by rigidifying it in a strict set of decrees (*Love's Labour's Lost*, act 1, sc. 1). Effective control of the present requires a suppleness. Petruchio tames his shrew in part by speeding up the customary pace in wooing her, then by slowing down and at times halting the pace of wedding and bedding her.

Shakespeare delights in such comic distortions of customary rhythms. *A Midsummer Night's Dream* is full of transformations, and it is their suddenness—the jerkiness with which the gears are shifted—that is a prime source of its humor. When the lovers aren't running, it seems, they are sleeping; and their changes from love to hate are equally abrupt and complete, as when Lysander awakens in mid-couplet to declare to Helena, whom he formerly despised: "And run through fire I will for thy sweet sake" (2. 2. 103). Titania's infatuation with Bottom begins and ends instantaneously. On the other hand, part of Bottom's charm is that although his outer being is translated in one stroke, his inner self only gradually metamorphoses. Not until his second translated appearance has he begun to express the appetites of an ass or put on the airs of a queen's consort (act 4, sc. 1). And when untranslated, Bottom's dream lingers: "Methought I was, and methought I had . . ." (4. 1. 205).

At the other extreme, *Much Ado about Nothing* makes the most of the comic slowness with which Beatrice and Benedict recognize and declare their love. Even to the end they hold back, claiming that they are marrying one another only out of pity. The tardiness of their hearts syncopates the quickness of their wits and tongues. But throughout they perform their unique mating dance in step, as when in parallel scenes they are brought to recognize their love for one another (act 2, sc. 3; act 3, sc. 1).

One of the joys of these two comedies is that they create worlds in which such amusing distortions can be allowed and still produce happy outcomes. But in each play there is a supervising Oberon or Don Pedro to control the rhythms that in the lovers are so entertainingly inclined to run wild. In *The Merchant of Venice* Portia is both lover and controller.

No less bright than Beatrice or Benedict, she applies her presence of mind to the immediate needs of the moment. Without hesitation she sends Bassanio on his way to join Antonio, even though that interrupts the consummation of her marriage (act 3, sc. 2.). Yet she also knows how to bide her time. She holds out at the end until Bassanio has apologized properly for giving away her ring (only his third and last apology is without excuse) and until Antonio has given his surety that it will not happen again.

Rosalind is another who is both a lover and a controller. But she seems to me more self-indulgent in her timing. She herself cannot bear to be out of the sight of Orlando, rebuking him for being late ("I had as lief be woo'd of a snail") and sighing until he comes again. Why then does she hold back from revealing her true identity to him? Perhaps she wants to test his love. Chiefly, I suspect, she wants to prolong the delights of being wooed exactly as she likes it, and without the need for committed response.

Nonetheless, events play perfectly into Rosalind's hand, with the conversion of the two bad brothers in the last act. And this is often the case with Shakespeare's masters of timing. In *Measure for Measure*, Barnardine has no sooner declined to be executed (until he has "more time to prepare me") than the Provost reports the death of Ragozine, at which the Duke remarks, "'Tis an accident that heaven provides!" (4. 3. 74). Such collusion is especially disturbing when it favors a villain. "Edgar," says Edmund, and Edgar immediately appears; as Edmund notes, "Pat he comes like the catastrophe of an old comedy" (1. 2. 130). Iago is also favored in this way, particularly whenever the fatal handkerchief is involved. Certain situations seem to invite villainy. "Th' occasion speaks thee," says Antonio, as he begins to persuade Sebastian to let him kill sleeping Alonso (*The Tempest*, 2. 2. 201). As Lucrece explains at length (*The Rape of Lucrece*, 869–924), Opportunity conduced to Tarquin's rape.

In general, Shakespeare's villains until their final undoing are among his keenest masters of timing. Richard III is a classic instance, being full of ambition—the conventional incitement to rapid action—and unhampered by either conscience or cowardice—the conventional impediments to it. Beyond these traits, his characteristic "bustling" pace seems systemic, a part of his nature. He is acutely conscious of timing. He repeatedly asks "What is't o'clock," hastens his servants, slows down the women he woos (1. 2. 116; 4. 4. 361), chides himself for running "before my horse to market." Only toward the end of the play does his mastery of pace break down. Instead of his earlier spontaneous dispatch, Richard now must spur himself from "fearful commenting" to "fiery expedition" (4. 3. 51–56). When Richard now tries to hurry a messenger, he forgets to give him a message to deliver (4. 4. 442–48). It is Richmond who moves with natural dispatch: "True hope is swift, and flies with swallow's wings" (5. 2. 23).

So much for the secrets of successful timing in Shakespeare. He seems still more interested in characters whose timing is tragically off, especially those who with integrity keep pace to a different drummer.

Probably the most common dislocations are those of haste, and of these the most violent are occasioned by anger. "Barr'st me my way in Rome?" Titus cries, slaying a son (1. 1. 291). Not until his sufferings have brought him to an utter standstill (3. 1. 252–64) and his paralysis has then been broken by his laughter, does he begin methodically to go about the "Task I have to do." King Lear is another exploder. He does have a fuse, but it is a short one. He is able to contain his wrath long enough to invite Cordelia to "mend her speech a little," but soon it breaks forth: "thy truth then be thy dower!" (1. 1. 94, 108). The same is true of his outburst against Goneril (act 1, sc. 4). Coriolanus has a longer fuse that he consciously tries to control at the urging of his mother and Menenius; as she tells him "I would have had you put your power well on / Before you had worn it out" (3. 2. 16–17). But his fury cannot finally be contained and bursts out disastrously in his final diatribe against the taunting plebs:

> You common cry of curs, whose breath I hate
> As reek the rotten fens, whose loves I prize
> As the dead carcasses of unburied men
> That do corrupt my air—I banish you!
>
> (3. 3. 121–24)

These characters shock by the unrestrained violence of their reactions. The power of Macbeth's imagination carries him into the realm that might be called preaction. Several critics have seen Macbeth as one of those who "place a great store by the future" and thus try "to forestall, as it were, their own compulsions and fears; to get ahead of events, almost as if they were running a race with them." [2] I would add that Macbeth's problem is that his will is too weak to keep pace with his hopes. The rate of his physical actions lags behind his purposes, despite the goadings of the weird Sisters and Lady Macbeth. Malcolm is named heir, Fleance escapes, so does Macduff. Macbeth's rhythm fluctuates between feverish activity and burnt-out lassitude, but he does seem to gain in the race, until with the slaughter at Fife the very firstlings of his heart become the firstlings of his hand (4. 1. 146–48). To the end, however, he seems unable to act without external instigation. Even his last stand is prompted by Macduff's accusations of cowardice, charges that recall those with which Lady Macbeth first tried to screw his courage to the sticking place. Lacking anyone else to do so, Macbeth cheers himself on with his final battle cry: "Lay on, Macduff, / And damn'd be him that first cries, 'Hold, enough!'" (5. 8. 34).

Moments when a character is slow to act stand out in most of Shakespeare's plays, full as they are of action and of characters who are too quick to act. In *Hamlet* and *Troilus and Cressida*, such slowness is a general malaise verging on paralysis. Virtually everyone in Elsinore is prone to delay in much the same way that Hamlet is. They are all given to ringing declarations of purpose that in fact are soon halted or deflected before, finally and unexpectedly, reaching fulfillment.[3] *Troilus and Cressida* is pervaded by the atmosphere of a long siege in stalemate. But where the delays in *Hamlet* are largely involuntary—the result of dead-locked inner and outer forces—the holdings back from action in *Troilus and Cressida* are largely deliberate, often willful, even spiteful.

Usually when Shakespeare's characters change their pace, they do so in a clear progression. Richard II may be alone in being alternately too slow and too hasty. When it comes to performing acts that would save his reign, he is fatally slow. As the Gardener points out, the king in his "waste of idle hours" missed his moment to order his garden-realm and now suffers a "disorder'd spring." Richard finally comes to the same awareness: "I wasted time, and now doth time waste me" (5. 5. 49). Thus in the opening scene, he lets the quarrel between Bullingbrook and Mowbray go too far before trying to intercede. But when it comes to acts of self-destruction, Richard's pace is precipitate. All is haste for his campaign to Ireland; Gaunt is no sooner dead than Richard is seizing his possessions. As a result Richard has shipped for Ireland when Bullingbrook breaks exile and returns (2. 2. 42–51). He is away just a little too long, causing the Welsh troops to disperse (act 2, sc. 4). And so it goes. At his return (act 3, sc. 2), Richard's inclination is "to sit on the ground / And tell sad stories of the death of kings" while Bullingbrook marches. Carlisle sensibly rebukes him: "wise men ne'er sit and wail their woes, / But presently prevent the ways to wail." Yet at Flint castle, when a holding action is needed—Aumerle to no avail at one point advises: "let's fight with gentle words, / Till time lend friends and friends their helpful swords (3. 3. 131–32)—Richard far from temporizing races ahead of necessity. Bullingbrook's defiance of his banishment and claiming of his inheritance make him feel as if deposed, and so he enacts a symbolic fall: "Down, down, I come; like glistering Phaethon" (178). His actual deposition seems to him a crucifixion, and so he enacts it.

Richard is no match for Bullingbrook, who times his ascent to power so adroitly that he almost always appears to have what he wants fall into his lap.[4] He gets ahead of himself only once, when he takes it upon himself to execute Richard's followers before he has officially assumed royal authority (act 3, sc. 2). Prince John is more overt. He times his trap for the rebels to spring immediately after they have dismissed their troops (2 Henry IV, act 4, sc. 2).

Of all the Lancastrians, Henry Monmouth has the surest, and deadliest, sense of timing. His only lapse comes when he mistakes his father's sleep for death and dons the crown a little too soon. Even so he recovers so well that his father feels:

> God put it in thy mind to take it hence,
> That thou mightst win the more thy father's love,
> Pleading so wisely in excuse of it!
>> (2 Henry IV, 4. 5. 177–79)

In general Henry's timing is as skillful as that of the masters of timing in the comedies already discussed. His way with the three traitors (Henry V, act 2, sc. 2) recalls Portia's way with Shylock. He delays his condemnation of them until they have in effect condemned themselves:

> Thy mercy that was quick in us but late,
> By your own counsel is suppress'd and kill'd.
>> (2. 2. 79–80)

His most daring piece of timing is his delay in assuming kingly grace, playing the prodigal son for maximum effect.

Falstaff is a fascinating study in pace and rhythm. Most basic is the fact that this "old fat man" has so nimble a wit. The timing of his wit is consummate. In fact, as long as they are at the tavern, Falstaff can more than hold his own with the Prince. When the Prince springs his Gadshill trap, Falstaff pops out of it with his brilliant topper, "By the Lord, I knew ye as well as he that made ye." When the action moves to the battlefield or the court, however, Falstaff still clings to his tavern-scenario. That is why his gag-substitution of a bottle of sack for a pistol misfires with the Prince, who really wants a weapon: "What, is it a time to jest and dally now?" (*1 Henry IV*, 5.3.54). And that also explains why, when the king is crowned, Falstaff could feel that he is "Fortune's steward" and ride all night—"the young king is sick for me"—to commit so colossal a piece of mistiming as calling out on the king ("God save thy Grace, King Hal!") when he comes in procession from his coronation.

Like Falstaff, Shakespeare's tragic figures are often "out of sync" with their surroundings. Richard III is a born warrior in a piping time of peace; the go-it-alone fury that carried the day for Coriolanus on the battlefield (act 1, sc. 4) undoes him in Rome. Yet some of them meet their doom because they follow prevailing rhythms. As mentioned, that is true of delaying Hamlet amid the general impasses of Elsinore. At the other extreme, as Brents Stirling has shown, haste like that of Romeo and Juliet is a way of life for most everyone in Verona.[5]

Because Romeo and Juliet are so young and the consequences of their mistakes so far exceed their deservings, their sufferings seem more than usually cruel. One wishes that they might have been given a second chance. In his last plays, that is what Shakespeare gives certain of his characters. Even though they carry their untimely acts to tragic extremes, they are allowed to mend their ways and come out on the other side of tragedy. Rash Leontes is permitted to learn patience, to wait on the workings of nature and Apollo. Preoccupied Prospero, who neglected his "temporal royalties," learns to exercise vigilance, seeing to the exact timing of the love relationship of Miranda and Ferdinand and frustrating the counter-rhythms of his adversaries. In both plays, however, the overall movement seems artificial and contrived, determined by exterior forces rather than the free, touch-and-go interplay of personalities in action.

The death of Cleopatra comes as close as Shakespeare convincingly came to transmuting the destructive rhythms of tragedy into those of a new kind of life. When we first meet her, Cleopatra seems to have the presence of mind and resource of a Shakespearean comic heroine. In the opening scene she daringly keeps Antony from hearing the Roman messengers simply by insisting that he must hear them. But before long it becomes clear that she is running a desperate and losing race against time, as events have their way and take Antony from her. When he returns, she makes two terrible blunders in timing. The first is in the sea-battle with Caesar. Scarus's report says it all:

> Yon ribaudred nag of Egypt
> (Whom leprosy o'ertake) i' th' midst o' th' fight,
> When vantage like a pair of twins appear'd,
> Both as the same, or rather ours the elder—
> The breeze upon her, like a cow in June—
> Hoists sails and flies . . .
> She once being loof'd
> The noble ruin of her magic, Antony,
> Claps on his sea-wing, and (like a doting mallard)
> Leaving the fight in heighth, flies after her.
> I never saw an action of such shame . . .
>
> (3.10.10–21)

The other blunder comes when Cleopatra sends Mardian to tell Antony that she has killed herself. The news arrives when Antony is at his lowest point, unsure of his own identity (act 4, sc. 14), and it occasions his own suicide. For, as in the sea battle, Antony is impelled to "fly after her"; he vows: "I will o'ertake thee, Cleopatra . . . ."

Antony has spent the play trying to catch up with Cleopatra, who has made it a policy always to be where he isn't; she instructs Charmian, "If you find him sad, / Say I am dancing; if in mirth, report / That I am sudden sick" (1.3. 4–5). Even at their first meeting, it was he who went to her:

> Upon her landing, Antony sent to her,
> Invited her to supper. She replied,
> It should be better he became her guest;
> Which she entreated. Our courteous Antony,
> Whom ne'er the word of "No" woman heard speak,
> Being barber'd ten times o'er, goes to the feast . . .
>
> (2. 2. 220–25)

After his suicide attempt his painful ascent to join her in the monument is the most graphic and touching example.

After his death, it is she who is going to him: "Husband, I come!"

Elsewhere I have called Cleopatra's last speech (2. 278–313) one of Shakespeare's "moments of stillness,"[6] It has a hushed, trancelike quality. Her physical movement is minimal and formal: once she is attired in her regalia, she kisses her attendants farewell, applies an asp to her breast, adds another asp, and dies in midsentence. Yet the movements she imagines are free and fluid. It is as if she has already entered life after death, vanishing like fire and air into a future where Antony is her husband and she has a baby at her breast.

She hurries to join him. Antony felt:

> Since Cleopatra died
> I have liv'd in such dishonor that the gods
> Detest my baseness.
>
> (4. 14. 55–57)

Now when Iras dies first, Cleopatra declares:

> This proves me base.
> If she first meet the curled Antony,
> He'll make demand of her, and spend that kiss
> Which is my heaven to have.
>
> (5. 2. 300–3)

And, it seems, their reunion is consummated: "As sweet as balm, as soft as air, as gentle—O Antony!"

As she realizes, her pace also serves to make "great Caesar ass / Unpolicied." Six lines after her death Caesar's guard comes "rustling in," but is "too slow a messenger"; he concludes: "Caesar's beguil'd." Here too her timing is perfect, though fatal.

This rapid survey is obviously not meant to be exhaustive.[7] It does no more than call attention to salient traits in the leading characters it includes; and it omits a number whose pace and rhythm are no less interesting: the dislocation in Othello's sense of timing is a study in itself. Furthermore, the distinctive tempos of individual characters should be seen in the context of other features of Shakespeare's choreography, particularly the tempos that he creates for the whole play. And these are interrelated with the tempos with which a spectator is allowed to understand and respond to what is happening. All of these matters are only beginning to receive critical attention. For too long, critics have been preoccupied with that moment during the finale in which Shakespeare invites us to step out of time, look back over the whole, and reflect on its meaning. As a result the dynamism that inspires all the other moments in the plays tends to go unconsidered. It is time for concern with "spatial values" in Shakespeare to be balanced by an awareness of sequential ones. This essay is intended to contribute to that process, and hasten it.

NOTES

1. In addition to the studies cited later, a number of recent commentators have been much interested in time as a theme. See the text and notes of Kenneth Muir, *"Troilus and Cressida,"* *Shakespeare Survey 8* (1955): 28–39, and of Douglas L. Peterson, *Time, Tide, and Tempest* (San Marino, Calif., 1973). Also David Kastan, "The Shape of Time: Form and Value in the Shakespearean Play," *Comparative Drama*, Winter 1973–74, pp. 259–77; David Kaula, "The Time Sense of *Antony and Cleopatra,"* *Shakespeare Quarterly* 15 (Summer 1964): 211–23; and Z. Stríbný, "The Idea and Image of Time In Shakespeare's Early Histories," *Shakespeare Jahrbuch*, 110 (1974): 129–38.

2. Frederick Turner, *Shakespeare and the Nature of Time*, (Oxford 1971), p. 143. See also Francis Fergusson, *"Macbeth* as The Imitation of Action" in *The Human Image in Dramatic Literature* (Garden City, N.Y., 1957), pp. 115–25; and Harold E. Toliver, "Shakespeare and the Abyss of Time," *Journal of English and Germanic Philology 64 (1965):* 247–50.

3. See my *"Hamlet* Nearly Absurd: The Dramaturgy of Delay," *Tulane Drama Review* 9 (1965): 132–45.

4. See Brents Stirling, "Bolingbroke's 'Decision'," *Shakespeare Quarterly* 2 (1951): 27–34.

5. "They stumble that run fast," in *Unity in Shakespearean Tragedy* (New York, 1957), pp. 10–25.

6. "Hearing Shakespeare: Sound and Meaning in *Antony and Cleopatra,"* *Shakespeare Survey* 24 (1971): 10–12.

7. See Bertrand Evans, *Shakespeare's Comedies* (Oxford, 1963). Marvin Rosenberg, *The Masks of King Lear* (Berkeley, Calif., 1972) suggestively assigns musical tempos to various parts of the play. For audience response to *Hamlet* see Stephen Booth, "On the Value of *Hamlet,"* in *Reinterpretations of Elizabethan Drama*, ed. Norman Rabkin (New York, 1969), pp. 137–76, and my reply, *"Hamlet* and its Thematic Modes of Speech," in *Perspectives on Hamlet*, ed. W. G. Holzberger and P. B. Waldeck (Lewisburg, Pa., 1975), pp. 29–47.

9

Shakespearean Playgoing Then and Now

BERNARD BECKERMAN

PLAYGOING IS A LITTLE LIKE CHURCHGOING. IT IS A PUBLIC ACT FOR private ends. It is a private act performed publicly. It is intimate and individual. It is impersonal and communal. It brings us nearer to the apprehension of our own godhood while at the same time it reinforces awareness of the transitory properties of our flesh. Yet likeness is not identity. Playgoing is surrender to illusion while churchgoing is a ritual embodiment of a higher truth. Through churchgoing we hope to step from one truth to *the* truth. Playgoing holds out the possibility that we can slip through fancy to a lookout upon truth. The fancy is the lure, however, and abandonment to its pleasures our reward. If we reach the lookout, so much the better. That intensifies and complicates the pleasure. It was so in Shakespeare's age; it is so today.

But this open and essentially child-like way of going to a performance is wrenched askew when we attend a play by Shakespeare. He possesses us in many ways. It is his language we speak. It is often his image of historical events that we accept for truth even when we know it not to be the truth. Will we ever imagine Cleopatra other than Shakespeare depicts her? Or will we ever surrender the delicious villainy of Richard Gloucester for the maligned figure, more like Sir Thomas More than Sir Thomas More himself, with which the rehabilitators of Richard III try to seduce us?

No wonder we cannot face Shakespeare without preconceptions and expectations. When we meet him in our rooms, reading his plays, our expectations are purely personal. No one is there to see how we do. If we nod, or rush to the dictionary, or intone his verse, there is no censor blue pencilling our act. But in the theater expectations are communal. We cannot shake off the sensation that something special is demanded of us—a depth of response, an acuity of perception, a verification of intellectuality, something to prove we deserve to be at a Shakespearean play.

Anyone who has ever directed Shakespeare cannot ignore the power of preconceptions in distorting audience response. This power is perhaps seen most nakedly when parent and child come to a play together. I particularly recall a moment during a performance of *The Tempest* that I had directed. I was sitting behind a mother and her ten-year-old daughter. Early in the play the girl was on the verge of laughing two or three times. The mother, however, had a firm grip on the child's arm, and so repeatedly the child's laughter sputtered out as suppressed giggling. At last though, during a bit of comic business involving Caliban and Trinculo, the girl guffawed in uninhibited glee. The mother hurriedly leaned over, and whispered: "Ssh, you shouldn't laugh. It's Shakespeare."

This remark is an illustration of a rather simple but perverted kind of reverence that besets Shakespearean playgoing. And silly though such reverence is, it is not essentially different from more subtle expressions of bardolatry. The scholar who, in attending a performance, calculates how many lines of the text have been omitted by the actors, the teacher who seeks confirmation of the themes he or she has stressed in class, the culture addict who pays homage to an established icon, all are worshipping the Bard in their own ways. Unfortunately, worship, whatever form it takes, is inimical to playgoing. It is the very thing that provoked Antonin Artaud's cry of "no more masterpieces!"

The initial impulse behind such reverence is healthy, I suppose. It comes from respect for the inimitable gift Shakespeare gives us. That respect, unhappily, has a tendency to be embalmed in fixed notions not only of what Shakespeare has to offer us but also of how we are to receive his gift. These fixed notions are communicated to us in our early years, through the way parents speak of Shakespeare, if they do so at all; through the treatment teachers accord him in school; and through the abstruse and never-ending commentary that scholars attach to his works. In time, the weight of these authorities bears on our own judgment so forcibly that we accept their inclinations as fundamental truths. We come to associate a high mindedness, a broad cultural uplift, and a remoteness with Shakespeare's plays. Instead of responding moment by moment to the dramatic event, we filter a production through the veil of a lofty and smug sentiment.

It may seem peculiar to stress the weight of reverence in Shakespearean playgoing at a time when so many recent productions seem to illustrate the opposite. We have had productions with lines rewritten, with rock music scores, with transposed speeches, with historical periods shifted, and with characters subdivided into multiple psyches. Do not all these alterations prove that it is not reverence but irreverence we have to fear?

Peculiarly no. These modernizations are symptomatic of the ways in which directors and actors have tried to cope with the oppressiveness of reverence, a reverence that turned theaters into museums. In effect, they are efforts to challenge the audience's preconceptions. When Peter Hall in January 1960 assumed the leadership of the Stratford Memorial Theatre Company in England, he insisted that the plays chosen for production be relevant to the concerns of the moment. As a gesture to the future, he dropped the word Memorial from the troupe, and in the new name, Royal Shakespeare Company, signalized a change of outlook.

Other companies paralleled his actions. The New York Shakespeare Festival under Joe Papp always resisted the reverential approach, but in the sixties and early seventies it went further than the Royal Shakespeare Company. It fragmented and politicized *Hamlet*; it turned *Two Gentlemen of Verona* into a rock musical about Puerto Ricans and blacks. The Stratford company in Connecticut, less adventuresome than either of the other organizations, nevertheless emulated the kind of relevance advocated by Peter Hall. All these efforts were—and to a degree still are—directed toward revitalizing the Shakespearean text and awakening a fresh view of Shakespeare. By considering him our contemporary, the directors and actors tried to evoke a spontaneous response from the audience. To do this they often had to outrage the audience on the assumption that only such measures could shatter the rigid yet shallow adoration that prevented people from seeing what is truly happening in a Shakespearean play.

Naturally, this approach necessitated a reverse reading of a play. Instead of proceeding from the text to the image to be projected through it, directors went from a new preconception—the demand for pertinence—to the reading of the text. Several ways of producing Shakespeare quickly became the fashion. One way was to give a play a topical slant. In an otherwise admirable production of *Timon of Athens* at Stratford, Ontario, Michael Langham introduced Alcibiades in khaki, with cigar and pistol, an afterimage of Fidel Castro. Another way was to present a play in modern dress, a practice that goes back to Sir Barry Jackson in the nineteen twenties but which became extremely popular in the last twenty-five years. Like any stylistic device, it has and has not proven effective, depending on how richly the modern motif illuminates the central events of the play. Still another approach was to see the play as an enactment of a mythic ritual. In a recent production of *Richard II* by the Royal Shakespeare Company (1973), the actors of Richard and Bolingbroke alternated roles in order to exemplify the cyclical struggle for power in which Death is the only winner. Identity disappeared in this struggle and puppets prevailed. And finally a fourth approach was to adopt one or more of the theatrical styles of the contemporary theater. During the height of the Berliner Ensemble's influence in the late fifties and early sixties, Brechtian productions filled Shakespearean stages. They were distinguished by costumes and settings in various shades of tattered brown burlap. The success of *Marat/Sade*, not too far removed from the Brechtian theater itself, spawned in turn its share of Shakespearean actors glowering at the audience as it dared to applaud them. These excesses are easy to satirize, of course. But we should also acknowledge that this shaking up of the text had and still has a beneficial side. It stimulated some magnificent productions of Shakespeare, such as Tyrone Guthrie's *Troilus and Cressida*, and Albert Marre's *Love's Labour's Lost*. It also served as a general corrective to decorative and empty performing.

Fortunately, this penchant for shaking up the text has reached its apogee. In its place there is a renewed interest in the traditional roots of theatre. Avant garde organizations like the Open Theatre and The Performance Group have rediscovered the dramatist's lines. Shakespearean companies are relying less on facile analogues and forced topicality, and although the mythic impulse is still strong, it too will fade soon. No new approach is on the horizon. The theater is free now to make a new effort, which is really the same effort in every generation, to find a synthesis between what is peculiarly Elizabethan in a Shakespearean text and what is suggestibly modern. Such an effort obliges the performer and playgoer to rebuild or rediscover their relationship in terms of the basic elements of theatrical art.

I

Of all these basic elements, I will concentrate on one of the simplest: how we perceive dramatic events. When we attend a play or film, we are aware of the unfolding incidents directly, that is, we pay attention to the realtionships between characters or the crises that they face. Occasionally we become aware of the illusory surface through which we are witnessing the event. In film we may become aware of the camera angle or the editing of a scene. In a play we may become conscious of the stage picture or the sheen of the dialogue. Both types of awareness are usually transitory. For the most part we accept the events as events while simultaneously enjoying the fancies that sound and sight produce. We thus have an experience in depth. Our attention is fixed on the event, but we approach the event through the visual, auditory, and kinesthetic pleasures that stimulate us.

In American playgoing the pleasures of vision and kinesis probably outweigh the auditory pleasures. We know from reports of anthropologists that in certain respects the organization of the senses is cultural. Peoples unused to reading the code of light and shade in a photograph do not recognize themselves in snapshots. This may seem incredible to us because we in the west have enjoyed an intense apprenticeship in visual perception. Film and television have cultivated a sophistication that enables us to read complex visual messages easily. Auditory response is not unimportant, of course. The spoken word or rather the utterance of sound is of vital concern. Don't we all use the telephone far more frequently than the mails? But in public performance today the utterance of sound rather than the formation of speech produces the greatest effects. The frenzied ecstasy of the rock concert is a response to the pulsation of rhythm and the wild leaps of tonal distortion. Rarely do we find performances that excite our ears through the interplay of spoken words. In the English speaking countries at least, poetry is more usually than not read silently and one's first meeting with Shakespeare is normally through the printed page. How many of us have reveled in the sheer exuberance of his language without having first served a long internship understanding the written word?

Because of this cultural emphasis on graphic rather than linguistic structures, the continuum between audience, language, and event, so central to Shakespearean theater, does not readily occur. There was a time when the actor did cultivate vocal skills, but that led eventually to an arty kind of poeticizing. Hollywood's version of a Shakespearean actor with a resonant voice, mouthing his speeches, is a parody of the once dominant style of spoken delivery. Such an actor communicates words and attitudes but seldom the event underlying them. That is why many directors now try to elicit an obvious contemporary relevance in the language or substitute a visual for an oral image.

As in all matters artistic, however, a delicate balance must be struck between contradictions. Given the disruption in our auditory tradition, it is unlikely that the unsullied innocence of the ear can ever be restored. Some compromise must be found. One of the most successful compromises was that achieved by Franco Zeffirelli in his noted *stage* production of *Romeo and Juliet* (1960). In the theater his experience as a director and designer of opera gave him the abilities to devise an interesting balance between speech and gesture. Always seeking a strong physical justification for a character's impulses, he encouraged an oral boldness in his actors while at the same time he helped them invent gestures and movements that reinforced the spoken word. Invariably, he stopped just short of elocutionary gesture. The Queen Mab speech is a case in point. Zeffirelli staged the speech as a performance that Mercutio gives his friends. This tack justified a bravura delivery. Yet Mercutio's histrionic gestures did not merely theatricalize the verse; they also counterpointed the thought, thus heightening and interacting with the words. Again and again throughout the production, Zeffirelli established a physical basis for intensified spoken expression: the summer heat of Verona's streets, the libidinous heat of the balcony scene, the heat of challenge in the duel between Mercutio and Tybalt. The physical basis of the scene generated the nervous energy out of which the language sprang. This approach stimulated the pleasures of Shakespeare's sound and images in an organic and convincing manner without relying on a delivery that was either too formal or too colloquial.

II

It is from the vantage point of these ideas that I would like to consider Shakespearean playgoing in its own day. Naturally, much of what I write is inferential. Evidence for playgoing in the sixteenth century is sparse, and what there is can be misleading. Scholars have regularly pointed out that much contemporary description of playgoing comes from the pens of men like Stephen Gosson, a professed enemy to the stage. For moral, economic, and civic reasons, the theater was the object of repeated attacks, and every disorder in the playhouse was relished by these foes. Yet without these antagonistic accounts, one is left with only fragments of direct testimony to playgoing and must thus rely on the clues that one can draw from a wide variety of sources, including the plays themselves.

My intent here, however, is not to recapitulate what others have said. Alfred Harbage's book on Shakespeare's audiences still tells us much of what there is to know about the composition of those attending his plays and the conditions under which they attended them.[1] In the last twenty-five years a number of scholars have carefully studied the original acting and staging of Shakespeare's plays, going over and over again the limited scraps of information about the Elizabethan and Jacobean theater. Although considerable controversy still remains, it is a controversy of details. On the basic arrangement of the stage there is broad agreement.[2] There is less agreement on the staging, however, partly because our evidence is limited and imprecise, but also because our conception of what constitutes staging is oversimple. It is not solely the way in which a theatrical company uses stage properties or how actors make entrances and exits. In fact, in Shakespeare's day these are only the incidentals of staging. More central are matters of how the players presented themselves to the audience, how and to what degree they related to each other, through what physical patterns they exhibited their skills. Only by gaining some clues to these matters can we begin to imagine playgoing in Shakespeare's day.

In a rather well known passage of his book on travels, Thomas Platter, a Swiss physician, recorded his visit to an English public playhouse on 21 September 1599. There he attended a performance dealing with Julius Caesar. Almost certainly, Platter is referring to Shakespeare's play and the playhouse he mentions must be the newly opened Globe. The passage itself is brief. Platter mentions the playhouse, the subject of the play, as well as an afterpiece in which two actors dressed as men and two as women danced. Elsewhere in his book, he describes a visit to another playhouse, probably the Curtain, this time giving fuller information about the play, apparently a comedy, and about the theaters in London together with a record of admission prices. He also notes the splendid dress of the actors and once again the dancing after the play. He concludes the passage on the theaters with the remark: "How much time . . . [Londoners] may merrily spend daily at the play everyone knows who has ever seen them play or act."[3]

While his deficiency in English—German being his native tongue—can explain why Platter did not say more about *Julius Caesar*, it is still somewhat surprising that he says so little about the production. During his visits at Court and to other parts of London, he gives considerable attention to ceremony, dress, and manners. Why does he say virtually nothing about these elements in the stage play? From English travelers such as Fynes Moryson, we know that the level of performing and staging on the continent, especially in Germany, did not match that of the English players. Yet only the dancing, at which admittedly the English comedians excelled, excited Platter's attention, that and the playhouses themselves.

Other foreign visitors besides Platter likewise include general descriptions about the public and private playhouses. When it comes to performance, however, they confine themselves to the music or the dancing. Even when Busino, chaplain to the Venetian ambassador, reports the occasion for the production of Ben Jonson's masque *The Vision of Delight*, presented to King James in 1618, he makes trifling reference to the antimasque and expatiates on James's irritation that the dancing is delayed.[4] His silence on the scenic dispositions along with the silence of other visitors on stage production generally make one wonder what were the distinguishing features of Elizabethan stage presentation.

Shakespeare, as we know, wrote only for the adult companies. The bulk of his work was first presented to a public playhouse audience. Repeated attempts have been made to prove that several of the plays, such as *A Midsummer Night's Dream*, were first offered to a private audience. These claims remain conjectural. Only with *Troilus and Cressida* and with the later plays of *Cymbeline, The Winter's Tale, The Tempest,* and *Henry VIII* is it possible that the first performances took place in a private theater before a more homogeneous audience than normally filled the Globe playhouse. And even in respect to these plays we cannot be certain. Consequently, where more than thirty of his works are concerned, Shakespeare had to speak to the animated, lively, and possible roisterous crowd that thronged the public playhouse.

Moralists describe the audiences as rowdy. We don't have to believe these charges to recognize that Elizabethan playgoers were not the subdued, polite, even intimidated folk who silently watch a contemporary play. W. J. Lawrence termed them the "nut-cracking Elizabethans," in honor of their inveterate habit of eating nuts throughout a performance. The crack of the shells could be heard during an entire play except, as Sir Thomas Palmer rhymed, when "Falstaff from cracking nuts hath kept the throng."[5] It it clear that the modern cinema theater has achieved a major breakthrough by substituting the relatively noiseless popcorn for the staccato crackle that competed with Shakespeare's verse.

Although writers mention the nut cracking scornfully, this habit was surely not the only disturbance in the playhouse. In fact, it is questionable whether disturbance is the proper word to describe such activity. Londoners came to the playhouses not only to see but, in Platter's phrase, ''to be seen.'' Daylight performance made the playgoer as visible as the player. The arc of auditors could readily view each other; groundlings could look up and around at the better sort, and gallery holders could gaze down at the commoners and across at their peers. Visitors to England are at one in noting how obsessed the English were by their love of dress, not hesitating, as Jakob Rathgeb reports, ''to wear velvet in the streets who can scarce afford a crust of dry bread at home.''[6] At the playhouse this mania for adornment had a marvelous outlet, spurring the young wits to show themselves and their feathers on the stage itself.

Some dispute exists over the presence of audience on the stages of the public playhouses. That members of the audience tried to insinuate themselves onto the stage itself, there is no question. From the end of the sixteenth century at least, young men sat on the stages of the private theaters. Once there, they saw no reason why they should not do the same at the public playhouse. Apparently, however, the adult actors resisted this incursion for a time, yielding to pressure probably about 1609 as soon as they themselves began performing in the private theaters. The impulse to sit on stage obviously had roots in the exhibitionism so dear to the London gentleman. It may also have endeavored to recreate the intimacy between player and auditor that existed in the great halls when the players brought their comedies, histories, and tragedies to the homes of great men.

This close commingling of noble, gentry, and commoner in the playhouse has been pointed out by Harbage and others. But it has not been stressed enough that the commercialization of playgoing provided a recurrent carnival atmosphere where class relationships were minimized and common humanity stressed. English society was at once stratified yet flexible. This anomaly is reflected in the arrangement of the playhouse. While the different admission charges divided the more affluent from the less affluent, all came through the same entry, save for the few who filled the Lord's rooms. Only the payment of successive pence at different doors separated one person from another. But not only did virtually all people come through the same door, the mass of two to three thousand were tightly packed together. Merchants and their wives peered at the players over the heads of apprentices and other standees in the central yard. Some jibes are occasionally launched at the common sort by Shakespeare as well as by other writers, but these are relatively infrequent. Far more often are there requests for understanding and sympathy from all members of the audience.

III

What Shakespeare himself thought of his audience is hard to fathom. We cannot take Hamlet's words on the judicious and the unskillful as the expression of Shakespeare's judgment. But if we do not know what he thought, we can get some idea of how he related to his audiences, and perhaps this is more important.

Both in his prologues or choruses, conventional though they may be, and in his dramatization of plays-within-plays, we learn directly and indirectly something of the theatrical event as Shakespeare pictures it. By noting what he stresses and particularly what matters he reiterates, we can gain an inkling of what he regarded as important features of a performance. I will consider two things in particular: the kind of perception Shakespeare sought to stimulate in his audience and the kind of empathy he tends to elicit.

Repeatedly during his career as a playwright Shakespeare employs the device of prologue or chorus. The Chorus appears first in the guise of Rumour in *2 Henry IV*. "Open your ears," he cries to the audience. In *Romeo and Juliet*, the Chorus is less an emblematic and more an impersonal voice. At the opening of the play, he assures the audience that "if you with patient ears attend, / What here shall miss, our toil shall strive to mend" (13–14). This request for patient ears echoes the conversation between Philostrate and Theseus in *A Midsummer Night's Dream*. Philostrate has already "heard" the play of Pyramus and Thisbe, and does not recommend it. Theseus insists that he "will hear that play" for himself. This manner of speaking about a performance is the norm in Shakespeare's early works. The Lord in *Taming of the Shrew* tells the players that

> There is a lord will hear you play to-night;
> But I am doubtful of your modesties,
> Lest, over-eyeing of his odd behaviour
> (For yet his honour never heard a play),
> You break into some merry passion
> And so offend him.

(92–97)

It is Shakespeare's capacity "to warme / Our eares" (45–46) that Ben Jonson praises so highly in his dedication to the First Folio.

It might be well to remind ourselves at this juncture that such a way of speaking about playgoing is alien to us. In common parlance we continually refer to plays we have or have not seen. It would never occur to us to say, "Have you heard *The Homecoming* or *The Iceman Cometh*?"

By 1599 the Chorus of *Henry V* indicates a change of perspective on Shakespeare's part. Deprecating the players as "flat unraised spirits," the Chorus pleads for the audience to "piece out [the players'] imperfections with [its] thoughts," concluding his first speech by invoking its humble patience, "Gently to hear, kindly to judge our play" (34). In the prologue to the third act, the Chorus asks the audience to imagine that it has seen certain offstage action. By the introduction to the fourth act the Chorus can invite the audience to "sit and see, / Minding true things by what their mock'ries be" (52–53). Though starting as "gentle hearers," the audience is gradually being transformed into "gentle spectators." Yet at this date Shakespeare knows that the transformation is mere fancy, that the visions he has to offer are visions of the mind rather than of the eyes.

A year or two later Hamlet invites Claudius and Gertrude "to hear and see the matter" of "The Mousetrap" (3.1.23). The matter to be seen must be the Dumb Show. The prevailing mode of speaking about playgoing, however, remains auditory. Hamlet asks whether the King will "hear this / piece of work?" (3.2.44). The Prologue, renowned for being as brief as woman's love, asks:

> For us, and for our tragedy,
> Here stooping to your clemency,
> We beg your hearing patiently.
>
> (3.2.140–42)

With Hamlet, who asks the player for a passionate speech, as with Polonius, who praises Hamlet's "good accent," a play is to be *heard*.

Several years later, sometime between 1606 and 1609, Shakespeare makes another attempt to relate the pleasures of sight and sound. Unlike the impersonal narrator who serves as chorus to *Henry V*, Gower in *Pericles* is the ancient storyteller come "to glad your ear and please your eyes" (4). He immediately asserts the primacy of vision. In the first chorus he tells the audience: "What now ensues, to the judgment of your eye / I give" (41–42). As prologue to Act 2, Gower states: "tid-

ings . . . / Are brought your eyes. What need speak I?'' A dumb show
follows. This confidence of eye over ear is somewhat qualified when
Gower introduces Act 3. Then he confides, ''What's dumb in show I'll
[make] plain with speech'' (14). Finally, before Act 5 begins, Gower
seems to be back where the Chorus to *Henry V* started. He urges the
audience to ''think'' the stage Pericles' ship

> Where what is done in action (more, if might)
> Shall be discover'd—please you sit and hark.
>
> (22–24)

Thus, Gower seems to reverse the progress of the Henrician Chorus. In
Henry V the Chorus asks the auditors to imagine they see until he directly
bids them see; Gower first mixes the pleasures of sound and sight, then
asserts the primacy of vision, only to retreat to the plea that the audience
imagine the stage a ship while it sits and hears.

So equivocal an attitude to the primacy of sound or sight soon
disappears. In *The Winter's Tale*, the chorus Time addresses the ''gentle
spectators'' (Prologue to Act 4). In *The Tempest* Prospero, serving as his
own prologue, bids Ferdinand and Miranda, ''No tongue! All eyes! Be
silent!'' (4.1.59). Earlier he had told Ariel that he must ''Bestow upon
the eyes of this young couple / Some vanity of mine art'' (4.1.40–41). It
is to the spectacle rather than to the speeches or songs that Ferdinand
responds: ''This is a most majestic vision'' (118), he says. By the time
Shakespeare wrote *The Tempest*, the elaborate masques of Inigo Jones
and Ben Jonson had begun to appear. The King's Men were regularly
performing at Blackfriars. A change of audience and theater may have
combined to encourage increased emphasis on the visual elements of
production. But as we can see, Shakespeare had been absorbed by the
question of visual and auditory balance as early as *Henry V*, and so the
changes in fashion could only have intensified a concern that already
existed.

In *The Tempest* the pleasures of sight are mentioned only in connection with the masque. In *Henry VIII*, on the other hand, the entire play is
suffused with that point of view. However much or little a share
Shakespeare may have had in the play, the sentiments reflect the pattern
already evident. Immediately, the Prologue tells us that ''Such noble
scenes as draw the eye to flow, / We now present'' (4–5). He then
divides audiences into two sorts:

> Those that come to see
> Only a show or two and so agree
> The play may pass—if they be still and willing,
> I'll undertake may *see* away their shilling
> Richly in two short hours. Only they
> That come to *hear* a merry bawdy play,
>
>   (9–14) (my italics)

will be disappointed. Yet later the Prologue addresses the audience as "gentle hearers" (17) and "the first and happiest hearers of the town" (24), urging them twice to "think [they] see" and finally to "see" how soon "mightiness meets misery" (30). This is a strange conclusion for Shakespeare to come to after so long a career as a warmer of ears. It suggests that Shakespeare was intrigued from his early days with how to hold the audience's attention and pierce its mind. From his writing it is obvious that Shakespeare never so shifted his priorities that spectacle outran verse. But we do find a tension between these two pleasures—a tension that found other expression than what I have cited in Shakespeare. Platter's delight in the dancing, Ben Jonson's rivalry with Inigo Jones, the flourishing pageants in the streets of London, all express one or another aspect of this tension. Fine clothing and elaborate ceremony appeal to the eye. Perhaps it is significant that puritanical enemies of the stage stressed plain dress and long sermons.

IV

Prospero, as we have heard, orders the young couple not only to see but "be silent." A glance at the earlier plays of Shakespeare indicates a different relationship between hearers and speakers. Besides *A Midsummer Night's Dream* and *Hamlet*, there are play-within-the-play scenes in *Love's Labour's Lost* and *Taming of the Shrew*. All of these plays-within-plays are addressed to hearers. These hearers are far from silent, however. Admittedly, the auditors are noble, the players plebeian. Nevertheless, the interplay between hearer and speaker has a wider application. Rather consistently we find the audience mocking or commenting on the play they hear. In *Dream* and *Love's Labour's Lost* the mockery is savage at times. It dramatizes the situation repeatedly alluded to by players and poets. In the Folio Heminges and Condell address readers who "arraigne Playes dailie." In the induction to *The Malcontent*, John Webster satirizes a gull who wishes to thrust himself

upon the stage of the Globe so that he can censure the play. Thomas
Dekker ironically urges gulls to do so, for in that way they can "engross
the whole commodity of censure." Is it not this kind of censure we
witness in *Love's Labour's Lost*? And is not the pain of the players
enunciated in Holofernes' admonition, "This is not generous, not gentle, not humble" (5.2.621). Oddly enough, the listening audience seems
to have been a speaking audience. Besides the cracking of the shells
there were the auditors' comments to rival the players' speeches,
whether these comments were caustic as in *Dream* and *Love's Labour's
Lost* or deprecatory as in Polonius's response to the Pyrrhus speech in
Hamlet. Spectacle, in order to weave its spell, seems to require silence,
and so Prospero bans "tongues" from his masque.

To what extent the speech of the player not only had to convey
character and emotion but also dominate the volatile playgoers is difficult to say. It is hard to believe that they were so noisy that they could not
hear Shakespeare's lines. Instead, there may have been running commentary that counterpointed the play, leading not to disturbance but a
vital kind of rapport. We have example of such commentary in Japanese
Kabuki production. We are so used to an audience being absolutely
silent during a performance that we find it hard to believe people can
both absorb complex verse and comment on it simultaneously. But I
would suggest that something of the sort went on, both in the public and
the private playhouses.

The nature of the plays and performances may have facilitated these
kinds of responses. About the same time Shakespeare was engaged in
writing *Henry VIII*, Thomas Middleton, in his prologue to *No Wit, No
Help Like a Woman's*, was asking:

How is't possible to suffice
So many Ears, so many Eyes?

He answers by listing the motives of the playgoers:

Some in wit, some in shows
Take delight, and some in Clothes;
Some for mirth they chiefly come,
Some for passion, for both some.

We have already encountered the audience's interest in clothes, whether
worn by the actors or the playgoers. Shows too we have met, either of

the mute kind evident in *Pericles* or the more marvelous in *The Tempest*. It remains to say something about mirth, wit, and passion.

Mirth has the connotation of merriness and farcing. An ancient word, first recorded in the ninth century, mirth initially had a religious association suggesting a spiritual joy. Gradually, it came to mean a merry diversion or entertainment. By the mid-sixteenth century, it was losing its positive meaning. George Whetstone in his dedication to *Promos and Cassandra*, 1578, remarks that contemporary plays "Manye tymes (to make mirthe) . . . make a Clowne companion with a Kinge." Little could he have imagined *King Lear*. The last reference in the Oxford English Dictionary to mirth as entertainment is drawn from *Antony and Cleopatra*. Octavius Caesar, speaking of Antony, concedes scornfully, "Let us grant it not / Amiss . . . To give a Kingdom for a mirth" (1.4.16–18). By the early seventeenth century Joseph Addison compares the word unfavorably with the word cheerfulness.

What we are tracing is how unselfconscious merriment came to be regarded as shallow farce. The turning point is smack in Shakespeare's day, and we can well imagine that for the popular audience mirth still retained a hint of its old meaning. To the extent that it did, the Londoner who came to the public playhouse for mirth expected something more than mere pratfalls, but a childlike and hearty joyfulness, perhaps.

Mirth, of course, is a matter of spirit. There were also those who came for wit. Wit is a consequence of the play of mind. The wild punning of Mercutio and Romeo, the wry or bitter commentary of Feste in *Twelfth Night* and of the Fool in *Lear* are expressions of wit. Middleton, however, is referring to the emergence of the fashionable young gentlemen marked for their quick apprehension. Dauphine, Clerimont, and Truewit in Jonson's *Epicoene* are fully formed figures, heralding the generation of wits we are to find in Fletcher, Shirley, and the Restoration dramatists.

Last are those who come to the playhouse "for passion," as Middleton writes. They are those who, like Hamlet, are apt to cry "come, a passionate speech" (2.2.421). Digges in his dedicatory poem to the folio refers happily to the "Passions of Juliet, and her Romeo." In his power to depict such passions, from the posturing laments of *Richard III* to the denuded anguish of Lear, Shakespeare outshone all rivals. As we read through his plays chronologically, we can appreciate how supple and intricate his depiction of passion becomes. He inherits from Marlowe and Kyd the freedom to display passion in a personal and operatic manner. In *The Spanish Tragedy* what impresses the King as he watches

Balthazar represent the Emperor Soliman, is "how well he acts [Soliman's] amourous passion" (4.4.20). Through the 1590s and the early years of the seventeenth century, it was still possible to present heightened passion as both bold and credible. In the hands of Beaumont and Fletcher, however, it becomes baroque, inflated, subservient to class manners. No wonder it becomes sensational and gives way to the exercise of wit as the fashionable as well as artistic expression of the Caroline theater.

In Shakespeare's day, however, hearing a player delineate a passion was one of the great pleasures of playgoing. Even when Shakespeare mocks the excessive or foolish display of passion in *Dream* and *Hamlet*, he does so to stress right display, a display that for the audience of his day must have appeared increasingly lifelike. Such passion, during the brief period when it could be purely expressed, must have been terribly exciting and novel. Remember, dramatic verse passed from a formal and measured expression to an irregular and personal revelation. In the same time that lies between us and Tennessee Williams's *A Streetcar Named Desire*—roughly twenty-five years—the vitality and imagination of the London stage had been transformed. Even in *Romeo and Juliet* some of the old formality hangs on though already the full-throated cry of love, sorrow, and rage bursts forth. The interweaving of such passion with mirth and wit fulfilled that aim of the stage so often enunciated: delight.

In the dedicatory epistle to the Folio, the plays are presented for the "delight" they offer. Shakespeare's prologues iterate the hope that the play has pleased. These are conventional phrases and, one might argue, not to be taken at face value. All the same, they are not to be lightly dismissed. Diversion, delight, pleasure were the commodities of the playing profession. Ben Jonson called Shakespeare "the delight [and] wonder of our Stage." These words can also be applied to Shakespeare's work. For not only was delight an expected reward of playgoing, so was wonder. In stressing the importance of wonder and delight for the Shakespearean playgoer, I do not wish to simplify the playgoing experience. I do, on the other hand, wish to put that experience in perspective. We too go to the theater for pleasure, but our attitude toward theatrical pleasure is perhaps different from the Elizabethan. If for convenience I can use the old Horatian dichotomy of profit and pleasure as the motives of drama, I would say that we along with the Elizabethans expect both profit and pleasure from play-going. We do differ, however, in what gives us pleasure as well as profit.

In most of our playgoing we separate profit and pleasure. A musical comedy is usually considered as mere entertainment, more suitable for the populace in general than for a true lover of theater. Especially when we attend a Shakespearean production we expect the profit to outweigh the pleasure, or rather the proof that we have had pleasure will reside in the profit we have gained. One of the great achievements of Peter Brook's *A Midsummer Night's Dream*, whatever else one might say about the production, was the unalloyed joy that it stimulated in the audience, especially the young audiences.

The kind of profit we expect to derive from Shakespeare changes with fashion. We have just gone through what one might term the Brechtian or relevancy fad. The profit we expected was insight into our contemporary condition, whether that be political or sexual. Just now we are in a "mythic" phase in which the links of Shakespeare's thoughts to the fundamental experiences of birth, rites of passage, and death are emphasized. In both approaches the fundamental assumption is that we present Shakespeare for the meanings we find in his work. By that measure, we stress the profit of intellectual apprehension to be gained and through which we hope to derive pleasure.

This relative weighing of profit and pleasure is, in my estimation, the reverse of what prevailed among Shakespearean playgoers. Pleasure came first, the pleasure of ear and eye through which they enjoyed the pleasure of the patchquilt narratives of the day. As I have argued, the pleasures of language as conveyor of witty duels and passionate reactions were most important for the greater part of Shakespeare's career. The pleasures of the eye received less emphasis, and as a result probably stimulated less inventive means of expression. These pleasures were the base upon which playgoing was founded. Larger meanings of existence and deeper insights into human action were there, but they were experienced by the audience as an overtone, as a fringe benefit to be appreciated by those of greater understanding, whether noble or commoner. We must remember that the playgoer then did not see the Shakespearean play as we do now, that is, either as one in a festival of his plays or as a single, long-running production. Shakespeare's plays were rotated in the repertory the same as any other. One day a person might see *Lear*, the next *A Yorkshire Tragedy*. Plays did not remain terribly long in repertory. With a few exceptions, two or three years would be all for the most popular plays, and even then the total number of performances would not exceed twenty or so. Shakespeare's plays were caught up in the business of theater just as the films of the twenties and thirties that we so admire now were caught up in the business of film making. As a result, they did not receive the self-conscious attention we bestow on emerging works of art. Playgoers went to see them for the excitement and pleasure not for the artistry, and that I would argue is a more fruitful atmosphere in which to attend a play.

Obviously, we can never return to that sort of unselfconsciousness. Shakespeare's plays will always excite unusual expectations. These expectations are inescapable. But if that is so, how can we ever enjoy the type of delight the Elizabethans expected and that seems to depend on spontaneous response? By clinging to our expectations, I would suggest. Since we can never return to a state of artistic innocence, we should move in the opposite direction. We should cultivate our expectations. We should examine them, add to them, enrich them. Above all, we should make them more detailed and precise—precise as to the quality of ideas we will accept from a production, precise as to the fullness with which events are presented, precise as to the connection between word, gesture, and situation we insist upon. For the more we the playgoers know about theater art, how it works, and how to apply its own critiques to Shakespearean performance, the more easily we can perceive those moments, rare enough it is true, when the performers achieve that nearly miraculous blending of fantasy and familiarity, of nature and art, which the Shakespearean playgoer took for granted.

NOTES

1. In a forthcoming study, Ann Jennalie Cook challenges Harbage's theory of a representative audience. She emphasizes evidence that suggests the overwhelming number of spectators were members of the gentry.

2. Ernest L. Rhodes in his *Henslowe's Rose: The Stage & Staging* (1976) adopts Frances Yates's argument for a recessed stage without adding materially to evidence for such a stage.

3. *Thomas Platter's Travels in England 1599*, trans. and intro. Clare Williams (London: 1937), pp. 166–67.

4. *Strange Island: Britain Through Foreign Eyes 1395*–1940, compiled and ed. Francesca M. Wilson (London, 1955), pp. 40–42.

5. Poem prefixed to the first edition of Beaumont's and Fletcher's *Works* (1647).

6. *Strange Island*, p. 26.

10

Beyond Words:
Shakespeare's Tongue-Tied Muse

TOMMY RUTH WALDO

"TONGUE-TIED" IS WITH GOOD REASON A WORD NOT USUALLY APPLIED to Shakespeare or his times. During the second half of the sixteenth century at least seventeen vernacular works on the art of rhetoric were published; one (Sir Thomas Wilson's) went through eight editions between 1553 and 1585. Almost as many treatises on poetic and educational theory appeared. An alphabetical table of English words was compiled. Poems were composed. Plays were written. To this verbal world, according to Spevack's *Harvard Concordance to Shakespeare* (1973), Shakespeare contributed 887,647 words. Many of these words concern language—"rhetoric," (used 8 times), "discourse" and its variants (used some 71 times), "language" and its variations (used some 47 times), "word" and "words" (used some 967 times), "speech" and "speak" in their several forms (used some 1,600 times). In contrast, "languageless" and "wordless" occur one time each, "tongueless" four times, "speechless" 15 times, and "tongue-tied" 12 times. As this token evidence indicates, contemporary interest in language ran high, and the prevailing focus centered on the potential of language, not on its limitations.

Analyses of Shakespeare's style have therefore usually stressed aspects of his language—its sound, its variety, its patterns, its poetics, its meanings, its interplay with action and theme, its rhetorical qualities.[1] On occasion, analyses have discussed the structural and atmospheric effects of words accompanied by music.[2] Sometimes they have studied the prosodic pauses in language, the limitations that language places on action or that action places on language.[3] But in general, stylistic analyses have not emphasized Shakespeare's dramatic use of the inadequacies of language, of halting speech or deep silence, of the wordlessness suggested by a few of the above figures. They have not attended the communication gaps that develop when a character under emotional stress attempts to express the inexpressible.[4]

This paper will therefore explore in several dramatic situations the faltering language which accompanies love and advancing death. It will notice reactions to love in the feeble love notes of Benedick, Orlando, and Hamlet, the feigned wordlessness of Cressida, and the defensive silence of Hermione; it will also consider the points of stillness and the audible music of the spheres that occur when death approaches King John (*King John*) and Queen Katherine (*Henry VIII*). It will observe, in conclusion, the effect on Pericles of both love and oncoming death. This paper will thus examine Shakespeare's[5] technique with what is beyond words, with what Sonnet 85 calls the "tongue-tied Muse."

I

The contemporary language code for young men in love—at least in literature—followed Petrarch and rhetorical theory.[6] Love, according to these traditions, inspired the creation of verse; verse, moreover, provided a way to put into words the ecstasy of the love passion. Yet when Benedick, Orlando, and Hamlet find love, they cannot discover the Muse. All try their hand at writing, but all grind out trite comparisons, jog-trot rhythms, and shallow sentimentality.

Benedick in *Much Ado About Nothing* comes to the world of poetry both suddenly and late in the play. The worlds he knows are the military and the court, and for these he needs the language of prose. Both require combat—one physical and one verbal. When he arrives in Messina fresh from triumphs as a soldier, he must immediately mount a new campaign—this one a war of wits with Beatrice, the "merry war" of which Leonato speaks in the first scene. In this word clash Benedick can barely hold his ground. If he labels Beatrice "Lady Disdain," she taunts him with "Is it possible Disdain should die while she hath such meet food to feed it as Signior Benedick?" (1.1.106–7). If he asks whether she takes pleasure in calling him to dinner, she quips, "Yea, just so much as you may take upon a knife's point and choke a daw withal" (2.3.233–34). Soon Benedick cries out in desperation, "If I do not take pity of her, I am a villain; if I do not love her, I am a Jew" (2.3.240–41). His battle, already weakened, is lost when his friends unite to play Cupid and when he joins with Beatrice to champion Hero; then he is forced to

declare, "By this hand, I love thee" (4.1.319). By the second scene of
Act 5 his love for Beatrice has brought him to the need for poetry: he
wants to praise her in verse.

Just a short time earlier Benedick was mourning the effect of love on
Claudio's language and wondering if he too will be susceptible to similar
charges:

> He was wont to speak plain and to the purpose,
> like an honest man and a soldier; and now he
> is turn'd orthography; his words are a very
> fantastical banquet, just so many strange dishes.
>
> (2.3.17–20)

Now Benedick has a like desire for the exaggerated phrases of love.

The verse that Benedick recites begins with an allusion to a poem
from *A Handful of Pleasant Delights* (1584)—to the title, "The joy of
Virginitie: to, The Gods of love," and to part of line three, "his
heavenly throne above." [7] Hyder Rollins explains that this poem "is a
moralization of William Elderton's famous ballad, 'The Gods of
Love,' . . . which was printed in 1562, but which survives only in the
snatch sung by Benedick in *Much Ado* . . . ." [8] Benedick's version
consists of a dimeter couplet half borrowed from the ballad, a repetitious
third line, and an off beat fourth line:

> The god of love,
> That sits above,
> And knows me, and knows me,
> How pitiful I deserve,—

After four brief lines Benedick breaks off. He confesses that Leander
and Troilus and other names that "yet run smoothly in the even road of a
blank verse, why, they were never so truly turn'd over and over as my
poor self in love." But though he feels love, he "cannot show it in
rhyme." His rhymes turn out to be "lady" and "baby," "scorn" and
"horn," "school" and "fool." All are faulty either in sound or meaning. "No," he concludes, "I was not born under a rhyming planet, nor I
cannot woo in festival terms" (5.2.26–38). Thus, Benedick must reject
the way of conventional love verse and, indeed, the articulation of his
feelings. Like the sonneteer he is absorbed by love but tongue-tied in the
experience.

Orlando in *As You Like It* is thrust into the need for poetry by the
eye-diet of Rosalind. He comes into the world of courtship unprepared

and unsophisticated. By nature (birth) he is noble, but by training he is rude and rough, as in his first meeting with Rosalind. By the time he comes to the greenwood, he is transformed by love. Like Benedick he has been accustomed to speaking in prose, but unlike Benedick he does not lose his voice in love. He tries it in an eight-line and then in a thirty-line unit. His poems, though, move in a hammering rhythm, and his rhymes increase the pounding effect, as Touchstone's "If a hart do lack a hind" parody is quick to point out (3.2.96–107). The ideas in the poems are as exaggerated as the sounds and rhythms are monotonous. Not even a jewel can compare with Rosalind; hers is the only face worthy to be remembered. Also, she surpasses the beauty of Helen, the majesty of Cleopatra, the fleetness of Atalanta, the modesty of Lucretia; indeed, she was devised by Heavenly synod (3.2.139–48). But with all his verbiage Orlando acknowledges the inadequacy of words. In answer to Rosalind's question "But are you so much in love as your rhymes speak?" Orlando responds in prose, "Neither rhyme nor reason can express how much" (3.2.375). Orlando too has tried words—especially conventional poetic expressions—and has found them inadequate.

Hamlet also finds that words fail to express the depths of his feelings. At the end of his first soliloquy he reveals that he is aware of circumstances that prevent even attempted descriptions of his emotions— "But break my heart, for I must hold my tongue" (1.2.159). By the time of his "O what a rogue and peasant slave am I" soliloquy, though still hemmed in by a time that is out of joint, he now wonders about a player who "but in a fiction" can imitate the words and actions of grief. Though with real cause for grief he "Like John-a-dreams, unpregnant of my cause, / Can say nothing" (2.2.534–53). When he speaks of love, Hamlet is again troubled by his inadequacy with words. What he discloses about his attitude toward Ophelia is often equivocal, but he has at some time written to her, making a straightforward avowal of his love, as Polonius reports to Claudius.[9] Part of Hamlet's expression is in verse:

> Doubt thou the stars are fire,
>   Doubt that the sun doth move,
> Doubt truth to be a liar,
>   But never doubt I love.

Like Benedick he finds himself "ill at these numbers"; "I have not art," he says, "to reckon my groans; but that I love thee best, O most best, believe it" (2.2.116–24).

Though Hamlet acknowledges his inability to find words for his emotions, he is more effective than Benedick and Orlando. He conveys his meaning by four commands about doubt—three positive and one negative. The things to be tested by doubt, moreover, are not open to question—the stars, the sun, truth; by placing his love on such a level Hamlet emphasizes its strength and sincerity. In addition to his effective repetition of the word "doubt" and its connotations, Hamlet makes subtle use of alliteration ("stars," "sun," "liar," "love"); one pair occur in the middle of the first two lines, and the other two at the end of the second two lines. The rhymes he chooses include the frequently coupled "move" and "love," but also the slightly more original juxtaposition of "liar" and "fire." Even the rhythm he selects, which at first blush seems jog-trot, shows a degree of inventiveness—for example, the varying initial patterns, two trochees, a spondee, and an iamb. Thus, Hamlet is not as verbally inept as he thinks or pretends he is, and, in keeping with his more complex nature, he is more articulate and at the same time more aware of the discrepancy between words and feelings than are his counterparts Benedick and Orlando.

Petrarchan convention offered models and rhetorical books instructions for amorous verse. When Benedick, Orlando, and Hamlet attempt to follow the traditional advice, however, they fail. Their words perhaps are artificial in the Renaissance sense of "improved by art," but, more important, they are artificial in the modern sense of "unnatural," "simulated," "affected." They fail to express the true feelings of the lovers. Instead, the lovers are inarticulate in the all encompassing experience of true love. Like Shakespeare in Sonnet 85 they have discovered the distance between the word and the feeling. Yet in spite of their awareness of the gap between word and thought, in spite of their tongue-tied condition, Shakespeare in the sonnet and the young men in the plays breathe sincerity and depth of emotion. It is the same honesty which emanates from the conclusion of Sonnet 130; after twelve lines of anti-Petrarchanism the poet concludes, "And yet, by heaven, I think my love as rare / As any she beli'd with false compare."

II

Whereas apt words were expected from young men in love, amorous declarations were denied their feminine counterparts. Though she does not speak of language, Helena defines the code. "We cannot fight for love, as men may do. / We should be woo'd and were not made to woo" (*A Midsummer Night's Dream*, 2.1.241–42). Both Cressida and Hermione are caught by these limitations, one out of wedlock and one in marriage; one reacts by pretending to bow to custom, the other by waiting in silence for heaven to justify her position.

Although Ulysses sees that "There's language in her eye, her cheek, her lip," and even her foot and implies that she is "glib of tongue" (*Troilus and Cressida*, 4.5.55–58), Cressida plays—at least for a while—the role of the decorous lady, restrained by convention from expressing her love. She is hardly one of the "tongue-tied maidens" of whom Pandarus speaks in Act 3—but she pretends to be. When she is viewing with Pandarus the procession of Trojan warriors returning from battle, she is witty but noncommittal, even with this man who is a member of her family. Her uncle, determined to move her, laces his dialogue with phrases designed to glorify Troilus. "Would I could see Troilus now! You shall see Troilus anon." "I marvel where Troilus is." "I marvel where Troilus is. Hark! do you not hear the people cry 'Troilus'?" "'Tis Troilus! There's a man, niece! Hem! Brave Troilus! the prince of chivalry!'" "Mark him; note him. O brave Troilus! . . . O admirable man!" (1.2.205–25). Cressida answers indifferently: "For then the man's date's out" (244); the time is not right for Troilus. When Pandarus accuses her of lying, she accepts his bawdy pun and transfers it to mean a defense of her good name. Alone after her uncle's departure, however, Cressida reveals her strategy. Although Troilus has indeed caught her eye and her passions, she holds her distance in word and deed. "But more in Troilus thousandfold I see / Than in the glass of Pandar's praise may be; / Yet hold I off" (1.2.270–72). Thus, Cressida can articulate her feelings, but hides behind convention.

In a later scene Cressida's dissembling is intensified, now with the aid of Pandarus. Like Theseus's poet giving "to airy nothing / A local habitation and a name" (*A Midsummer Night's Dream*—5.1.16–17), Pandarus builds in the imagination of Troilus, already giddy and wordless, the picture of a girl who does not exist—a blushing and breathless maiden, too shy to show her face or even to speak:

> She's making her ready, she'll come straight . . . . She does so blush, and fetches her wind so short, as if she were frayed with a spirit . . . she fetches her breath so short as a new-ta'en sparrow.
>
> . . . .

> Come, come, what need you blush? Shame's a baby . . . What, are
> you gone again? . . . Come your ways, come your ways; an you draw
> backward, we'll put you i' th' fills . . . . Come, draw this curtain, and
> let's see your picture.
>
> (3.2.28–32, 38–46)

Playing her part with skill, Cressida gives the appearance of having
trouble with her words. When Troilus exclaims over being admitted to
her presence, she responds with a question and the start of a seemingly
unguarded admission. "Wish'd, my lord? The gods grant—O my
lord!" Troilus is quick to catch the apparent slip. "What should they
grant? What makes this pretty abruption?" (3.2.59–61). But Cressida
cannot maintain her pretense for long. Only a few lines later she is
avowing boldness and revealing how easily Troilus won her. "Boldness
comes to me now." "Hard to seem won; but I was won, my lord / With
the first glance that ever— . . ." "Why have I blabb'd?" (3.2.106,
121–32). Her release into speech and love receives applause from
Pandarus, who wishes the same for all young women:

> And Cupid grant all tongue-tied maidens here
> Bed, chamber, Pandar to provide this gear!
>
> (3.2.201–2)

For the rest of the play Cressida is anything but tongue-tied. Her vows
to Troilus stress her intended constancy at the same time that they
suggest, through her repeated use of the word "false" and of conditional
sentence structure, her lack of faithfulness. Seeming to believe her own
words, she contributes to what Ann Barton in the introduction to the play
in *The Riverside Shakespeare* calls "the hiatus between a character's
words and actions, between the verbal formulation of intent and subsequent behavior." During the beginnings of her association with
Troilus, Cressida was aware of the relationship between her seeming
speechlessness and her feelings. In her passion for Troilus she loses for a
little while her self-insight. With Diomedes, though she breaks faith,
she acquires anew a clear view of herself. "I will not keep my word."
"The error of our eye directs our mind" (5.2.94,106). With her eyes at
last open to herself and her future Cressida has no more reason to play
the tongue-tied maiden.

Hermione in *The Winter's Tale* is all the things which Cressida is
not—a loving wife and mother, a steadfast friend, a gracious hostess, a

majestic queen. Yet her virtues do not save her from false accusations; in her husband's eyes she is as faithless as Cressida. Driven by Leontes' irrational jealousy, Hermione assumes a defensive silence. At first she is quiet from courtesy. When her husband, entreating her to persuade Polixenes to prolong his visit, asks, "Tongue-tied, my queen? Speak you," Hermione responds, "I had thought, sir, to have held my peace until / You had drawn oaths from him not to stay" (1.2.28–30). Later she remains quiet because she cannot communicate with her husband. Seeing that he is deaf to her words and blind to her character, she becomes the tongue-tied queen he has labeled her. Then she says axiomatically, "One good deed dying tongueless / Slaughters a thousand waiting upon that. / Our praises are our wages" (1.2.92–94). Although "tongueless" is here glossed in *The Riverside Shakespeare* as "without praise," it carries a reflection of Leontes' epithet. Also, it gathers importance when later in the scene Camillo urges "forsealing [silencing] / The injury of tongues in courts and kingdoms / Known and allied to yours" (1.2.336–38). Hermione's tongue is tied, while slanderous tongues are loosed, though a few tongues move to speak in her defense.

When, however, loyal Paulina raises her voice for the Queen—"I'll use that tongue I have," she says (2.2.53)—and for her efforts becomes in Leontes' view "a callet [scold] of boundless tongue" and Antigonus's "lewd-tongu'd wife" (2.3.90–91,172), Hermione still prefers the defense of silence. Uncomplaining endurance is her way. In spite of her long speeches, which at first blush seem to contradict the description "tongue-tied" (act 2, sc. 1 and act 3, sc. 2), she places her faith not on a factual or legal basis but on her integrity and signals from heaven—on silence. Heaven has brought misfortune; heaven will take it away:

> There's some ill planet reigns:
> I must be patient, till the heavens look
> With aspect more favorable.
>
> (2.1.105–7)

> Being counted falsehood, shall as I express it,
> Be so receiv'd. But thus: —If powers divine
> Behold our human actions, as they do,
> I doubt not then but innocence shall make
> False accusation blush, and tyranny
> Tremble at patience.
>
> (3.2.26–31)

Hermione's confidence appears justified when the oracle sends down the verdict proclaiming her innocence. As Paulina says when she presents the baby Perdita to Leontes, "The silence often of pure innocence / Persuades when speaking fails" (2.2.41–42).

In spite of the voice of heaven, true restoration for Hermione is sixteen years in coming. When she does reappear, she is revealed as a statue in an awesome and absolute silence. Paulina describes the scene. "I like your silence; it the more shows off / Your wonder" (5.3.21–22). Leontes responds to the marvelous likeness of his queen, "O royal piece, / There's magic in thy majesty." "I am content to look on" (5.3.38–39,92). Only one barrier remains between husband and wife; Paulina defines it for Leontes: "It is requir'd / You do awake your faith" (5.3.94–95). When Leontes acquiesces, "Proceed; / Nor foot shall stir" (5.3.97–98)—, Hermione has no need for words. Still in silence, she steps down from her pedestal and embraces her husband in forgiveness and reunion. When she does speak, she addresses the gods and her daughter, not her husband:

> You gods, look down
> And from your sacred vials pour your graces
> Upon my daughter's head! Tell me, mine own,
> Where hast thou been preserv'd? where liv'd? how found
> Thy father's court?
>
> (5.3.121–29)

Hermione's long ordeal is concluded and with it her defensive silence. Now if she is tongue-tied, her difficulty with speech must come from a heart full of love, not grief and fear.

III

Characters in love, then, according to several Shakespearean plays, may find themselves at a loss for words. Characters approaching death, charged with a different kind of emotion, may suffer from a similar difficulty. Though some (like Gaunt) react by articulating great truths in their final hours, a number of others respond in reflective quiet, with increased sensitivity but decreased verbal powers. In their stillness they are apt to think of music or to hear music—probably the music of the spheres. Several examples come to mind. Hamlet's last words are "The rest is silence"; Horatio's farewell is "And flights of angels sing thee to thy rest!'' Emilia in *Othello* dies saying, ''I will play the swan, / And die in music,'' and like her mistress she sings ''Willow, willow, willow!'' Lear, hovering speechless between life and death, awakes to the sound of music, and just before his death suggests to Cordelia, ''We two alone will sing like birds i' th' cage.'' Shakespeare's depiction of King John (*King John*) and Queen Katherine (*Henry VIII*) near death demonstrates the technique in depth, as in their transitional state they partake of two worlds—the earthly and the heavenly. Their experience brings them both the silence of death and the sound of music.

In the final scene of *King John* Prince Henry and Pembroke discuss the condition of the king, who is dying of poison. Already caught by the silence of death, the king has rallied in his final moments to break forth into song. His reaction is compared to the swan, which, according to mythology, sings only at death, and also to the organ, which speaks (sings) body and soul to eternal rest:

PEMBROKE.   He is more patient
Than when you left him; even now he sung.
PRINCE HENRY. O vanity of sickness! . . .
. . . .
'Tis strange that death should sing.
I am the cygnet to this pale faint swan
Who chants a doleful hymn to his own death.
And from the organ pipe of frailty sings
His soul and body to their lasting rest.

(5.7.11–24)

Here Prince Henry combines the concept of swan song and funeral music. If his analogy follows Plato,[10] it means that John like the swan is expressing in music his joy at being transferred from the flesh to the spirit. The organ pipe stands for the human voice—John's and also a choir's; in addition, it refers to the pipe of an organ that speaks or sings to the vibrations of air columns. Both connote the Requiem (''Grant them eternal rest, O lord—Requiem aeternam dona eis, Domine''). As the Prince blends the two concepts, the song of the swan becomes the funeral hymn and the voice of the king the organ and choir for the last rites. The combination of elements emphasizes the dual status of the King, more in the next world than this, yet hanging precariously to life on earth. In his condition he has lost the power of speech and gained the power of music.

In *Henry VIII* the ill Queen Katherine, also on the borderline between life and death, retains her ability to speak and uses it to articulate her

anticipation of the peace and ethereal music of eternity. Her thoughts
alternate between earth and heaven. At her funeral, she says, she wants
only one tongue in eulogy—Griffith's. During her time of waiting she
will listen to music—music that will both sound her knell and prepare
her for entry into another world. Always responsive to music, she had
after her trial requested a song to help disperse her troubles; the result
was "Orpheus with His Lute" (3.1.1–14). Now she prefers a sad note:

>   Good Griffith,
> Cause the musicians play me that sad note
> I nam'd my knell, whilst I sit meditating
> On that celestial harmony I go to.
>
>   (4.2.77–80)

As the music plays, she has a vision of "six personages, clad in white
robes, wearing on their heads garlands of bays, and golden vizards on
their faces, ..." and dancing around her. At the sight she shows signs
of rejoicing, so that after the dream is over she feels deprived:

> Spirits of peace, where are ye? Are ye all gone
> And leave me here in wretchedness behind ye?
> . . . .
>
> Saw you not, even now, a blessed troop
> Invite me to a banquet . . .?
> . . . .
>
> They promis'd me eternal happiness,
> And brought me garlands, Griffith, which I feel
> I am not worthy yet to wear. I shall, assuredly.
>
>   (4.2.83–92)

After the vision her thoughts become more and more set on heaven. Now
in comparison with the celestial harmonies she has heard, human instruments seem inadequate. "Bid the music leave," she says, speaking
of the court ensemble; "They are harsh and heavy to me" (4.2.94–95).
Katherine is now ready for death—for earthly silence and cosmic
sounds.

IV

Part of Shakespeare's technique, then, as seen above, is to reveal that
characters in plays like characters in life are often caught in emotions

which words cannot express. Such involuntary curbs on language often arise from feelings of love and anticipation of death. In *Pericles* Shakespeare shows both reactions in one character. During the play, sprawling as it does over time and space, Pericles experiences the coming of love and just escapes knowing the coming of death. In both cases his language is impaired and eventually is taken away altogether.

When false love (infatuation for Antiochus's daughter) afflicts Pericles, he pours out his ecstasy in a flood of words, filled with farfetched images. Antiochus has begun the exaggerated language in his command for his daughter's entrance. His words at the time seem like those of an over-fond father; later it becomes clear that they are heavy with implication of incest. "Bring in our daughter, clothed like a bride / For the embracements even of Jove himself" (1.1.6–7). Pericles takes his cue from Antiochus and from the girl in front of him. He compares her to the spring, her thoughts to a king, her face to a book, her love to the fruit of a tree; he ranges from the heights of the gods to the depths of the grave in his attempt to do justice to the girl who fills him with desire. "See where she comes, apparell'd like the spring, . . . her thoughts the king / Of every virtue . . .! / Her face the book of praises." He appeals for help to the gods "That have inflam'd desire in my breast / To taste the fruit of yon celestial tree / Or die in the adventure . . ." (1.1.13–25). In his emotional state Pericles sees only as far as appearances permit. Because the girl has beauty of body, he takes for granted that she has beauty of soul, that the beautiful must signal the presence of the good and the true. He believes also that his feelings are heaven-sent, inspired ("inflam'd") by the gods. His language reflects the swirling emotions of his false love.

In the face of true love, however, Pericles is strangely tongue-tied. At the court of Pentapolis with Simonides and Thaisa, even when asked to identify himself, he has been sparing with his words. "A gentleman of Tyre; my name, Pericles; / My education been in arts and arms" (2.3.81–85). He praises Thaisa only at the prodding of her father. She is "a most virtuous princess"; she is "as a fair day in summer—wondrous fair" (2.5.34,37). His avowal of love takes only one line—a fragment of a sentence. He loves Thaisa "Even as my life my blood that fosters it" (2.5.89). Not until the recovery scene in Act 5 does he reveal the extent to which he has noticed and held details of sight and sound from Pentapolis. Then he remembers Thaisa's brows, her stature, her voice, her eyes. In courtship, however, Pericles is inarticulate.

Only in defense of his honor does he find his voice. Simonides, like

Prospero, pretends to disapprove the match and, like Brabantio, accuses Pericles of bewitching his daughter. The incensed Pericles answers vehemently, "By the gods, I have not. / Never did thought of mine levy offence; / . . .My actions are as noble as my thoughts" (2.5.51–52,59). He has words when his good name is questioned.

If we may count on the text in this part of the play, Pericles' unusual quiet and also his staunch self-defense are devices of characterization. In the face of real love he is unable to put his feelings into words. In act 2, scene 5, with a total of ninety-three lines, Pericles speaks only thirty-two lines (or parts of lines), in contrast to the King's fifty-eight; seventeen of Pericles' lines pertain to the defense of his honor. When he tries to convey his love, he can only deliver one line (2.5.89).

The emotion of love, thus, seems to diminish his ability to speak. Certainly the emotion of grief in the final act of the play reduces him to a state of complete wordlessness and death-like numbness. In Helicanus's words he is "A man who for this three months hath not spoken / To anyone, nor taken sustenance" (5.1.24–25). Pericles, who has withstood the external dangers of false friends and stormy seas, finally succumbs to the internal attacks of emotion. Early in the play he acknowledged the devastating effects of "the passions of the mind"[11]—of fear that "makes both my body pine and soul to languish" and of melancholy, "dull-ey'd Melancholy" (1.2.1–33). In Act 1 Pericles controlled the problem of fear for himself and for his people by appointing a deputy ruler and by making himself a running target. By Act 5, with the reasonable and sensible aspects of his tripartite soul gone, he has lost control of himself and of his kingdom. He is reduced to being "heavy Pericles" (Gower's description—Prologue to Act 5) with "deafen'd parts" (Lysimachus's words—5.1.47), silent tongue, and insensitive senses. Sadness and despair have altered his mind and body so that he is near death—a speechless shell of a man.

In this condition Pericles' responsiveness to music links him to two worlds. The voice of his daughter Marina anchors him to this world and causes him to utter sounds—first just a "Hum, ha!" (5.2.84),[12] then faltering questions about what she is saying. His increasing ability to articulate marks the renewal of his life and ultimately the resumption of his place in his family, his kingdom, and his universe. Then the authority in his voice gradually increases. With the rediscovered Thaisa he still has need for only a few words: "O come, be buried / A second time within these arms" (5.3.43–44). To Lysimachus he grants permission to woo and wed Marina and to reign in Tyre; he and Thaisa, he announces, will rule in Pentapolis (5.1.262–63; 5.3.79–82). He comes to the restoration of his faculties and his realm with sharpened perceptions; he has endured the ravages of time and tragedy.

Although Pericles returns to this world in response to Marina's song, he has been near enough to death to identify the music of the spheres and to hear the voice of the goddess Diana. "But hark, what music?" he asks Helicanus. At the response, "My lord, I hear none," he describes the sounds: "The music of the spheres!" "Most heavenly music! / It nips me unto listening, and thick slumber / Hangs upon mine eyes. Let me rest" (5.1.225–34). In a vision, then, Pericles sees and hears the goddess Diana. What she reveals to him eventually drives him completely back into the world of the living, for she leads him to Thaisa. Through his submission to divine will, Pericles has regained his temporal position and at the same time obtained an insight into eternity. Silence and music have made both possible.

V

Shakespeare, then, has experimented with techniques for conveying what is beyond words. He has shown that three young men cannot compress their love into lines of verse or harness their feelings within verbal patterns—especially when they are such inept lyricists. He has, in addition, exposed the shallowness of Cressida's affections by revealing that her speechlessness is feigned, that her language parallels her actions. He has, in contrast, emphasized the steadfastness of Hermione's devotion by displaying her silent acceptance of false accusations, years of waiting, and final reunion with her husband. Matters of the heart, if genuine, he seems to suggest, defy expression.

Shakespeare has also explored the relationship between language and emotions aroused by the approach of death. Where words fail now, he uses music for a pivot, as in the death scenes of John and Katherine. John's song thus signals the departure of his soul from his body ("this muddy vesture of decay") and his entry into spiritual realms. Katherine's perception of celestial sounds and sights indicates her readiness for eternity, though she remains for a while suspended between two worlds, aware of both. In her case as in John's, silence provides access to the next life and allows heavenly music to penetrate mortal ears. By drawing on the old Pythagorean notions of cosmic harmony Shakespeare has created the dramatic illusion of heaven and earth.

Because of its epic scope Shakespeare in *Pericles* can follow a man from young love to the threshold of death. Pericles jousts for Thaisa's hand, wins under adverse circumstances, and also earns praise for his musical performance. ("My education been in arts and arms"— 2.3.82). But he cannot speak his love. Years later, after repeated blows from Fortune, he again loses his voice, this time from the proximity of death. Like John and Katherine he hears, because of his increased receptivity, the far-off music of the spheres. In this play as elsewhere Shakespeare has witnessed the distance and paradoxically the connection between language and emotion.

Of course, Shakespeare's experiment with expressing the inexpressible includes other emotions beyond those aroused by romantic love and encroaching death. In Cordelia he shows the language difficulties of filial love: "Love, and be silent." "I am sure my love's / More ponderous than my tongue." "Unhappy that I am, I cannot heave / My heart into my mouth." In Othello, especially in his fragmented trance speech, and in Leontes he displays incoherence born of jealousy: as Othello exclaims, "It is not words that shakes me thus." Similarly, by distorted language—ranting, loud singing, then loss of speech in deep slumber—Shakespeare projects the degree of Lear's madness. Sometimes his characters find evils too horrible to label. Othello in agony at the murder scene cannot give a name to the cause: "It is the cause, it is the cause, my soul; / Let me not name it to you, you chaste stars." In a different kind of horror the witches chant to Macbeth about "a deed without a name."[13] And grief for Richard's young queen is "nameless woe." Shakespeare's experiment thus extends to various indescribable things.

In general, Shakespeare, in a manner reminiscent of Aristotelian precepts, brings his characters to self-examination and reflection. He creates for them lofty measures built in part on rhetorical tradition and received beliefs about the power of the word.[14] Yet even his soaring blank verse falls short of giving full expression to their emotions. For these feelings which are beyond words, then, Shakespeare sometimes reveals his tongue-tied Muse.

My tongue-tied Muse in manners holds her still,
While comments of your praise, richly compil'd,

Reserve their character with golden quill
And previous phrase by all the Muses fil'd.
I think good thoughts whilst other write good words,
And, like unlettered clerk, still cry "Amen"
To every hymn that able spirit affords
In polish'd form of well-refined pen.
Hearing you prais'd, I say, "'Tis so, 'tis true,"
And to the most of praise add something more;
But that is in my thought, whose love to you,
Though words come hindmost, holds his rank before.
Then others for the breath of words respect;
Me for my dumb thoughts, speaking in effect.

(sonnet 85)

NOTES

1. See, for example, Edwin Abbott, *A Shakespearean Grammar* (London, 1901); Richard D. Altick, "Symphonic Imagery in *Richard II*," *Publications of the Modern Language Association* 62 (1947): 339–65; Edward A. Armstrong, *Shakespeare's Imagination* (London, 1946); Paul E. Bennett, "The Statistical Measurement of a Stylistic Trait in *Julius Caesar* and *As You Like It*," *Shakespeare Quarterly* 8 (1957): 33–50; Muriel C. Bradbrook, "Fifty Years of the Criticism of Shakespeare's Style: A Retrospect," in *Shakespeare Survey* 7 (Cambridge, Mass., 1954); Delores Burton, *Shakespeare's Grammatical Style* (Austin, Tex., 1973); Wolfgang H. Clemen, *The Development of Shakespeare's Imagery* (Cambridge, Mass., 1951); Oliver Elton, *Style in Shakespeare* (London, 1936); B. I. Evans, *The Language of Shakespeare's Plays* (London, 1952); Robert O. Evans, *The Osier Cage: Rhetorical Devices in "Romeo and Juliet"* (Lexington, Ky., 1966); Hilda M. Hulme, *Explorations in Shakespeare's Language* (London, 1962); Sister Miriam Joseph, *Shakespeare's Use of the Arts of Language* (New York, 1947); Milton Boone Kennedy, *The Oration in Shakespeare* (Chapel Hill, N.C., 1942); Mikhail Morozov, "The Individualization of Shakespeare's Characters Through Imagery," in *Shakespeare Survey* 2 (Cambridge, Mass., 1949); Caroline Spurgeon, *Shakespeare's Imagery and What It Tells Us* (Cambridge, Mass., 1935); Robert Weimann, "Shakespeare's Wordplay: Popular Origins and Theatrical Functions," in *Shakespeare 1971*, ed. Clifford Leech and J. M. R. Margeson (Toronto, 1972).

2. See, for example, Sir Frederick Bridge, *Shakespearean Music in the Plays and Early Operas* (London, 1965); G. H. Cowling, *Music on the Shakespearean Stage* (Cambridge, Mass., 1913); Louis C. Elson, *Shakespeare in Music* (Boston, 1900); Phyllis Hartnoll, ed., *Shakespeare in Music* (New York, 1966); John H. Long, *Shakespeare's Use of Music . . .* I, II, III (Gainesville, Fla., 1955, 1961, 1971); A. H. Moncur-Sime, *Shakespeare: His Music and Song* (London, n.d.); Edward W. Naylor, *Shakespeare and Music* (London, 1931); Richard Noble, *Shakespeare's Use of Song* (Oxford, 1923); Peter J. Seng, *The Vocal Songs in the Plays of Shakespeare* (Cambridge, Mass., 1967); F. W. Sternfeld, *Music in Shakespearean Tragedy* (London, 1963); James J. Wey, "Musical Allusion and Song as Part of the Structure of Meaning of Shakespeare's Plays" (Ph.D. diss., Catholic University of America, 1957).

3. See, for example, James L. Calderwood, *Shakespearean Metadrama* (Minneapolis, Minn., 1971), pp. 9, 20–21, 149–86; Alfred Harbage, *Shakespeare Without Words* (Cambridge, Mass., 1972), especially p. 11; M. M. Mahood, *Shakespeare's Wordplay* (London, 1957, 1965), pp.

176–85; Ants Oras, *Pause Patterns in Elizabethan and Jacobean Drama* (Gainesville, Fla., 1960).

4. For a related discussion—concerning Romeo's character and style—see Leo Kirshbaum, *Character and Characterization in Shakespeare* (Detroit, Mich., 1962), pp. 111-18.

5. For this paper I ignore the authorship problems and assume that Shakespeare wrote all of *Pericles* and *Henry VIII*.

6. See George Puttenham, *The Art of English Poesie* (1589), ed. Gladys D. Walker (Cambridge, Mass., 1936), pp. 44–45. Puttenham devotes chap. 22 to the subject "In what forme of Poesie the amorous affections and allurements were uttered."

7. Clement Robinson and Divers Others, *A Handful of Pleasant Delights* (1584), ed. Hyder E. Rollins, (New York, 1965); pp. 42–43.

8. Ibid., p. 101.

9. For a brief comment on and slightly different viewpoint about this passage see Kenneth Muir, "Shakespeare's Poets," in *Shakespeare Survey* 23 (1970): 91.

10. See *The Philosophy of Plato*, The Jowett Translation, ed. Irwin Edman (New York, 1928), p. 147. Also see *The Bestiary: A Book of Beasts*, ed. T. H. White (New York, 1954, 1960), pp. 118–19; William Meredith Carroll, *Animal Conventions in English Renaissance Non-Religious Prose* (1550–1600) (New York, 1954), pp. 116–17; Kathi Meyer-Baer, *Music of the Spheres and the Dance of Death* (Princeton, N.J., 1970), p. 68.

11. My paper for the 1973 meeting of the Southeastern Renaissance Conference suggested Thomas Wright's *The Passions of the Minde* as a possible analogue for *Pericles*. See Thomas Wright, *The Passions of the Minde* (1601, 1604) in *Early English Books*, 1475–1640 (Ann Arbor, Mich., University Microfilms, Reel 1225 and Reel 1125).

12. See James O. Wood, "Humming Water," *Notes & Queries*, n.s. 13 (1966): 293–94— about Shakespeare's tendency to cluster images of sleep, death, riches, and music.

13. For "the idea [in *Macbeth*] of deeds which are too terrible for human eyes to look on," see Spurgeon, *Shakespeare's Imagery*, p. 331.

14. For discussions of the word *Logos* see Mahood, *Shakespeare's Wordplay*, pp. 169–81. Also see James Muilenburg, *The Way of Israel* (New York, 1961), pp. 31–43.

11

The Visual Powers Denied and Coupled: *Hamlet* and *Fellini-Satyricon* as Narratives of Seeing

W. R. ROBINSON

FELLINI-SATYRICON OPENS WITH THE LEADING FIGURE, ENCOLPIO, ON A stage of sorts, decrying in a Hamlet-like soliloquy the time's being out of joint, his own solitude, and the sad state of his affairs. The movie thus insists on being compared to Shakespeare's play. Besides, beyond that common feature, the two works also share an historical setting, a protagonist who was just recently a student and is thrust alone into the cauldron of public affairs to complete his education, a conflict between the restlessness of the younger generation and the staid heads of the older one, a central concern with spectacle (obvious in the movie's baroque images but also throughout the play), and a common overall action. Both works dramatically posit a disjunction among the vital powers (between the individual and authority, or a house divided against itself, in *Hamlet*, and between the light and dark selves, the "ego" and the "alter ego," in *Fellini-Satyricon*) that poses a problem of action. Both enact a cure aimed at reunifying what had been set asunder and restoring to normal the powers of action.

These superficial similarities suggest the remote possibility that the two narratives are basically the same story told under different guises— even perhaps that *Fellini-Satyricon* is essentially a cinematic adaptation, though admittedly a bizarre one, of *Hamlet*. But a cursory glance at the protagonists, their situations, and what happens in the two narratives quickly dispels such a possibility. A talker who is most graphically delineated in soliloquies during which he withdraws to the furthest possible remove from the visible world in order to indulge his reflective powers, Hamlet tries to think out his predicament but fails. As a paragon of verbal articulateness, intellectual sophistication, and ethical self-consciousness, Hamlet's facility with words perfectly equips him to be the agent of the play's verbal action. But even more than that, words are the milieu of his dramatic life. Originating from the words of the script, he lives inevitably in and through them. And completely encompassing his life, their "primordiacy" dooms him from the outset of his story to being haunted by authority—the monolithic voice of his dead father whose spirit walks the night and whose "commandment," Hamlet acknowledges, "all alone shall live / Within the book and volume of my brain, / Unmixed with baser matter" (1.5.102–4). The isolation of Hamlet's brain from the baser matter of his life catches him up in an inescapable fate that "cries out" (1.4.81). His conscience is captured by the past and he spends himself in ancestor worship and service to the dead. He is absorbed in his inherited role of prince and is required to attend to the family and state affairs of "emulate pride" (1.1.83), land, and ambition or election. His mind is distracted from his life or from the pragmatic question, to live or not to live, which he scorns when he exclaims, "I do not set my life at a pin's fee" (1.4.65). Instead, that mind is concentrated on the "essentialistic" concern of "To be or not to be"—that is, on the social and metaphysical identity that men and God respectively pass judgment upon. Hamlet is motivated by revenge and tasked to set right an imbalance in the scales of justice that existed before he comes on the scene. He must counter a past crime with a fit and present punishment. And he is sent on a quest for truth that requires him to put a theory of his uncle's guilt, inherited from his idolized father, to empirical and pragmatic test. This entails his inevitable fall from the innocence with which he receives the ghostly abstraction of his father's spirit and words into the treacherous confusion that reigns in the climax of that quest. In this intricate way the authoritative voice maintains control over everything that Hamlet does. His will is "not his own" (1.3.17). It is just a formality when he, the extravagantly reflective individual, serves as the expendable sacrificial victim for cleansing the state of its moral rottenness.

Encolpio, in contrast, has no past—no family, no father, and no station—except for Giton, the young boy who is the image of his childhood slipping away. Despite his natural reluctance to let go of his past, that past abandons him, cutting him loose and attaching itself to Ascylto, the cynical alter ego that cannot grow. And all subsequent attempts to institutionalize Encolpio by assigning him a role, such as that of the husband of Licas, or by hooking him on the past, such as Eumophio's two bequests, come to nothing. Born simultaneously with the light and images of the movie, he is no more than what is seen in action on the screen. And since, except for the light, he is the first thing to move in his world, the action springs from him. He is on his own, self-motivated, his future indeterminate. At first, like Hamlet, Encolpio is utterly alone; words also divide him against himself in painful self-consciousness; and he, too, is uncomfortable with the individuation to which his growth subjects him. But while capable of being verbally articulate, Encolpio prefers to look rather than talk. The unnatural state of Rome—a human artifice like Denmark, dominated by males and especially by poets, who are men of words—offers him a place in its hierarchical structure. Though for a moment he sits atop that structure as the husband of Licas, the pressures of change, active *about* and well as *in* him, spring him free of the artifice of the rational state and its land economy. With Licas's decapitation, Encolpio moves beyond the arbitrary authority of Trimalchio, amassed wealth, and the perverted chauvinistic power of the egocentric male (of which Licas is representative) into the mythic episodes of the third phase of his growth where a black slave girl, a nymphomaniac, a hermaphrodite, Ariadne, and a primitive earth mother of three visages equip him with the thread to find his way out of that maze of masculine egocentric individuality from which Hamlet also suffers. For Encolpio, a visual man, Hamlet's inescapable predicament is only an intermediate phase.

Encolpio's triumphant mythical rejuvenation consummates a regeneration process that sweeps through three phases, each of which contains a false and an authentic regeneration. In the first the severed hand of a dwarf, replaced with a metal hand in a theatrical illusion of regeneration, is opposed to a white horse scrambling out of the pool at the center of the crumbling Insula Felices. In the second Trimalchio's pretended resurrection from his grave is countered by the erotic revival of the widow of Epheseus in turning away from the corpse of her dead husband to her new lover. At the same time, and in a more profound authentic regeneration, her tale metamorphoses into a dramatic performance. When the words in which her story are told become flesh, the conventional formal lines that define genres are dissolved. And in the third the resurrection of the flesh of Eumolphus in the lives of his heirs who eat him contrasts with Encolpio's regaining of his potency at the alter of the goddess Oenothea. With the organic potency he lost through his masculinization now restored in this culminating authentic regeneration, Encolpio is able to bound beyond the heads and the hierarchy, the massive power and immobility of the land-based, agrarian culture that Rome shares with Denmark. Then in the company of an intellectually confounded Greek and an exuberantly active African he can sail the open seas in perpetual discovery of new places and new men. Instead of being haunted by the authority of a monolithic voice, Encolpio sees his life through, forgetting the past and "amorally" incorporating all the powers of life active in and about him. Words would work the same effects on him that they do on Hamlet, and momentarily did; but by undergoing all changes without intellectually or ethically judging them, he comes into his full capacities for change as a living individual, arming himself with a new potency and an increased mobility.

Despite the common overall action shared by the two narratives, the changes of which the two protagonists are agents are vastly different. More obviously, *Hamlet*, given over to cause and effect, tells a story of reaction dedicated to halting change. *Fellini-Satyricon*, on the other hand, narrates a story of growth. (Growth is the opposite of entropy: a self-generated increase in the total energy of a system and therefore of its capacity to act.) In Hamlet's story words have moral priority and life is a victim of their abstraction; in Encolpio's story images have moral priority and life breaks free of rational order. The former sacrifices the individual to the state, enacting a catharsis, a bloodletting of evil humors that purges the state of individuality. The other facilitates a mobilization of vital energies that empowers the individual to elude the state and launch off under his own power. Thus, whereas the first strikes back, the other strikes out through verbal barriers into the territory ahead. The simple dramatic fact is that whereas Hamlet dies and Denmark continues to exist, Rome collapses under the weight of its massive materiality and Encolpio moves on. That dramatic event entails the tottering walls of the monarchic state being shored up again in *Hamlet*, while the solid wall that Encolpio plays against at the beginning of *Fellini-Satyricon* ends in ruins, with only fragments of it left standing. Moreover, the surfaces of those fragments are not cluttered by the chaotic graffiti that appears on the original wall but rather are illuminated by brightly colored pastel portraits of single human beings comprising a visual community. The normal restored in *Hamlet* is that of the old order of the monarch and of the monolithic voice that is reinstituted with Fortinbras's arrival at the end of the play to claim the throne and terminate events by issuing a military command that "a peal of ordinance" be shot off. In contrast, *Fellini-Satyricon* restores to normal the primeval energies of the sea visible through the gaps in the wall and audible through the blowing of the wind. In the play a succession—the proper transference of the office of king—is accomplished; in the movie a passage from adolescent to mature individuality is negotiated. Clearly, from the initial divisions that incapacitates the powers of action in the two narratives, two radically different kinds of unity are won—an intellectual order in *Hamlet* that freezes the action into a resolidified state, an organic unity in *Fellini-Satyricon* that unleashes a whole new range of possibilities for change.

II

Yet Hamlet is caught up in the same creative process as Encolpio. He acknowledges the presence of the originating powers in his affairs when he describes what is to happen in the play with the words: "Foul deeds will rise . . . to men's eyes," (1.2.257–58). He also indicates their presence when he berates himself for being "unpregnant of my cause" (2.2.553). Thereafter he becomes pregnant by that cause, swells to a passionate fury under its fertile influence upon his mind, and eventually delivers what it has conceived in him—namely, his death! Moreover, the play announces right off, in Francisco's command in the second line, "Stand and unfold yourself" (1.1.2), that its dramatic intention is to bring the hidden into sight. The reaffirmations of that intention, in Horatio's subsequent profession of his belief in "the sensible and true avouch / Of mine eyes" (1.1.57–58) and Hamlet's supplanting of the vision of his father in his "mind's eye" (1.2.185) with "this vision here" of "an honest ghost" (1.5.137–38), establish it as the play's central concern—beyond the shadow of a doubt. And the promise to accomplish the feat of actualizing the potential in a visibly perceptible form is borne out at the end of the play in the final unfolding begun with Horatio's question, addressed to Young Fortinbras, "What is it you would see?" (5.2.351), the ambassador's indirect answer to it, "The sight is dismal" (356), and Fortinbras's summing up, in the play's next to last line, of the visible truth unveiled: "Such a sight as this / Becomes the field, but here shows much amiss" (390–91). The visual powers are obviously a primary force in *Hamlet*. They make things happen— indeed, they instigate all that does happen and bring the much that is amiss and the dismal sight to pass. Hamlet acknowledges the extraordinary ability of visual energy to excite profound change when he sets out to use the play-within-a-play to "tent [Claudius] to the quick" (2.2.583). He also recognizes that visual display unveils an extraordinary dimension of life when he reports having heard that "the very cunning of a scene" has "struck so to the soul" that guilty creatures have compulsively "proclaimed their malefactions" because murder, "though it have no tongue, will speak with most miraculous organ" (2.2.575–80). The springs of action, his statement admits, manifest themselves miraculously to sight.

This powerful stimulus, so arousing Claudius that all his royal power is unable to hold it in check, also moves Hamlet. For though the words of Hamlet's father direct him in pursuit of revenge, it is the vision of his father that most deeply agitates him, gives those words credibility, and generates the driving force of his passion to act. In fact, it is of such magnitude that it drives the play. Hamlet is aroused from the lethargy of his mourning and given a new passion, a new life, not only when his senses are pierced by the sight of his father's image, but when he turns to spectacle, to a dumb show and then action with words, to evoke from another man a display of that man's innermost passions in order to have unquestionable empirical proof of his guilt. He relies solely upon the evidence of his eyes to resolve the doubts of his mind. Besides awakening him, vision clears Hamlet's head, enlisting it on the side of the visual powers and further spurring him on to action. And the visual energies thus accelerated move to their inexorable climaxes. Ophelia cries out, "O, woe is me / T' have seen what I have seen, see what I see" (3.1.160–61). Gertrude, prompted by Hamlet, confesses, "Thou turnest mine eyes into my very soul, / and there I see such black and grainèd spots / As will not leave their tinct" (3.4.90–92). Laertes despairingly proclaims in reaction to Ophelia's madness, "Do you see this, O God?" (4.5.199). And Horatio sees, and would show to all the "unknowing" world, in the bodies of the dead "High on a stage . . . placèd to the view" graphic evidence of the rank confusion induced in the state and public mind: "carnal, bloody, unnatural acts . . . accidental judgments, casual slaughters . . . deaths put on by cunning and forced cause . . . purposes mistook / Fall'n on the inventors' heads" (5.2.367–74). Horatio's vision of the devastating confusion injected into the political affairs of Denmark caps a three-stage progress. An image of the father witnessed with awe and detachment by Hamlet is succeeded by a reflected, mirror image held up by the play-within-the play whereby Claudius's public responsibilities and his private passions are juxtaposed in turbulent conflict. That moral schizophrenia is in turn succeeded, in the final scene of the play, by an image of Hamlet's involvement in the moral confusion of the entire body public of Denmark. These three stages are the stations in Hamlet's enactment of his passion to see. A moral authority located outside the individual is first internalized in the individual, where it induces a moral divorce of his conscience from his vital passions; and then it completely expunges the individual except for his name.

More than simply being present in Shakespeare's drama, the visual powers infect his plot to the extent that its action arises from and turns upon them, proceeds in a manner and direction appropriate to their inclinations, and culminates in a climax of their doing. These visual powers are not just an adornment (if anything, the words are that, since they are an outer shell, an exoskeleton, encasing the play's life-generating vital organs); it is impossible for the full power of the drama to be felt apart from, in Aristotle's phrase, "representation and actors." Until its action is held high upon a stage for view, until its descent from theory into the empirical and pragmatic rises before the eyes, the play is at best a stillbirth. Thus spectacle, instead of being, as Aristotle insisted, the least artistic part of Shakespeare's play, is an inherent aspect of *Hamlet*. Indeed, it is the quick of his drama, and the interaction between the spectacle and words is the life blood of the play. Unavoidably, *Hamlet* is a narrative of seeing at the same time that it is a narrative of speech. It remains substantially unacted until it comes alive as a spectacle.[1]

But the visual powers and spectacle are not free within the play to move as they are inherently inclined to move. At every turn they are checked in their progress by the compulsion Horatio acts under when he imperiously orders the ghost, "Stay. Speak, speak. I charge thee, speak" (1.1.51). This injection of the compulsion to speak does not arise naturally from what is seen. The visible could be simply looked at, in awe or terror or otherwise, for its visual qualities and what it is doing. The injection of the compulsion to speak incongruously intercedes; it is a *non sequitor*. Ophelia's reaction to the dumb show, "What means this, my lord?" . . . "Will 'a tell us what this show meant?" (3.2.130 and 135), is the most blatant instance of the transmutation of a visual event into reflective concerns. But the verbalization of the visually perceived is the main enterprise of the play. It is responsible for the diverse strategies with which visual energy is counteracted (as it is when the youthful energies of Young Fortinbras are dampened by Norway's and Claudius's maneuvers to dampen Hamlet's). It is the source of Hamlet's elitism and idealism, and, above all, of his antipathy to change (repeated constantly but succinctly stated in his emphatic self-characterization, "Seems, madam? . . . I know not 'seems.' . . . I have that within which passeth show" [1.2.76 and 85]). And it is responsible for the sickness of heart that begins with Francisco (1.1.9); worsens through Gertrude's "thou has cleft my heart in twain" (3.4.156), Ophelia's "Divided from herself" (4.5.85), and Hamlet's "in my heart there was a kind of fighting" (5.2.4) and "how ill's all here about my heart" (5.2.201–2); and culminates in Horatio's characterization of Hamlet's death in the line, "Now cracks a noble heart" (5.2.348). Each and all undergo this incapacitating bifurcation of their vital powers. The verbalization of the visually perceived effects the cleavage in life that Hamlet recommends in his advice to Gertrude to "throw away the worser part of it, / And live the purer with the other half" (3.4.158–59) as well as the suffering of Ophelia when "Divided from herself and her fair judgment," she is no more than a picture of a mere beast (4.5.85–86). In this way the compulsion to speak divides and conquers the visual powers.

And this compulsion to speak determines that, while the visual powers ignited a "turbulent and dangerous lunacy" (3.1.4) that gets out of control and threatens to shatter the monolithic voice, in the final reckoning the verbal powers have the last say. At the end Hamlet's mind is totally occupied with concern for himself (his "wounded name" that "shall live behind me," the reporting of his "cause aright," and the telling of his story), the unknown being explained, prophesizing the election of Young Fortinbras, and passing on to him the legacy of his "dying voice" (5.2.328–45). By not heeding his own advice to Horatio to "let it be" (5.2.327) but, instead, overlaying the visually obvious with his self-centeredness, a redundant defense of himself and explanation of what has happened, and an attempt to control the future, Hamlet thoroughly squelches the passion to see that has been active in him. He is nothing but a creature of speech in the last analysis. Originally he thinks that the enactment of "the motive and the cue for passion / That I have" will "amaze indeed / The very faculties of eyes and ears" (2.2.545–50), but in the end of his story only his voice and hearing are active, and without amazement. All that is left of him—all that he has to save him—when he is face to face with the ravages of change wrought by the visual powers are his words. Like Oedipus, he is led into confusion and slaughter by his physical eyes, and when those eyes have wrecked their havoc, he, too, in his indirect way, expunges them in order that his mind's eye can resume control over change. And what Hamlet ignores his designated spokesman Horatio, in proposing to lecture the unknowing world to be sure it understands correctly the sight before it, would turn into a moral lesson. He can no more let it be than Hamlet can, but rather must reinstate the hegemony of words over their lives.

In doing that Horatio reverts to ethical judgments, the use of abstractions to get a detached perspective upon the "warlike" (5.2.341) visible world and from that distance to assess the degree to which it is amiss. Because the verbal filter that Hamlet and Horatio hold between themselves and the dismal scene polarizes the visual and the verbal powers, the filter enforces an uncompromising assessment in which not just the scene is dismal. Sight itself is! The foul deed that rises to the eyes in the play is, finally, the deed of seeing. In the final reckoning the eyes don't just initiate the mind into the evil world; they are themselves the source of evil. By means of Hamlet's and Horatio's lens of reflection the eyes, which saw no evil in the beginning of Hamlet's story and were opened by the sight of another's miraculous confession of his malefactions, in the end see nothing but evil. The visual powers, eye to eye with themselves, behold not only the maliciousness of the visible world but their own abominable vileness. Then all change—the source, means, and consequences of it—is known to be vicious. This viciousness is all that anybody sees when their eyes are opened—Hamlet's to Claudius's malefaction, Claudius's to his guilt, Gertrude's to her black and grainèd spots, Laertes's to Ophelia's madness, as well as everybody's to the dismal scene at the end. It is this very detection of evil that Hamlet said seeing can beget when he set out to "observe [Claudius's] looks" (2.2.582) while the play within the play worked its effects upon the guilt at the core of Claudius's life. Then he relied upon the extraordinary power of visual stimuli to penetrate to the springs of Claudius's passion to flush his evil out of its hiding. In turn, the visual stimulus of Claudius's miraculously confessed malefaction in an eyeball-to-eyeball exchange explode in him the will to murder. And it is precisely this feat that is narrated in his story. The visual powers, by arousing Hamlet's passion to act, manifest his potential for evil, involve him in it, and demonstrate that all acting, whether or not harnessed by reason, can come to nothing but evil. This is the import of the fact that all those who act in *Hamlet* die while only the passive Horatio survives; in its dramatic version of original sin, all action is dedicated to destruction and death. Hamlet sets out to catch the conscience of a king but ends up catching the visual powers in a net of conscience. In the final reckoning of his story, his verbal conscience, spurred into action by the visual powers against its normal inclinations, reasserts its prerogatives once more. This verbal conscience is his legacy for Young Fortinbras and the spectators of his tragedy.

But what is entailed in the translation of the visual into the verbal is most decisively revealed in the play-within-the-play, and the events directly connected with it. A self-image of sorts since *Hamlet*, along with it, is "a fiction, a dream of passion" (2.2.536), the inner play provides the outer play with the opportunity to establish the fact that the story it tells is not a whimsical choice of Shakespeare's but the narrative capabilities of dramatic form. In the sequence of events beginning with the lines recited by the player and running through the dumb show, "The Mousetrap," and Claudius's soliloquy, the same event, the murder of the dominant male in his various guises of father, older brother, and husband, is renarrated three times over—or four if the encompassing action of the outer play is included. However, a change occurs over the course of the repetitions. This change is most apparent in Hamlet's tears, in response to the player's recital of Pyrrhus's slaughter of Priam, giving way to the rage with which he instructs Lucianus to begin his speech. But it also entails Hamlet's passive suffering and his personal emotional reaction to a fictional telling—or simply the thought of the murder— giving way to his aggressive assertion of wit and will in directing its dramatic performance as a public event involving the life of the mind of the premier public figure, "That spirit upon whose weal depends and rests / The lives of many" (3.3.14–15). And it also involves Pyrrhus's unconscionable, rebellious murder of "father" Priam leading to Claudius's conscientious scrutiny of the eternal prospects of his soul. An action that initially occurs only in the head is generalized until it becomes a reality within the body politic and its public head, and this happens solely by means of a succession of narrative forms. A literary narration is followed by a mime and the two of those succeeded by a drama, a form that combines the first two. That drama in turn affects the imaginary action of the outer play.

At the center of the imaginative development accomplished through these narrative transformations occurs a startling jump from the apparently irrelevant dumb show to the dramatic performance of Hamlet's lines written for "The Mousetrap." To the narrative fact of the dumb show, whose action is sensed by both Ophelia and Hamlet to be incomplete, his lines attach a meaning. In the light of his remark to Ophelia, "I could interpret between you and your love, if I could see the puppets dallying" (3.2.237–38), Hamlet's completion of the dumb show with an interpretation indicates that he thinks he sees the mechanical forces controlling others, has selected the instrument that will operate the strings to which they are attached, and can manipulate them. To do that he compulsively overlays a meaningless visual spectacle with ethical idealism. Hamlet's extraneously inserted words here, as throughout the sequence of events connected with the inner play, are his means of exercising control over the action with his intelligence. But the crucial fact in the imaginative development through the narrative forms is that while the dumb show, imaging the powerful passion Claudius acted upon in gaining the throne, has to stir him to the quick, he remains outwardly unmoved until Hamlet's lines introduce the principle of eternal fidelity sworn to by the "Queen." Lest what she has done be missed by the play's audience, and because of his compulsion to speak and repeat, Hamlet underscores the injection of intellectual principle into her affair with the intellectual supplement, "If she should break it now!" (3.2.216).

This introduction of the reflective intelligence into the imaginative development arouses Claudius's intelligence only to the extent, however, that he asks, "Have you heard the argument? Is there no offense in't?" (3.2.224–25). His conscience is caught only, as Hamlet redundantly notes, "Upon the talk of the poisoning" (3.2.279). Without talk Claudius's guilt would never have surfaced. His guilt had emerged earlier when Claudius confessed to himself in response to Ophelia's talk, "How smart a lash that speech doth give my conscience!" (3.1.50). Hamlet's own talk both in the inner play and about it flushes Claudius's guilt out into the open. It repeats the effects of Ophelia's words, but, in addition, it springs the trap that catches Claudius's conscience in the net of public affairs. Hamlet can bring that result about because, while the spectacle of the dumb show tents Claudius to the quick, the cunning of his scene in "The Mousetrap" strikes so to Claudius's soul that his vital passions and intellectual spirit are radically severed from one another. Only the words tell Claudius that he did wrong. Only because of them does the mirror of dramatic form held up to him enable Claudius to perceive his moral vileness and provoke him to cry out, "Give me some light" (3.2.259). But there is none other than Polonius's simple-minded kind. Claudius's visual powers have been blackened out by verbalization. The division between the spectacle and thought in the drama have infiltrated Claudius's consciousness; Hamlet has captured Claudius's mind and made Claudius into a copy of himself. Hamlet succeeds to such an extent, in fact, that Claudius employs a Hamlet-type reflective soliloquy and Hamlet's imagery to judge his offense as "rank" and smelling "to heaven" (3.3.36) and to confess himself caught, like Hamlet, in a state of inaction where "like a man to double business bound / I stand in pause where I shall first begin, / And both neglect" (3.3.41–43). The moral discordance between the intellectual and visual narrative dimensions in the dramatic performance of Hamlet's lines consummates the rebellion of son against father, or of reckless passion against reason, in Pyrrhus's story. But where passion prevailed over reason in his tempestuous story, here by means of dramatic form reason presides over Claudius's passion and he is momentarily impotent.

Hamlet's idealism is the pivotal force in the process that produces Claudius's deactivation. By means of it the passions of life are made to serve a purpose. That purpose governs what happens in *Hamlet* is evident from the fact that Hamlet, although he is awakened from his melancholy by the vision of his father's ghost, cannot move without being assigned the verbal motive of revenge. And *Hamlet*, although it would stir its spectators to the quick with a vision of Hamlet's death, must look into the future to the purposes of the state and mankind, as the play obviously does in the Prince's prophesizing, his request to have his story told, Fortinbras's succession, and Horatio's promise to provide answers to the "bloody question" "to th' yet unknowing world" (5.2.364 and 368). Hamlet's addition of the extraneous intellectual purpose of catching the conscience of the king to the aesthetic phenomenon of the inner play explicitly proclaims that purpose controls even the creative powers once they are aroused. For that inner play is performed only because it is useful beyond itself in carrying out Hamlet's revenge. That same addition also gives the distinct impression that the injection of purpose generates a meaningful change at a time when nothing much was happening. But that is an illusion. The subtlest effect of Hamlet's idealism is to overrule those powers of division and generalization, promising proliferation and expansion, with the powers of redundancy.

The redundant enactment of the dumb show in the dramatic performance of Hamlet's lines, by substituting concepts for percepts, overlays the transitory with the immutable. And that overlay is doubled by the inner play itself when the "King's" statement that "even our love should with our fortunes change" (3.2.193) is countered with the "Queen's" own "deeply sworn" (3.2.217) fidelity. Measured against the ideal the "Queen" swears to honor, the innumerable possibilities of the natural powers of the pure action in the dumb show are rejected as unworthy of man and are sacrificed for an intellectual certainty that precludes all subsequent changes. (Which is what the inner play in its entirety is designed to do—to demonstrate the viciousness of change and serve Hamlet's purpose of putting a stop to the change that Claudius had brought about both in the power structure of Denmark by murdering Hamlet's father and in the affections of Gertrude.) Since her words don't make anything happen but rather only reflect what has already happened—in this case, her existing marriage—the "Queen's" words are inherently redundant. They merely repeat an event of the senses in the realm of thought on thought's own terms; they institutionalize a change enacted in the past. This redundancy is operative in the opening lines of the outer play when Francisco turns Bernardo's question "Who's there?" back upon him and in the ghost's repeated appearance, and is rampant thereafter in endless variations, such as Hamlet's pun in his first words, "A little more than kin, and less than kind" (1.2.65), his first complete public statement, "Seems, madam? Nay, it is. I know not 'seems'" (76), and his characteristic exclamation, "Words, words, words" (2.2.191).

Redundancy provides the device whereby the visual powers are kept from passing on through intact into the subsequent event and from completing the natural course of their passions. For although its form combines thought and spectacle, the innerplay does so in a manner that divides them against one another even as it sets the "King" and "Queen" on opposite sides of the issue in their argument and assigns hegemony to thought. The path of the organic energies of the dumb show is blocked and those energies split in two, not only by the "Queen's" words, but also by the extremely formal verse and rhymes of Hamlet's lines, which truss the subtle living language of the outer play up in a straitjacket of rigidly stylized poetic conventions, and thereby force the fractured vital powers into lateral diffusion. As exemplified by the unhappy, unshriven authoritative figure of the ghost, who, unable to forgive and forget, passes its misery on down the line to and through Hamlet instead of transforming it into beneficient vitality, the powers of redundancy disseminate their divisive effects until both inside and outside, heart and head, are sick with it. In the inner play they spread the disease of the order of dominance that begets Pyrrhus's animosity. In the outer play they spread the disease of Hamlet's "melancholy" (3.1.165) abroad until it infects even Claudius, the moral innocent who acts uninhibitedly and who even in his darkest hour can maintain, as no other in the play ever can, "All may be well" (3.3.72).

"Purpose," the "King" notes, "is but the slave to memory" (3.2.180). Hamlet's purpose in introducing a meaningful change weighs the present and the future down with the past, limiting the action to a quantitative change, an amassing of the truth, in which the compulsion to speak has a vested interest by its reiteration. The extrinsic and intrinsic redundancy that results from Hamlet's purpose, by keeping the potential for development in check, keeps anything significant from happening. It eventually catches everybody in the mousetrap, a system in which men, as Claudius observes of himself, "struggling to be free / Art more engaged" (3.3.68–69). With each redundancy yet more inclusively enlarging and perpetuating its dominion over life, that system confines the action of *Hamlet* to clarifying and perpetuating the given state of affairs, namely, the status quo of Denmark and the rational order it exemplifies. The given predicament cannot be eluded (the action can be no more than a momentary perturbation in the enduring order), but only expanded horizontally to its ultimate implications.

The action of the dumb show is not developed but is put in perspective by Hamlet's purpose and idealism and then suspended, like his father's ghost between life and death, in a limbo of irresolution that stops it from proceeding any further. (The dramatic performance of the inner play embodies that irresolution by itself being no more than a fragment.) And unable as well as unwilling to open the way out of this impasse, the powers of redundancy successfully close off the possibility of novelty by channeling the active powers of the dumb show into definition. Just as the "Queen's" oath of eternal fidelity fixes limits on what she can do in life as a wife or woman, so the powers of redundancy on every occasion in *Hamlet* truncate the potent, integral, complex motions arising from its visual center. They short-circuit those motions initially by focusing the play's three main visions of the ghost, Claudius's "bosom black" (3.3.67), and the dismal scene itself on death, life's terminus and the end of action. Then they prescribe perception further by limiting the mind's deliberations to one facet of the image's multiple potentiality and by assigning ends that put an end to experience. After all is said and done, both inner and outer plays are ruled by this passion to define. Hamlet exerts his control over the events of the play-within-the-play sequence by dictating a manner of dramatic performance midway between the extremes of whirlwind passion and being too tame, and by conceiving of drama as an instrument of reflection "to show the very age and body of the time his form and pressure" (3.2.22–23). Similarly, the outer play's opening question, "Who's there?," asks for a definition, but since the simple identity that would satisfy that definition is never explicitly given, the opening question, left open, catches Hamlet up in a pursuit of who he is. That quest leads beyond his obsession with defining others— in, for example, his line, "The king is a thing—" (4.2.27)—to his self-definitions in his impetuous assertion, "This is I, / Hamlet the Dane" (5.1.244–45) and his curious, repeated words near the end that make no sense apart from the passion to define, since they could not be spoken and be true: "I am dead" (5.2.322 and 327).

In enlarging the animosity between son and father in the Pyrrhus story that issues from a dominance relation and is the reverse of Hamlet's reverence for his ideal father, the inner play draws a line that the creative powers of spectacle are forbidden to trespass. In addition, *Hamlet*, itself a redundant expansion of the inner play, its dramatic "heart of heart" (3.2.70), elaborates this categorical discrimination of speech against spectacle into a "dissociation of sensibility" within its own dramatic form that denies the validity of its own creative powers. The compulsion to speak, to "unpack [the] heart with words" (2.2.571), directs everything that happens in *Hamlet*, finally, toward the end of its own self-definition. On the very occasion that it holds before itself the opportunity to look into the springs of its own creative potency and unite with them, *Hamlet* not only steers the inner play's dream of passion away from its visually exciting source and organic impulses toward the external considerations in which thought specializes, but also chokes off the dream of passion welling up from within its own narrative eye. That self alienation is explicitly evident in the fact that dreaming and the imagination are always associated with disastrous consequences. Hamlet is a victim of "bad dreams" (2.2.254), fears the dreams he theorizes may come after death if he commits suicide, and insists that "A dream itself is but a shadow" (258). And when his imagination is active within the world of shadows, it "waxes desperate" (1.4.87), finds Yorick's skull "abhorred" (5.1.175), and traces "the noble dust of Alexander till 'a find it stopping a bunghole" (5.1.191–92). His fear of the dark and obsession with death saps his creative faculties. Hamlet himself acknowledges his exclusion from the organic matrix in bewailing the contrast between the ease with which the player can suit "his whole function... With forms to his conceit... And all for nothing" (2.2.540–41) and the difficulty he has in getting under way in the serious business of revenging his father's murder. His candid acknowledgement that the player is more immediately and completely involved than he himself is able to be admits that while the fiction of the various inside narratives' dreams of passions are freely and fully alive, his is bound up in self-alienating and inhibiting external limitations. Hamlet's admission of his inability to invest all of himself in his dream of passion emphasizes his suspension from the matrix of action in a self-conscious theoretical isolation. Like Hamlet throughout his soliloquies, Shakespeare's larger dramatic form defines itself by concentrating upon the outer differentiation at the expense of its inner ties. It thereby posits the definitive boundaries that it cannot trespass narratively and also acknowledges that it is not the sum of life, not even the "essence" of it—that something crucial lies outside its realm, beyond its powers of assimilation and therefore enactment.[2]

But despite the fact that words do have the last say in *Hamlet*, they do not rule supreme over the visual powers in it. Dramatic form traditionally, by keeping spectacle thoroughly subordinated to the control of thought, had exclusively devoted itself to developing the potentialities of its more or less self-enclosed system of words (those inherent not only between words but between them and silence, or between essences and nothingness). Shakespeare's great feat, as a narrator, was to incorporate two wholly distinctive systems of change into dramatic form on an equal footing. Within the walls of its arena he allowed thought's domain and method of change to be challenged by life's organic powers and method of change. The dramatic manifestation of his incorporation of the two systems as moral counterparts is to be found in the fact that Hamlet and Claudius, who respectively embody the reflective powers of thought and the decisive powers of action, opposite aspects of the king that were united in Hamlet Senior, are bound in eternal enmity, mutually caught in one another's traps, and destroy one another. But the mutual incompatibility and destruction of Hamlet and Claudius merely reflects the fundamental incompatibility between speech and vision, the play's opposed modes of narration. The words of the play have the first and the last say, squelching the visual powers that generate its motion. But at the same time life overwhelms the words that would strap it into their straitjacket of perspective, purpose, and definition. The three intellectual quests launched in Act 3—Polonius's to learn the true character of Laertes, Hamlet's to determine the guilt of Claudius, and Claudius's to decipher Hamlet's madness—conclude ambiguously. Laertes proves to be a man of honor in his passion to revenge his father's murder but engages willingly in Claudius's blackguard scheme to kill Hamlet and, "almost against [his] conscience" (5.2.285), dishonorably wounds Hamlet when Hamlet is off his guard during the dueling match. Claudius's guilt, proclaimed so absolutely by Laertes's remark, "The king, the king's to blame" (5.2.309), is undercut by the naiveté of Laertes's begging off of any responsibility for events, the emulate pride that infects everybody, Hamlet included, and especially by the exorbitant superiority of Hamlet Senior that inspires even Old Fortinbras to war. Above all, Hamlet's madness, which seems to be dispelled when the climactic action begins, is reembraced by himself when he disclaims any "purposed evil" (5.2.230) and attributes his action to a madness that is "poor Hamlet's enemy" (228).

Even more crucially, when after long reflection and increasing sickness of heart, Hamlet finally acts, he is lost. At first Hamlet thinks of nothing but his mother's incest and his father's revenge. In preparing himself to act upon these matters, however, he increasingly allows his self-interests, such as his "advancement" (3.2.326), to occupy his mind and fight in his heart. His growing assertion of his own interests finally blots out his penchant for self-effacement and his oath of allegiance. When he becomes "incensed" (5.2.291), he acts solely for himself, manifesting the "something dangerous" (5.1.249) in him and being completely oblivious of his father and his cause. His remark to Laertes, "Was't Hamlet wronged Laertes? Never Hamlet. / If Hamlet from himself be ta'en away, . . . Then Hamlet does it not, Hamlet denies it" (5.2.222–25), restates his own theory uttered in a line spoken by the "King": "Our thoughts are ours, their ends none of our own" (3.2.203). And he proves his theory when he acts impulsively to kill Laertes, as he had done earlier in blindly killing Polonius. His actions when he is incensed are not his own doing. His behavior is no longer controlled by thought as it is in his soliloquies or dialogue. Abandoning reflection for politics, theory for empiricism, he is sucked into "the corrupted currents of this world" (3.3.57).

The play-within-the-play sequence Hamlet managed had been an intellectual event, the thought of Hamlet working upon the thought of others. It allowed him to remain detached from and on top of the current of events. When he acts out of vital impulsion, he obliterates his identity, becoming mad the moment his passion catapults him into taking up arms against the sea of troubles. Within the system of redundancy and definition of the play, all that can actually happen is that the sensory disguises that keep things from being seen for what they truly are be removed. For Hamlet this means that all he can do is clarify his identity. But he knows his identity ironically in the vision of death he reveals, shortly before his own death, in his speculative remark about Caesar: "O, that that earth which kept the world in awe / Should patch a wall t' expel the win'ters flaw" (5.1.202–3). A victim of change all along, Hamlet sees that in the final change when he is conclusively defined as a man, and not simply as a prince, he comes to nothing. All he has left when his worldly position and power are dissolved back into the earth is the hollow shell of his name. His final self-definition is possible only when he has seen through the facade of his identity and reached the furthest limits of his life. Nothing remains of Hamlet to go on when he knows the eternal truth of "that which passeth show" in himself.

During the opportunities provided by his soliloquies to withdraw from the world at large and give thought to his personal predicament, Hamlet's attempts at insight stop short of penetrating to the active center of his own living individuality. The best he can do in such attempts is to unite his intelligence with his vital powers in the manner indicated in his resolve, "O, from this time forth / My thoughts be bloody, or be nothing worth" (4.4.65–66). In this kind of union, instead of thought being infused with the fluid of life and functioning as an agent of the living process, it presses the vital energies into serving its own destructive ends. All that Hamlet's thought can allow blood to be is deadly. Or his thoughts can be bloody only in the sense of being splattered with blood. One result of his vital superficiality is that Hamlet fails to unify the mythic and monistic powers in himself. The mythic powers have already been emasculated into an abstract supernatural ghost incapable of enforcing the dominance of its monolithic voice at the beginning of his story. The banishment of the mythic powers with the suicide of Ophelia and the death of his mother completely drains not just him but his entire world of generative power. What little is left of him after Gertrude's death is thoroughly ensnared in the arid perspective and succession of the monolithic voice. Another result is that Hamlet's thought, his intellectual hold on life, is thoroughly infused with life's vital fluid to the point of its annihilation. Because of his naiveté about life, Hamlet not only fails to unite the mythic and monistic powers in himself, he also fails to experience the classical enlightenment of the tragic hero that Oedipus exemplifies with the expunging of his outer physical eye and the opening of his intellectual eye, and that Aristotle designates the moral climax in a narrative of thought. Though Horatio, a holdover from an earlier era, experiences it in his intellectual surrogate capacity as one who is not a participant in the action of Hamlet's story, that intellectual vision is closed to Hamlet at the same time that he closes his mind to the possibility of the life before him. His exclusion from both suspends him in a narrative limbo between the story of thought and of spectacle, of the verbal and visual powers, of the act of speech and the act of seeing. But the crucial fact is that life possesses him to such a degree that he cannot sustain the classical stance of being intellectually on top of it.

III

The play can no more maintain an intellectual authority over life than Hamlet can. The words of Hamlet, consistent with Ophelia's desire to know the meaning of the dumb show, and in accordance with Horatio's intentions of explaining the dismal scene, would tell what life means. But they do not. Life, the play admits, will not submit to a meaning. The play confesses its exclusion of the subtler powers of change in Hamlet's reaction to the skulls he examines, "Here's fine revolution, an we had the trick to see't. Did these bones cost no more the breeding but to play at loggets with 'em? Mine ache to think on't" (5.1.84–86). Lacking the trick of seeing the fine revolution of living individuals into decaying skull bones, Hamlet cannot see new life forming from death. And unable to determine the strings that control love or any passion, the would-be puppeteer not only fails to interpret the action but becomes himself the puppet! The play's determination of who's there falls far short of incorporating the full panoply of the powers of change that it admits are there. Like its protagonist, its virtue lies in the forthrightness with which it "denies it," with which it admits its inability to assimilate the organic powers. The play's detachment from these powers leaves it with nothing more than the ache of thinking about them. Though the play can speak of the "fine revolution," it cannot enact that revolution. It cannot go beyond its verbal perspective; it cannot self-destruct and continue to exist as drama. The play can only assert its dramatic form. And so it is of necessity stuck with its own definition—with its self-conscious limitations and impotence. The compulsion to speak, as revealed by Francisco's "Nay" in the second line of the play and confirmed by Hamlet's repudiation of responsibility for his acts, is ultimately ruled by the passion to negate. The play turns that passion to negate upon itself. In affirming itself, which it does by the fact of its creation, it denies itself. Thus by its own doing it is restricted to recording the attainment and impending disintegration of its self-consciousness.

Shakespeare brought dramatic form and verbal narration in general to self-conscious awareness of its limitations as a vehicle of creative change. Drama had, of course, always been potentially capable of directing its powers of reflective thought away from the world in general and upon itself, but it remained for Shakespeare to hold the mirror of reflection before the face of drama and deliver it into self-conscious autonomy. An organic narrator, a narrator of life rather than of thought, as is amply attested to by the history of Shakespearean criticism, he stretched dramatic form to the limits of its capacity to incorporate the passion for seeing, the individual, and life. The result was to sever the umbilical cord that bound drama to the womb of abstraction and entrap it in its own particularity. *Hamlet* does not narrate the birth of the word—much less that of the brave new world; instead, it tells the story of drama's old age, of its spending itself as the entrenched older generation in the rearguard action of holding the line against the new generation's relentless challenge to its narrative hegemony. Horatio claims, "All this [meaning the significance of the dismal scene] can I / Truly deliver" (5.2.374–75). Shakespeare surpasses Horatio's promise; he truly *delivered* drama. Shakespeare's delivery of the truth of drama not only marks its end but also its end as a narrative power (and historically as well as theoretically, since not too long thereafter it yields to the novel as the major mode of narration). He saw that drama could not deliver the actual successor in Hamlet's line, that *Hamlet* and its protagonist define the limits of vision, individuality, and life attainable through dramatic form. Its dreaming power squelched by itself, "the

rest,'' as Hamlet sees when his noble heart cracks, ''is silence''
(5.2.347). Whatever more can happen has to happen beyond the narrative reach of words and dramatic form.

IV

Fellini-Satyricon is as self-centered an art about art as *Hamlet* is.
Indeed, it dwells even more than *Hamlet* does upon the forms of art,
mainly upon the spectacle of architecture, sculpture, painting, dance,
and the theater, but also upon poetry, story, legend, and music. As a
consequence, it too is devoted to clarifying its narrative capabilities. But
in contrast to *Hamlet*'s fixing its narrative limitations by defining dramatic form, *Fellini-Satyricon* evolves itself from that form. It does not
narrate the process whereby, as in *Hamlet*, the past rules over creative
energy, or history over the work of art. Instead, it narrates the process
whereby art feasting upon art generates itself out of art, specifically a
movie by Fellini from Petronius's prose narrative. The range of art
encompassed by *Fellini-Satyricon* suggests that the movie draws its
strength for performing its self-generation from fusing all the arts
together in its encompassing unitive form rather than by distinguishing
itself as an exclusively separate genre. But it is of crucial significance for
the movie as a narrative that the initial instrument of that self-generation
is dramatic form. The juxtaposition of a scene of high tragedy (Encolpio's soliloquy and his passion to murder Ascylto, his darker side) with
the low comedy of Vernacchio's farce theater reflects Encolpio's opening verbal bias and the split between himself and his alter ego. But in
addition it casts the movie's action in the mold of the Greek categorical
separation of tragedy and comedy—or of thought and spectacle, reason
and passion. Like its protagonist, the movie begins with its powers of
action divided against themselves. However, it then drives the divisive
tensions inherent in dramatic form beyond the breaking point to which
Shakespeare took them. *Fellini-Satyricon* negotiates a cinematic leap to
a picture gallery from the collapse of the massively immobile structure
of the Insula Felices and the destruction of the pyramidal stage upon
which both the tragedy and the comedy are performed. Thus, it transfers
the action of its story from dramatic to visual form. Thereafter in the
movie dramatic form steadily declines in power. It is always relegated to
a subordinate function, as it is at Trimalchio's banquet, where Greek

tragedy is played by blinded actors and pretty much ignored amid the festivities.

The polarized conflicts of the dramatic forms carry over into the subsequent section in Encolpio's complaint that "I have taken into my house a cruel guest" and in the atavisim of Eumolphus, who defends the classical commitment to thought with his protest, "What has happened to logical argument? Where is astronomy? Where is the honorable path to knowledge?" But Encolpio's remark as he walks around the statue of Psyche and Eros, "All myths speak to us of love, of unparalleled couplings," introduces the mythic powers into the movie and indicates that from there on the movie's action, under the auspices of the visual powers, will be taken up with eliminating and dissolving the walls that segregate the powers of action into two classes of narration and with accomplishing an unparalleled coupling of them. Along the way the breaking of the hold of the rational powers over the active ones is imaged in the decay of the head of static sculptures. The decay is first evident in the gold head in the museum that appears to be riddled by maggots and so devoured by a life from within itself. That decay increases when Encolpio passes in the street the monumental head whose jaw is partially broken away. Then the demise of the dominance of the rational powers is imaged in the abstract heads and decapitated figures toward the end of the movie, culminating in the final almost unrecognizable shrunken and featureless head on the statue in the anteroom to Oenothea's house. At the same time the emergence of the active powers is imaged by the enlargement of the phallus, beginning with the numerous small urns in the burial cave of the Widow of Ephesus scene and ending with the huge one present in the open countryside as Encolpio walks away from the dead Ascylto.

But the turning point in the evolution of narrative form occurs in the Labyrinth scene, itself in structure a dramatic form with, however, the spatial dominance in the relation between the audience and the stage reversed so that the audience controls the stage. In this dramatic performance Encolpio is cast in the role of the sacrificial victim who is paid as tribute to the Minotaur, the mythical beast that monolithically presides at the center of the rational maze and that at the expense of the sacrifice of life will guarantee the survival of the existing social order. Encolpio finds his way out of the maze into the open and into an enlargement of vision; when this occurs, the mythic figure unmasked is revealed to be an ordinary human, and a new friendship is formed.

But Encolpio fails as both the tragic and triumphant hero that ritualistically insures the perpetuation of society. His failure at the dramatic game of killing or being killed, or of total dominance or submission, costs him his potency. But more, the inherent redundancy of the dramatic form of the event proves itself to be utterly useless. For Encolpio's inability to make love to Ariadne is not just his personal failure; it is, at the same time, a failure of that coupling in which a dominant male and a submissive female ritualistically confirm the hierarchic structure of society and, instead of reproducing life, publically enact a symbolic regeneration. The kind of relation that dramatic form authorizes, whether it be between lovers, the audience and the play, or elsewhere, cannot bring off the unparalleled coupling toward which Encolpio as lover is moving. It can do no more than perpetuate the existing state. By finding his way out of the labyrinth not by the thread of his powers of thought but by his ordinary humanity and will to live ("I'm not a Theseus worthy of you . . . . I will love you if you'll let me off with my life"), Encolpio achieves a new union between the mythic and the human in himself, one that links him personally with the Minotaur at the same time that it dissociates him from the impotent state represented by the effete Proconsul and the lame Eumolphus. Encolpio fails to save society and society does not save him. But in eluding the *cul de sac* of dramatic form, he prepares himself for the more complex and subtle organic coupling that occurs when he unites his vital powers with the three faces of Oenothea—the beautiful phenomenon, the ultimate death, and the generative mother.

In this unparalleled coupling—in both senses of the phrase: not consisting of paired opposites, as well as being unique—the more subtle and complex organic unity that has been the moving force of the movie all along through its visual images emerges to the fore. And after the death of Ascylto, the divisive dramatic principle that afflicts the movie's powers of action and holds them back is superceded by Encolpio's new-found potency. When he heads out to sea in an exuberant living coordination of an African's primal energy and a Greek's baffled intelligence combined with his own new imaginative enlightenment, the new integration of the powers of change in Encolpio clearly breaks out into the open. His running toward the fluid, open form of the sea in the company of the antithetical Greek and African fuses the tragic and the comic powers of action into a new narrative synthesis, taking them the next step beyond Shakespeare's combination of them in *Hamlet*. That next step integrates comedy and tragedy in an organic unity free of their categorical identities.

Encolpio's new powers of action are not debilitated by intellectual self-consciousness but build upon that self-consciousness to evolve a creative consciousness, an awareness that focuses upon and issues from the creative matrix at the center of the powers of consciousness. Accordingly, they do not wantonly shatter order into chaos as the visual powers threaten to do in *Hamlet*. It is true that Encolpio, in ignoring the will of Eumolphus, his poetic senior, abandons his poetic heritage. Actually, he had begun to abandon it immediately after the collapse of the Insula Felices, or as soon as dramatic form is eclipsed by visual form as the vehicle of his story. Then he ignored Eumolphus's negative criticism of contemporary Roman art in the picture gallery and a short time later shunned Eumolphus's maudlin bestowal of his poetry and the human voice upon him in the tilled field at the end of the Trimalchio episode. Just before the collapse of the Insula Felices, Encolpio refers to Ascylto and himself as men of letters, but thereafter he makes no such profession. While Eumolphus's first words, "I am a poet," link him to the intellectual structure defined by Trimalchio's material wealth and masculine authority and qualify him for the later worldly success he inexplicably comes by, Encolpio regards indifferently the attempts of others who say they have heard he is a poet to identify him by that role. And when he regains his potency he moves beyond poetry, indeed all literary art. With its protagonist's refusal to eat the body of Eumolphus and thereby pass up the opportunity to perform the simple succession Hamlet performs, *Fellini-Satyricon* does not define itself but instead gives birth to the new form of visual narration. In doing that, it enacts its own phylogenetic evolution, assimilating the old forms of narration into a living narrative art and thereby revising the relation of the old forms to the new, including that of death to life. Whereas the illusory "transformation" (2.2.5) in *Hamlet*, that Claudius's political realism leads him to doubt, proves to be spurious, a genuine transformation—a rearrangement in moral structure that qualitatively alters the capacity for enacting change—is accomplished in fact in *Fellini-Satyricon*. In contrast to *Hamlet*'s narrative of reaction and truth, *Fellini-Satyricon*, following Encolpio's lead of blithely sailing out to sea beyond the substantial categories and classes of a land-based agrarian order, narrates an increase and expansion of the powers of life.

V

Despite their numerous common features, *Fellini-Satyricon* begins where *Hamlet* stops. The latter perpetuates the conventions of thought; the former passes along the generative potency of life. *Fellini-Satyricon* can perform this exceptional feat because it works with the created and creative bodies of the visible creation, which always consist of the components and coherence necessary to the creation—for otherwise they would not exist—and are perpetually pregnant with creative potency. It lets the light latent within the dark inexplicably shine forth and then transmits the powers of creation inherent in its images along intact throughout its story. On the dramatic level the difference between the two narratives is simply that Hamlet dies in the course of his transition beyond the adolescent stage of a school boy—literally, from a prince to a king—and Encolpio successfully negotiates his growth beyond that stage. But on the narrative level the difference derives from elementary moral properties of the media in which they are narrated. *Hamlet*'s powers of narration derive from a medium that is set in motion by percussion, the impact upon air by an aggressive act that by means of cause and effect initiates a vibration that is impossible in a vacuum. *Fellini-Satyricon* issues from a self-generating source that overflows from the combined total internal stresses of an electromagnetic field and is self-sustaining and self-transporting—darkness being not a medium but only the absence of an interaction that transforms the radiant energy with which it is replete with illumination. Not hobbled by redundancy and definition, not bound up in remembering and appalled by the incongruity of the ideal and the real that results in confusion in the visible world and the visual powers, it is empowered to flash forth in brilliant hue and potent vitality. Inherent in its medium is the capacity to carry out transactions in which the powers of growth, expansion, and coupling are present and perpetuated in a continuous sequence of vitally charged inner and interactive discrete entities. When Encolpio, seeing clearly, is full of life, so is the movie. It, too, has gathered and activated its vital power and moved out into the open beyond the divisive walls. Blessed with this greater power of action, and through its version of the birth of the movies that realizes its own inherent potency, it celebrates the freedom of self-generated action in which every event is not an end, not a closing off, but a beginning. Its feat is not, as *Hamlet*'s self-professed one is, to be a mirror of the times that reflects the change present in its day. Rather, the movie offers a direct enactment through its various specific and overall transformations of the powers and potentialities now for vision, for carrying on the metamorphical possibilities natural to the creation and ever-active in the pregnancy of images.

Wallace Stevens noticed that from within the literary perspective, "It is one of the peculiarities of the imagination that it is always at the end of an era. What happens is that it is always attaching itself to a new reality, and adhering to it."[3] *Fellini-Satyricon* demonstrates that in the movies the imagination is always at the beginning of an era and is always detaching itself from an old reality, or just from reality. This is the first fact of light and images with which the cinematic imagination must reckon. Although it had been obscured for a time by the verbal bias of black-and-white "talkies," *Fellini-Satyricon*, along with the color movie in general, revives the discovery of the silent movie that the medium of the movies is not just a new gimmick for telling the old story but rather opens up wholly new prospects for narration. Like the addition of time to the dimensions of Newtonian space by the theory of relativity, the movies' addition of self-generating and self-sustaining motion to art does more than throw a new datum on the table for analysis; it expands consciousness to the awareness of a greater aesthetic complexity and subtlety that entails a radical revision of the traditional sense of art—and also, it might be added, of criticism.

Allardyce Nichol spotted a crucial aspect of the new narrative possibilities opened up by the movies and explored by *Fellini-Satyricon* when he observed, " . . . practically all effectively drawn stage characters are types and in the cinema we demand individualization . . . and impute greater power of independent life to the figures we see on the screen."[4] He correctly detected the commitment of the movies to a greater individuation and greater power of independent life than were hitherto accessible to narration. But *Fellini-Satyricon* demonstrates that that commitment is to more than just the figure of man; consisting of nothing but concrete particulars, it grants greater individuality and independence to everything it surveys, to places and things as well as persons. In focusing its eye upon the light of everything that exists and isolating that aspect of the universe man inhabits for concentrated attention, it practices an existential egalitarianism by allowing all that exists (and existence occurs only in individuals) to exist equally in its sight. Since its camera eye does not and cannot shoot generalities (unlike the intellect, which can think alone in the darkness abstracted from the visible creation), *Fellini-Satyricon* lives only in beholding the life of another, only through concrete and specific relations. Accordingly, it specializes in cultivating the conjunctive, as opposed to the disjunctive, forces that prevail in the universe of relativity among inescapably related individuals. In that way, *Fellini-Satyricon* demonstrates that the movies are an art of inclusion rather than exclusion and that they are devoted to assimilating and transforming all the other arts as well as drama along with everything else that can be photographed or recorded on their sound track. In helping to open up these new prospects for narration, *Fellini-Satyricon* testifies that the movies emerge in the history of narration when, as has happened in the twentieth century, the study and rendering of change switches its concentration from the extrinsic, mechanical motions (to which the classic rational bias restricted Shakespeare) to the development of the media and the formulation of the method required for more completely liberating those unitive and generative powers shared by all that exists. The movies thus activate the processes of life and growth.

This greater power of relating and assimilating and this expanded ability for a more independent, unified, and powerful narration establishes that the movies are the crucial tool for imagining the momentous evolution presently in progress from a monistic to a monomythic culture. In the latter culture the randomly explosive energies of myth and the vectoral, linear thrust of thought are united into a vision of organic process and potentiality—whether it be that of the universe, the stars, the earth, its vegetation and creatures, man himself, or the life of the mind.

NOTES

1. Shakespeare's narrative form, of course, was drama, the classical vehicle for enacting the emergence and development of rational man. And no one before or since has so thoroughly and eloquently rendered the act of speech. Yet his is a language of spectacle. It is replete with literary imagery and tropes, pictorial descriptions of people, places, objects, and events, and vividly active verbs. And that language issues from the mouths of sharply delineated, rounded, individual dramatic personae in great variety and number, personae who are caught up in the treacherous counterforces of life that Hamlet refers to as godlike reason and the passions that enslave (the stamp of one defect, a particular fault). Very decidedly, Shakespeare's drama burgeons with life. His language of spectacle is pregnant with action. Its fullness of becoming in its every word, line, and personage sets Shakespeare's drama head and shoulders above all other literary achievements, not just all other drama, as a literature of life and living art. And this fullness of becoming not only

charges his language with vitality and his character with organic complexity but, surging through the separate lives of individuals and the collective life of the body politic, also bursts the seams of the classical unities of time and place with the inclusive sweep of its vital action.

The presence of that fullness of becoming manifests itself most decisively, however, in the growth of Shakespeare's narration over the course of his career. Among the abundant signs of that growth are such developments throughout his canon as: the decline of "monarchy" through the erosion of the power of the authoritative figure, whether king or nobleman, who presides over the given order of things; the transfer of the locus of decisive power from the court and the city to the wild energies of the heath in _Lear_, the woods of Dunsinane in _Macbeth_, and Prospero's island; and the emergence of figures of life, like Falstaff, who ignore the code of honor and of men endowed with extraordinary personal power (such as Prospero's natural magic) rather than that of station. Yet these specific alterations are but dramatic instances of more inclusive narrative transformations. Verse forms become less formal and more open and flexible, prose more frequent, and the categorical separation of tragedy and comedy, class differences, and double plots less pronounced. The logos and cosmos—the reign of words in, for instance, the conventional wit of the early comedies—disintegrates into Macbeth's sound and fury signifying nothing. And, most crucially of all, Shakespeare's imagination turns from the periphery of its subjects—the external reality denoted by words in their referential function, specifically, the state and public order—to a self-centered view wherein all the world becomes a stage. In this latter narrative transformation the world becomes a projection of dramatic form and thus a theater of action in which the imagination, enjoying Prospero's isolation, tapping the magical, living potential at the center of words, and moving under its own powers, affirms its creative energies, its urge toward more fully unified individuation, and its autonomous creations.

In every respect Shakespeare's drama is shot through with visual energy. In it the empirical exerts relentless pressure upon intellectualism to break the hold of the monolithic voice over the creative potency of life and to give birth to Miranda's "brave new world." From the point of view of the verbal powers, or in the dramatic aspect of the plays, the creative powers on the loose confirm Socrates' claim that in vision "every sort of confusion is revealed within us; and this is that weakness of the human mind on which the art of painting in light and shadow, the art of conjuring and of deceiving by light and shadow and other ingenious devices imposes, having an effect upon us like magic" (Jowett, p. 860). That power leads inexorably and unutterably into Lear's madness and the public chaos that runs rampant in, for instance, _Measure for Measure_. But from the perspective of the visual powers, and thus in the narrative aspect of the plays, the onslaught of that creative powers upon the closed system of thought prepares the way for discrete, vitally charged, self-centered units to perform as agents of living action. Instead of passively submitting to being fragmented into frames and brief acts, the visual powers turn the tables on the monolithic voice, breaking it down into the proliferating eccentricities of the living voices and making room for the emergence of an organic language. Reversing Aristotle, they reconnect words with their vital source and restore to them the powers inherent in speech—those powers that begot words and that endowed them with the power of action. And with that feat they evolve a language of life that, despite its being obscured under a mask of dramatic disruption and negation, is positively empowered to enact living changes.

2. Nor was Shakespeare able to imagine that method in any of his other plays, including _The Tempest_. Prospero's fabulous magic would seem to be an infallible instrument of organic transformation, since it is a natural power, mediates between the angel Ariel and the beast Caliban, sets the tottering social order aright, and performs a marriage of youths who have all the qualifications to be the heirs of the older generation's powers. But Prospero's power is a vestige of the monolithic voice, an authoritative power by which he manipulates events toward a preconceived end. Thus it cannot be transferred; it is his own, a feature of his role and singular thought. Moreover, though he generously uses the power of his monolithic voice to save Milan from its inherent viciousness, he admits, in his epilogue, that he cannot save himself. Because Prospero's own "strength . . . is most

faint," he cannot be free unless "Mercy itself," begotten by the audience's prayer and extended to him by its indulgence, pardons him. The powers of his own salvation do not lie within himself.

And that is the case in all of Shakespeare's comedies. For example, in *Twelfth Night* sick Illyria cannot cure itself but must be rescued by a saving grace introduced from outside it in the disguised form of Viola. The same holds true for Shakespeare's tragedies as well as his comedies: without a force from without to intercede, the action of his tragic plots, as illustrated by *Hamlet*, runs its doomed course to catastrophic purgation. No matter how far he stretched dramatic form, Shakespeare could not incorporate that aspect of phenomena Galileo called motion without a cause. Even the theatrically and rationally preposterous magical feats of *The Tempest* are part of a system of entropy in which motion cannot be self-initiating and self-perpetuating. Instead, the motion can only be a secondary change in reaction to disturbing causes; all action is therefore diminishment.

Nor has drama since Shakespeare been any more successful at incorporating motion without a cause into dramatic form. The tragicomedy that immediately followed Shakespeare's drama enlarged into baroque distortions the internal tensions threatening *Hamlet*'s dramatic form with disunity. The love-and-honor drama that succeeded the tragicomedy polarized the dissociation of personal passion from public conventions in stilted artificiality. And then the implacably cynical Restoration drama and the sentimental drama that emerged later in the seventeenth century as its polar opposite completed this amplification of the internal disunity and the dissociation from the springs of action by dividing the head from the heart of drama in two completely separate kinds of dramatic form. That disunity and dissociation become even more pronounced later in Ibsen's tragedies of the *joi de vie* and Shaw's renderings of the Life Force in a drama of ideas. Both in the name of creative power—embodied in an artist like the masterbuilder and in the historical evolutionary agent St. Joan—explicitly attack the callousness and visciousness of bourgeois society in particular and social order in general. Their attack on the rational structures that rule the external relations between men called for a revolutionary reform that would assign moral priority to life over order. But in turning the moral tables of *Hamlet* 180° they were as guilty of excluding life from art as the rational social order they castigated was of excluding it from society. For, though they could speak sympathetically for life, they could not forge in dramatic form the viable relation between the rational and the creative powers necessary for enacting it. Itself an instrument for promulgating the values of a rational society, the dramatic form they employ to accuse society of being intolerant of the creative individual could not itself directly accommodate the creative powers. Inevitably, their fervid criticism of the rational structures that have succeeded in encasing life in Western civilization by means of one of the those structures not only perpetuated the adamant hostility between the rational and creative powers inherent in dramatic form from the monolithic voice but also enlarged the gap between them. In fact, that was their achievement: to intensify the tension between the rational and the creative powers beyond the point where the relation between them could be housed within traditional dramatic form.

Shaw's innovations in dramatic form already signal the fundamental revisions in dramatic form required by the emergence of the creative powers, and the theater of the absurd, which gave dramatic form over to articulating the disruption of the rule of the rational powers, carries that revision its next inevitable narrative step. As in Beckett's *Waiting for Godot*, where the absence of the monolithic voice results in absurdly arbitrary and polarized authority, so the method of thought is without a moral center in the theater of the absurd. Without a viable basis for motivation and for integrating a coherent action (the latter immediately evident from the disappearance of the third act, or the resolution, from the theater of the absurd), dramatic form cannot resist and negate creative energy, but rather can only submit to its disintegrative effects. This ultimate futility of dramatic form is manifested in Beckett's thirty-eight-second play, *Breath*. Here the creative action occurs in the prerational spectacle of inarticulate organic sounds and then the play is over, the creative event stopped, when the voice is born with the first cry. *Breath* also exemplifies the recent upsurge in emphasizing the theatrical over the literary aspect of drama. To remain viable when thought fails to provide a unifying center of action, dramatic form has been forced to turn to spectacle. But, as illustrated by Happenings, the more dramatic form relies on spectacle the more incoherent it becomes.

It is true that twentieth-century fiction, emulating dramatic form, has evolved the pluralistic voice to supercede the monolithic voice in literary narration. The multiple voices of William Faulkner's *The Sound and the Fury* sufficiently illustrate that tendency. Nevertheless, dramatic form itself, plotless in effect, has been restricted to recording from its inescapable intellectual perspective the dissolution of thought's cherished essential structures into discontinuous random events. The attempt to reconceive the theater as an arena and to break down the barriers to a new communication between the stage and the audience has not gotten any closer than *Hamlet* did to the development of a plot capable of enacting the powers for organic change inherent in spectacle. The career of drama since Shakespeare has amounted to a continuous confession that the growth of the living individual beyond Hamlet's self-conscious individuality cannot be achieved in the "dying voice" of dramatic form.

And today, with causality no longer a tenable view of change and with the theater unable to gather its resources into an organic force, dramatic form can only be the victim of the impact upon it of a motion that is too subtle to be narrated in its essential form. Words had their story to tell, and although that story had numerous variants, it was over and done with as a positive creative force when Shakespeare wrote *Hamlet*.

3. Wallace Stevens, *The Necessary Angel* (New York, 1965), p. 22.

4. *Film and Theatre* (New York, 1936), p. 165.

12

The Filmed Shakespeare: From Verbal to Visual*

SIDNEY HOMAN

I WANT TO EXAMINE HERE FIVE GENERAL THEORIES ON THE POSSIBILITY of translating Shakespeare's plays to a primarily visual medium such as the cinema. But this topic is not exclusively theoretical. The history of Shakespeare on the screen is strewn with actual failures, successes, or moderate successes. The discussion can therefore blend conflicting aesthetic theories with the admittedly conflicting but hard practical evidence—the nearly one hundred examples of Shakespearean films produced from the earliest silent movies to this day. After the five theories are presented, I will make some personal observations.

I

The extreme right position, that of conservative purists both in the theater and the cinema, holds that it is impossible to translate any play into a movie while retaining the aesthetic integrity of both media. The cinema, the argument has it, is nothing if not visual. And while originating as a physical experience when we watch live actors playing in a definite space, the theater ultimately moves to the abstraction of words. As Jackson Cope argues persuasively in his *The Theater and the Dream*, the theater on Shakespeare's level is constantly invoking a platonic or cerebral world beyond our physical existence.[1] A primarily verbal medium, the stage thereby "gives voice to the mind's lust for meaning."[2]

The cinema, conversely, celebrates not meaning but actuality. Properly speaking, one cannot film an abstraction. W. R. Robinson, one of its best spokesmen, contends that movies are a "visual medium in

*Parts of this article appeared earlier in *Literature / Film Quarterly*, 4 (1976): 176–86.

which the word is complementary and dispensable," that "the movies illuminate sensory reality or outer form . . . [and] . . . are empirical revelations lighting the things itself."[3] Movies are about the here and now, about what we can "see" in life. A play such as *Hamlet* is ultimately about the there and hereafter, or the for-all-time, pressing us on to what we can *know* about life. Pure cinema cannot admit pure theater. A multimedia production complete with nonverbal effects such as background projections, strobe lighting, and a mixture of words, music, and dance (as in the works of John Cage) might survive in the cinema—but not Shakespeare. By committing his vision to the theater, as opposed to the epic or sculpture or music, Shakespeare determines and defines the meaning of his vision. Reversing the dictate of Mr. McLuhan, the message here is the medium.

Curiously, when directors call attention to the camera's principles or techniques by redoing Shakespeare in terms of the cinema's own aesthetics, there is invariable conflict. One literary critic complained of Olivier's *Hamlet* (1948) that the film by necessity magnified the figure of the Prince, showing him full-size on the screen (as opposed to his smaller dimensions on stage) and thereby twisting Olivier out of all importance.[4] The "world" of the play—Hamlet against the many or Hamlet representing the many—became the private domain of whatever screen actor happened at the time to be photographed. Peter Alexander objected to the Ophelia in that same movie throwing herself "on the pavement writhing and howling horribly" after the disastrous interview with the Prince. Now, her lines in the play may indeed suggest a restrained choral response at "The glass of fashion and the mould of form, / The observ'd of all observers" (3.1. 153–54) reduced to his present sorry state. And yet if the cinema is perforce a visual medium, where emotions are expressed best by action rather than verbal reaction, perhaps what Mr. Alexander saw as a "sad misunderstanding of the character of Ophelia" was dictated by film aesthetics, not fidelity to the theater.[5]

Listen to the film director speak honestly, I believe, and without prejudice, indeed, with a healthy respect for the demands of both the theater and the cinema. Renato Castellani, whose movie of *Romeo and Juliet* appeared in 1954, explained to a London reporter:

> Shakespeare's play was not real enough for the vast cinema audiences. Certain dialogue written by Shakespeare was too theatrical. I want the public to believe that Romeo and Juliet really existed.[6]

Accordingly, he minimized the dialogue and concentrated on spectacular still and action shots of Verona. But many reviewers, perhaps with first loyalties to the play, argued that he had substituted a shallow "sumptuous travelogue" for what they took to be an early tragedy full of meaning.[7] These charges would be repeated years later against another Italian, Zeffirelli, in his *Taming of the Shrew* and *Romeo and Juliet*. Are we perhaps back to this conflict, one of both medium and message, between a cinema stressing what we are and a theater concerned with what we mean? A vicious triangle suggests itself. Worlds very different in meaning and priority are envisioned by the artist using the camera's "eye," the artist using the pen, and the spectator watching the performance. And the latter is forced to choose between media whose message is inextricably linked to the artist's choice of a vehicle of expression.

II

As we move toward the left a more liberal position emerges, although this second stand is still closely related to the opening one: Shakespeare *can* be translated to the screen but the resulting product can at best only be inspired by the play. Filtered as it is through the meaning inherent in the second medium, the screen "play" may not even overtly resemble Shakespeare's original. Shakespeare here becomes a point of departure. For example, one of the most successful films using Shakespeare as "source" but not as final authority was the Russian ballet of *Romeo and Juliet* (1954). Here the play was first translated into dance and then into the cinema. Actually, the media of music and film, as Ingmar Bergman has maintained, may be closer than any other potential pairing involving film:

> I would say that there is no art form that has so much in common with film as music. Both affect our emotions directly, not via the intellect. And film is mainly rhythm; it is inhalation and exhalation in continuous sequence. Ever since childhood music has been my great source of recreation and stimulation, and I often experience a film or play musically.[8]

The response of the critics to this *Romeo and Juliet* was predictably enthusiastic. One observer, Gavin Lambert,—and he is representative, I believe—speaks of how the camera "records this dance with perfect fluidity,'' of how the ''film also creates an imaginative moment in its own right.''[9] Indeed, the essence of youthful love embodied in Juliet, caught both in dance and camera-work, overcame the physical fact that the prima ballerina, Galina Ulanova, was anything but youthful in 1954.

Orson Welles has been condemned because he insists on making the plays into vehicles for his own private notions of the tragedy in human interactions. But he has also been roundly praised by commentators who might feel most at home in this second category. Claude Beylie commended the Welles *Macbeth* (dismissed by other reviewers as a bestial redaction of Shakespeare's poetic symphony of evil) because the director ''refuses the mediocre compromises habitual in attempts at realism (principally in matters of decor, but also in a certain theatricality in the gestures of the actors).'' Beylie's argument is that the realism of the stage must give way to the palpable unrealism of the cinema. There is a ''secret substance'' or essence in literary works, an imaginative ''reality'' residing beneath the physical reality of the stage; this essence can shine forth in the unreality of the film world since that world, one eternally dead, is fictive by definition. The film is therefore the perfect medium for Shakespeare's world, but only when the director, ''rather than treasonously seeking cinematic equivalents'' for the language, chooses instead ''to *exaggerate the theatricality*.''[10]

Youtkevich's *Othello* was similarly praised because it too used the play only as a point of departure. One critic saw in it ''no calculated transference of a stage classic to the screen, but a total reconsideration of the subject from first to last in terms of the cinema.''[11] One might also mention the Japanese director Kurosawa, whose film version of *Macbeth* retitled *Throne of Blood* (1957) was celebrated as an instance of ''constructing a film from an idea and using appropriate dialogue.''[12] In point of fact, *Throne of Blood* was influenced as much by his earlier *Seven Samurai* as by Shakespeare's play.

A more mundane alternative to this use of Shakespeare as inspiration is to write an original script suggested by Shakespeare's basic story, thereby not even attempting to translate his actual language to the screen. At times the mere idea of the play, less than the actual plot, has been the source of such inspiration. One thinks here of movies such as Ken Hodges's *Joe Macbeth* (1955), which transferred Shakespeare's story to the hoodlum underworld of Chicago, with Macbeth as gangster and Lady Macbeth metamorphosed into his gun moll. Or of Delmer Daves's *Jubal* (also 1955), loosely based on *Othello*. An imaginative recreation using *The Tempest* as background was *Forbidden Planet* (1955), where Prospero becomes a scientist presiding over a planet that once flourished as a center for advanced technology. Shakespeare's visitors are a crew of space men who land there by error and are quickly involved in the nightmarish adventures perpetrated by the "creature of the id," an insuperable monster who materializes, with the help of a futuristic machine, from the scientist's own brain. The Prospero here is disturbed because the visitors threaten his private world—not to mention his attractive daughter. In *Men Are Not Gods* (1936) both movie script and Shakespeare's play rested uneasily together. Here a husband and wife acting team played by Sebastian Shaw and Gertrude Lawrence confuse their roles as Othello and Desdemona with a real-life situation involving adultery.

There was perhaps even less sense of fidelity to Shakespeare in the silent cinema; and, of course, there dialogue was not an issue. The adaptations ranged from Asta Nielson's *Hamlet* (1920), in which the Prince's secret was that he was a woman parading as a man for reasons of succession, to such lunatic adaptations of *Romeo and Juliet* as *Romeo of the Coal Wagon* and—if you will—*Romeo in Pajamas*.

This second category, where Shakespeare becomes the source, seems to have spawned the greatest variety of attempts, ranging from serious efforts to extract the "essence" of the play residing beneath its language to adaptations employing the story and not the essence, to shameless capitalizations on Shakespeare's name. This latter practice was most prominent in the silent cinema where it was assumed the name of Shakespeare would lend a certain needed dignity to the struggling new medium.

One of the problems, aesthetic as well as moral, with this attempt to adapt is that the film will invariably call to mind the play; no matter how dazzling the cinemagraphic technique, the audience will have a peripheral theatrical preoccupation. One cannot employ a complete filmic technique and keep Shakespeare's full intention. On the other hand, the Shakespearean origin of the film, however distant or camouflaged, is there. In the same way that our next-door neighbor boasts of having read the novel before having seen the film, and goes on to judge one by the other as if no change of media were involved, so the movie audience, consciously or unconsciously, will pass judgment. Here the judgment will most likely flow from the play of a dead author to the live film director's work struggling for birth as its own entity.

III

One step to the left of position two is the belief that Shakespeare *can* be translated to the cinema, not just adapted, but that everything verbal must find a filmic or visual equivalent. The question here is: should every image be translated? Can the director substitute equivalent images? That is, do some images work better in the blank verse of Shakespeare's theater than they do on film? Extremes are to be avoided. Olivier, for example, was generally criticized for using symbolic tableaux shots while retaining Shakespeare's original description, such as showing in *Henry V* a painted backcloth of the destruction of the French countryside while an off-camera voice spoke of "Her vine, the merry cheerer of the heart, / Unpruned dies" (5.2. 41–42).[13]

Clearly, every and all of Shakespeare's images cannot be made visual. Robert Richardson illustrates this convincingly by putting side by side a prose account of a scene from Pudovkin's *Mother*, where a boy in prison receives a note telling him that he is to be released the next day, with Claudio's speech in *Measure for Measure*, "Ay, but to die, and go we know not where" (3.1.118–32). The prose description—"shots of a brook, swollen with the rapid flow of spring, of the play of sunlight broken on the water, birds splashing in the village pond, and finally a laughing child"—sounds amateurish, mawkish, when in reality the sequence is most effective on film. On the other hand, to give visual equivalents for every image of Claudio's speech—"To bathe in fiery floods, or to reside / In thrilling region of thick-ribbed ice, / To be imprisoned in the viewless winds"—would be impossible. Even if the director managed to find equivalents on screen, no audience could take in the dazzling number of images in Shakespeare. Mr. Richardson comments: "Each scene works in its own medium; neither would work in the other medium; yet the technique is virtually the same in both."[14] If it is true that the medium in part determines the message, it may hold equally that the nature and scope of the imagery is similarly predestined.

One bright suggestion comes from the stage and film director Peter Brook. After remarking on the sense of alienation we get in the theater, that feeling of being engaged and disengaged with respect to the actions on stage, Brook touches on the catholic nature and the speed of Shakespeare's imagery. He argues that the screen as presently constituted is not fast enough, or wide enough, or plural enough to convey the richness and mobility of imagery delivered on stage. Brook then points to Francis

Thompson's film documentary for Johnson's Wax at the last New York World's Fair, a film studying young children growing up in various parts of the world. Thompson used the multiple-screen technique, three screens side by side but with a clear break between them. That is, as audience we are sufficiently alienated by the break, being aware of the three-fold projection; and yet we know that the three parts are also part of a larger collage. Brook then "stages" two well-known scenes from Shakespeare, but scenes as visualized on the multiple screen:

> You can show Hamlet in the battlements of Elsinore on the right-hand screen, and the other two screens may just show a rampart and the sea. Or to return to Gloucester, you can have a heath, and the moment that a soliloquy begins you can drop the heath out of your picture and concentrate on different views of Gloucester. If you like, you can suddenly open one of your screens to a caption, write a line, write a subtitle. If you want, in the middle of a realistic action in color you could have another or the same in black and white.[15]

Would this be a way out, assuming it is important to do more than adapt or to find equivalents for all, most of, or some of the imagery of the play?

The experience with Shakespeare in the silent film may be instructive here. In general, the silents closest to what was taken as Shakespeare's original conception were the most ridiculous; the more sweeping the change to visual, the better the film. Accordingly, Buckewetzki in *Othello* of 1922 was roundly praised, for there the screen actor playing Iago found that quick movements and bizarre leapings about the castle seemed to suggest the quick, irrational, malignant mind of the villain.[16]

Years later Castellani would include shots of Romeo running about the city, and up and down almost endless stairs. To more than one viewer this effectively suggested the "harassed, compulsive, joyless sort of haste, the urgency of something which neither understands" that also pervades the opulent imagery of Shakespeare's balcony scene. There the lovers make equally frantic attempts to convert day into night, larks into nightingales, and so on.[17]

In this practice the film director does not try to duplicate visually Shakespeare's images. Instead, he picks equivalent filmic images, that is, images that work best with his own medium. Of course, he risks the wrath from purists of the theater, Welles's case being the most glaring evidence here. Eric Bentley, for example, complains that in the Welles Shakespeare the lead actor is merely photographed but doesn't really "act" in the sense of stage acting.[18] Even Olivier, who seems considerably distant from Welles when it comes to Shakespeare on film, is criticized for being more conscious of traditional cinema than traditional theater.[19]

A minimum for successful cinematic equivalents may be Youtkevich's *Othello* where he used close-ups of hands as a recurring image, an image coming from the director, not the playwright. We see Emilia's arm twisting across the screen, taunting her husband with the purloined handkerchief, then Othello's hand desperately demanding that same handkerchied, and at last Cassio's raising the handkerchief to his lips.[20] Note here that a static image in Shakespeare is combined with a purely cinematic image, the hand being the very essence of movement, that surface or "flesh," as a colleague calls it, so essential to the cinema. In Mankiewicz's *Julius Caesar* (1953) the Cinna episode was cut, but its essence was sustained. The irony of the episode in the play is that the first act of violence committed by the enraged mob is against a poet. There is a mistake of names, a simplistic abuse of language. When Cinna protests that he is not Cinna the conspirator but Cinna the poet, the mob, indifferent to his pleas, uses as justification a black parody of Juliet's "What's in a name?" Appropriately, this linguistic element is eliminated from the screen version, the director not wanting to incorporate words, the mainstay of the stage. But he does retain Shakespeare's larger emphasis by cutting to the crowd as Antony concludes his oration, a call to anarchy if there ever was one, and by showing the first sporadic acts of violence as the crowd pushes and shoves. With mounting hysteria they lash out indiscriminately—as, indeed, the killing of Cinna in Shakespeare is indiscriminate—at each other and at passersby. Still, this conversion of verbal to visual raises some questions regarding both the definition of conversion (correlatives or equivalents?) and the degree (how often, under what circumstances?).

IV

The fourth category is probably the most inclusive. The assumption here is that in the cinema words and vision are not inimical, that a proper combination of the two allows for fidelity to Shakespeare's intentions.

Still, the balance has to be a delicate one. In 1935 Max Reinhardt tried to strike such a balance in his *A Midsummer Night's Dream* between generous passages from Shakespeare's text and the imaginative scenery of the Hollywood dream factory. Great hope was held out for the picture, Allardyce Nicoll, among others, observing that the "future of Shakespeare in the films seems to rest pretty heavily on [its] shoulders." Nicholl's basic contention was that Shakespeare needed the extensive scenery possible in the cinema, the "imaginary world" that the visual medium could invoke, since the present age had lost its "alertness to spoken speech." He argued that the "psychological penetration rendered manifest through a realistic method" such as the cinema was the twentieth-century surrogate for the verbally complex, symbolic stage of the Renaissance.[21] The common judgment, however, was that the film was a failure—at the box office and aesthetically. The words were lost amidst the scenery; the scenery failed to carry the suggestiveness of the words. A year later MGM's *Romeo and Juliet* (1936), with Norma Shearer and Leslie Howard, fared even worse. Diminishing the scenery, keeping the text more intact, did not seem to solve the problem.

Still, theoretical arguments would suggest a happier future, a happier blending of words and sight. Henri Lemaitre speaks of Shakespeare, unique among the Elizabethans, as a master of "aesthetic illusion," and distinguishes this illusion from that "intellectual illusion that was [the] literary ideal" of his fellow playwrights. As a playwright Shakespeare offers to "the inner eye of the spectator the rich unreeling of an imaginary film."[22] Since his verse appeals to this mental or mind's eye, the step to the film ought to be a relatively easy one.

Yet purists of either extreme will never be satisfied. John Mason Brown complains of the time wasted in Olivier's *Hamlet* in getting about the complicated set of the castle.[23] Someone else praises Barrymore's part in *The Show of Shows*, where he recited a passage from *3 Henry VI*, by reminding us that "good speaking is important in any type of motion picture." Such praise, however, appears contrary to the advice of most film actors, who point out that the laws of stage acting do not fully apply to the screen.[24]

The argument here works both ends. *Hamlet*, one director contends, is really a "series of pictures, vivid, brief, isolated," lacking a wholeness or consistency; and thus Olivier in filming the play gives tangible expression to a symbolic statement implicit in the play's version.[25] The director here selects the words that are most essential, which will hold their own amidst scenic profusion and camera perspectives. Castellani's *Romeo and Juliet* is praised because with its few words the director has extracted the "quintessence of Shakespeare's poetry."[26] Constance Brown admires Olivier's *Richard III* because "Every ounce of linguistic fat is removed," thereby clearing the stage for the swiftly moving plot. Part of the text exists happily here with visual equivalents selected from the poetry, and with images peculiar to the film, such as the twitching, writhing body of Richard as he dies. This visual action implies, "as the play does, that a portion of Richard's destructive impulse is self-directed." Brown also calls attention to the shadows cast by Richard that serve as dissolves to subsequent scenes, or the descent from the bell rope, a cinemagraphic equivalent for Richard's malignant strength.[27]

The film that seems to satisfy most, though not all proponents of this fourth category is Olivier's *Henry V*. Much of the poetry is intact; it is delivered by skilled actors with backgrounds in the legitimate theater. The movie, we will recall, begins on a reconstructed Globe stage, gradually broadening out to vast battlegrounds possible only in the movies. Camera techniques are conspicuous, among them Olivier's trademark of using close-ups with voiced-over soliloquies. The Saint Crispin's Day speech starts with a close-up of Olivier, but slowly moves back so that at the end, while we hear this voice as clearly as ever, Olivier himself is a small figure surrounded by a field of soldiers. The battle of Agincourt is actually shown, not merely described in language. Many spectators defined the film as filmic poetic drama with no clear tension between words and cinema images. The "style or manner of pictorial presentation . . . [was] in accord with the richness of the verse."[28]

Film directors themselves have suggested this essential compatibility between Shakespeare and the movies. Eisenstein argues that all literature, "Dickens and the whole ancestral array, going back as far as the Greeks and Shakespeare," is the true heritage of the cinema—not Edison.[29] Herbert Read maintains that "To project onto that inner screen of the brain a moving picture of objects and events, events and objects moving toward a balance and reconciliation of a more than usual state of emotion with more than usual order" is a "definition of good literature as well as the ideal film."[30] The supposed dangers of bringing a verbal piece into a visual medium may be imaginary. Far from a clash, the merging of Shakespeare and the cinema may be a proper return to some golden age or conception of art where what is verbal is mentally visual. And as perceptual psychologists would hold, what is visual gives way to cerebral connotations inherent in any serious act of perception.

It is interesting that when a record was made from the sound track of Olivier's *Richard III*, the effect was mere chaos. The recording seemed full of gaps; words were ripped from their "literary" context and voices clashed at different tones and levels of emphasis. But in the movie, with sound in lively combination with the visual, no such chaos existed— except in the eyes or minds of purists of either side. David Bradley's two low-budget films of *Macbeth* (1948, directed by Thomas Blair and starring Bradley) and *Julius Caesar* (1950) were shot with considerable fidelity to the text, but with the sound added afterwards. Shakespeare's language here complemented a series of sophisticated shots of Chicago scenery. Bradley generally was commended, though mixed with the praise perhaps was a certain sympathy for the underdog, the non-Hollywood producer working on a limited budget and not "tainted" by the professionals. Welles in *Othello* took caution to record all the dialogue ahead of time; the verbal took precedence over the visual. Budget considerations also entered here since Welles was forced to spend valuable time scurrying about Europe for backers. Perhaps what is called for, then, is a new aesthetic, one not coming exclusively from either medium.

V

The argument here verges on the thoroughly practical; from another perspective, it may even be thought of as a cop out. One should just film the play, perhaps taking some advantage of the camera's ability to provide close-ups and other cinematic tricks to heighten tension. The advantages brought by the cinema to Shakespeare are not primarily aesthetic but social: more people can see the play, exceptional performances can be captured "for all time." With several takes a certain state of perfection can be achieved. Curiously, this simple transference from stage to screen—if it *is* just that—is the way Shakespeare first entered the movies when on 20 September 1899, part of Max Beerbohm Tree's production of *King John* was filmed. In our time one might point to the Tony Richardson film of Nichol Williamson's 1969 production of *Hamlet*.

This last category allows for a little variation. Listen to Oliver talk about his filming of *Henry V*: "You don't need tricky shots . . . . In many of our scenes the camera hardly moves."[31] The next logical step would be to plant the camera stationary in the audience and grind away—and this has been done. The Soviets, particularly, were once given to televising cultural events in this fashion, a seeming negation of the camera's mobility and "piece" of the metaphor.

The evidence seems to suggest, however, that this bare bones approach is not very successful. The Maurice Evans–Judith Anderson *Macbeth* (1960), filmed for television presentation on the Hallmark Hall of Fame, was soundly denounced as dull, and yet the fault surely was not in the quality of the lead actors. And I have heard viewers complain of a series of filmed plays for the American National Theater because the camera tried to move about, offering shots (sudden exteriors, for example) that smacked of filmic technique. The viewers apparently wanted the "illusion" of live theater to be preserved by the camera, but would at the same time deny the flexible reality of the film medium. This method also tends to debilitate the plays themselves. Markiewicz was chided for his close adherence to *Julius Caesar* since the camera only managed to highlight the "weaknesses" of the play that apparently would be nonexistent in the stage version.[32]

Yet the practical side cannot be entirely dismissed. In the movies microphones can be used judiciously, and the improved quality of sound, not to mention its range, can be a potent factor. Nor have the heroes of the cineasts been insensitive to the importance of a stage conception for the cinema. Welles toured with *Macbeth* as a stage presentation before filming; one certain virtue here was that the actors were better prepared than are most screen actors doing Shakespeare.[33] Indeed, if for the actor the insistent chronology of a Shakespearean play is an aid in the "growth" of a character, one practical problem presented by filming is that the product is usually not done as a consistent evolving piece, but rather in many pieces, and often out of order. That order of filming is subject to weather conditions, the location (all scenes of one locale are usually shot at once for economy measures, whether or not they occur concurrently in the play itself), the budget, the availability of actors (stars tend to want to do their scenes all at once, and the producer wants to cut down on inactivity, expensive both for stars and the studio).

Yet one might add: is not the present-tense nature of a stage production, the fact that we are witnessing current, albeit fictive events, itself part of the metaphor? If so, this dimension is automatically negated in a filmed version. Until recently, when we have begun to develop on a broad front some aesthetic principles for the cinema, most reviewers of Shakespeare's films have seen them as if they were filmed plays. When a call is made to use theatrical producers as directors of filmed versions of Shakespeare, we may have cause either for comfort or alarm.[34]

VI

There is always the danger that purists in the theater or the cinema are talking about an art form that not only never existed but may be indefensible even on purely aesthetic grounds. I would hope that no one reading the several essays in this volume could totally dismiss this concern for the nonverbal or visual dimensions of Shakespeare's plays. The words are paramount; but are they really paramount on their own? That is, would a concert reading or a radio presentation of *Hamlet* be the same, aesthetically, as a performance by actors even on a bare stage? On stage actors *do* make entrances and exits witnessed by the audience, and with appropriate physical movements *do* complement the language. The Elizabethans themselves were certainly not all purists about their theater. It is true that Jonson championed the three unities, but he says nothing about eliminating scenery or the physical dimension of the stage.

Excluding Shakespeare—and even he must rank as a minority dramatist today in terms of frequency of performance—we don't really see many Elizabethan plays. They "exist" by virtue of our literary criticism, and that existence is properly in a theater of the mind and, more specifically, a theater eminently verbal. But the actual theater is anything but that.

To be sure, the theater often has unconsciously parodied and even abused the visual. Consider the awkward sets of the Restoration, where perspective was carried to an extreme, or the staggering opulence of the nineteenth-century theater and its insistence on absolute "realism" in stage sets. In that period directors wanted real panes of glass in stage windows, and the actual food on the plate that the character was said to be eating in the script. With the growth of acting schools and theories of acting, the bodily and facial complements to the actor's voice have at times been ludicrously systematized. It was the nineteenth century, that extremist in so many things theatrical, which saw the publication of actor's manuals giving "proper" facial settings for the various emotions and reducing hand movements to the level of a mechanic's repair manual.

Yet at its best times, in Shakespeare's or our own, the theater seems a happy combination of verbal and visual. And if the visual must be subordinate, it still seems indispensable to the verbal. Indeed, the essence of the verbal seems to exist by reason of its antithesis to the visual. In much the same way Genet in *Our Lady of the Flowers* suggests a kinship between police and criminals, each owing his existence, his definition as a member or antimember of society, to the other. Our contemporary theater appears willing to go to any lengths to stress the visual. Beckett himself has progressed or regressed (depending on one's point of view) from absurdist dialogue as in *Endgame* or *Waiting for Godot*, to a combination of actual and recorded dialogue in *Krapp's Last Tape*, to a flirtation with radio plays like *All That Fall* and *Embers*, to the purely visual drama of his *Act Without Words I* and *II*, to the screenplay *Film*. Our own living or open theater underscores this flirtation with the visual, as dance and mime enter in increasing proportions, and as directors rely on other media, particularly the cinema.

In Grant Duay's *Fruit Salad*, for example, three Viet Nam soldiers (Banana, Melon, and Cherry) occupy front stage, while we watch on a screen at back stage a silent commercial in which a home economist demonstrates the proper technique for dicing fruit for a combination salad. As she moves toward success—the perfect salad revealed in all the glossy tones of an industrial technicolor film—the three soldiers destroy themselves, their petty rivalries a vicious little island amidst the tragic rivalries of war. Thematically, of course, we are meant to grasp the ironic juxtaposition between the "destruction" of fruit for the ends of the salad with the peer or self-destruction among the men. But there is also, unspoken, the tension between the faltering dialogue front stage and the triumph of the visual backstage. The theater of war—how interesting that we give that word, as in "Asian Theater" or the "European Theater," to such nonintellectual, physical activity—gives way to the cinema, with the cinema itself here falling to the low ebb of a commercial presentation.

The two, I would submit, are never independent on the legitimate stage. When we speak of the visual dimension of the drama, some distinction ought to be made between the visual elements (the amount of scenery and props, the gestures of the actors) and the theater's eternally visual dimension. The latter exists whether the stage is crowded or bare, whether the actors stand as statues before us or cavort about like monkeys.

In a real sense a Shakespearean play is purely visual in a way that the cinema can never be. What we see is what we see, whereas in the cinema what we see is doubly removed from actuality: there we see a fraudulent image of what the director wanted us to see, through the eye of an instrument that is not really equivalent to our eye or any other human eye. Lacking a universal eye, we ourselves with our naked eyes take in a "reality" peculiar to the beholder. The film experience is therefore three times removed from any physical actuality. It is Pirandello and his dilemma of what is real writ to the extreme.

Nor do theater audiences seem to be content to shut their eyes and, as one does with radio, merely listen to actors reciting lines. I refer here to my account in the Preface of Peter Schaffer's *Black Comedy* and the clash between a dark thematic world and the actual stage witnessed by the spectators.

I would think that the visual dimension of Shakespeare's plays has two effects so essential to the drama that their removal would invalidate the words and reduce the play to poetry of a nondramatic sort. There is, first of all, the sense of the present conveyed by the physical appearance of the stage and of actors moving across it. That active metaphor of the stage as a world and the world as a little stage, the double implications of Jaques's speech in *As You Like It*, may have been weakened or even lost entirely in our age. Yet we still *can see* the actors. We know without the makeup, without the lines that are not their own, that they are like us, that their present reality reduced to its simplest is that they too are momentarily housed in the same building. This "fact" enforces for us the relationship between the stage world and our own.

But it is the very presence of words that adds the vital dimension to this visual base of the theater. Our sense of actuality in seeing live actors before us creates a tension between what we see and a language moving toward an abstract dimension that ultimately dwarfs the visual. To paraphrase Hamlet, the question posed by the theater is: what to do as we crawl between earth and heaven, between what is solid and what is intangible? The metaphor so plentiful in Shakespeare is the passport to this larger world, for beginning in something solid—a metaphor cannot have as its base an abstraction—the metaphor implies something beyond, larger than, ultimately more significant than its substantial, earthly beginnings. Hamlet's "Oh, that this too too solid flesh would melt" (Q1, 1.2.129) signals, I think the way toward this issue. And as I have argued elsewhere, the preponderance of those theatrical metaphors in Shakespeare based on his craft, the stage, acting, actors, and audience reinforces this double implication of the theater as actual and yet as something with a "reality" that is only the first stage. The "seeming" is there primarily to admit a larger, intangible cerebral or imaginative world.[35] In a sense, physical vision gives way to a metaphorical vision that at length admits a metaphysical vision.

VII

It is, I think, the visual and the nonverbal dimensions of the theater that are at the source of this metamorphosis from physical to metaphysical vision. Now, curiously, it is the purists of the cinema who would, in their own medium, reverse the movement. The argument seems to be that words are not only unimportant but—to carry the argument to its extreme—actually hostile to the visual properties of the screen. Little wonder that Shakespeare with his well of English undefiled is seen as enemy. The cinema, the argument goes, is not symbolic, not cerebral, not abstract; it is relevant, about the here and now. It asks us to open our eyes to the present world; it is—in a phrase—where it's at.

I would not want to argue with this, but only to add that perhaps this argument addresses itself only to one kind of cinema. Surely this stress on seeing, as a pretext for criticism, works well with, say, a film like Mr. Kubrick's *2001: A Space Odyssey*. Listen to one of the best contemporary film critics speak about Bowman's voyage in the space pod, a voyage that the critic sees as the film's celebration of its own imaginative visuality and of the latent potentials in the liberated eye. Rationality is here, I must add, equated with the verbal, with words:

> The new story, and the difficult one, in "2001" is the further evolution of man beyond rationality. Reason plays only a small part in the overall movement toward the evolution of imaginative man, who sees and thereby synthesizes the world that words could only analytically polarize. For the bitter rational truth is that reason is merely a tool used to its limits by the eye and then, as with all tools, when its job is done it is disposed of.
>   The pressure of life within the wild eye seized the "I" of reason, which it drove to its ultimate polarization and annihilation, unfeelingly using reason to go on going on and cruelly discarding it when there is no good left in it. HAL looms as a sufficiently difficult obstacle for those who persist in demanding that "2001" satisfy the expectations and criteria of the literary sensibility. But when Dave

Bowman appears in the space "pod" (itself shaped like a giant eye and the carrier of the seed of new growth) at the beginning of the third phase in the purification of the eye—its transcendence of rationality as well as bestiality—the literary sensibility is nonplussed. Kubrick notes that "there's a basic problem with people who are not paying attention with their eyes. They're listening . . . and those who won't believe their eyes won't be able to appreciate this film." It is precisely at this point where the eye sets forth to transcend rationality as well as bestiality that the literary sensibility, which is phonetic or sound oriented, should it have stayed with the trip this far, bears out Kubrick's observation regarding the inevitable failure of listeners to appreciate "2001."

For his new story looks beyond exhausted verbal sources and values. It takes as its province visual relations, connections too subtle for verbal articulation.[36]

My complaint here is not that this criticism is wrong—it is eminently right, for Kubrick and for Fellini—but rather that it may be too exclusive. The salient fact is that our two most public forms of art have been the theater and the cinema. The theater makes room for a Shakespeare and a Jonson, and has included exquisite wordsmiths such as Lorca and Yeats. There is also the acrobatic, physical theater not only of our own day but of theater in its broadest sense (ballet, tribal dances, folk plays, happenings both then and now). Can that theater pretend to be anything less than inclusive? In practice the cinema has ranged from filmed plays to filmed abstractions (lines and form without clear reference to everyday actuality), from movies where actors predominated to those given to the director's vision. Does it follow, then, that the cinema may be no less inclusive? Some forms such as the sonnet or electronic music may, by definition, work themselves towards an increasingly exclusive aesthetic. But what of the theater and the cinema, and variations thereof—opera, ballet, not to mention the mixed media productions of our own century?

Listen to Bernard Shaw speak about that pleasure in Shakespeare's language that goes beyond meaning or abstraction:

That is what happened in a smaller way with *Much Ado*. Shakespear shews himself in it a commonplace librettist working on a stolen plot, but a great musician. No matter how poor, coarse, cheap, and obvious the thought may be, the mood is charming, and the music of the words expressed the mood. Paraphrase the encounters of Benedick and Beatrice in the style of a bluebook, carefully preserving every idea they present, and it will become apparent to the most infatuated Shakespearean that they contain at best nothing out of the common in thought or wit, and at worst a good deal of vulgar naughtiness. Paraphrase Goethe, Wagner, or Ibsen in the same way, and you will find original observation, subtle thought, wide comprehension, far-reaching intuition, and serious psychological study in them. Give Shakespear a fairer chance in the comparison by paraphrasing even his best and maturest work, and you will still get nothing more than the platitudes of proverbial philosophy, with a very occasional curiosity in the shape of a rudiment of some modern idea, not followed up. Not until the Shakespearean music is added by replacing the paraphrase with the original lines does the enchantment begin.[37]

And recently, in a television documentary on well-known Hollywood directors, Howard Hawkes made the interesting observation that to him there is a sense of movement, of choreographed dance, even in screen dialogue. While primarily known as a director of action movies, Hawkes confessed to a partiality for the fast-paced dialogue of the madcap movies of the 1940s. In those films several people talked at the same time, each pressing an individual plea; the scene would often be a busy newspaper office, or some place of equally frantic activity. Hawkes's technique was to pad a simple sentence, fore and aft, with a fairly nonessential conversation so that the actors could step on each other's lines. They would thereby create the verbal cacophony to match the sense of chaos in the office and also supplement the seemingly chaotic lunges of the camera. Still, Hawkes allowed the audience to understand the basic point made by each of the speakers since it was securely sandwiched between the "padding" dialogue.

To be sure, the achievement of our own cinema has been to get away from the talkies. We all recall those movies of the early 1930s where too many directors, fascinated by the sound which had replaced silence, were content to bunch actors around a table with a microphone not so artfully concealed in a vase of roses. As the actors talked away the camera was relegated to a mere recording device. Yet possibly the fairest and most catholic definition of cinematic advances has been the movement not toward silence or the purely visual, but toward some decent, productive relationship between sight and sound. If the silent movies represented the ultimate stage in cinematic refinement, why was it that the people, the public trust of such public media as the theater and the cinema, quickly abandoned even the most sophisticated silent film for the most wretched talky? My hunch here is that the relation between sight and sound is essential to that human need that drives otherwise sane men and women into the theater, legitimate or movie. For here we watch on stage or screen an obvious fabrication in which grown men and women play at being something other than themselves. Still, a human need is expressed and satisfied.

VIII

I would argue that the most profitable question to ask is not whether the cinema is too visual for Shakespeare, or whether Shakespeare is too verbal for the cinema, but rather, are there any similarities of effect and therefore of meaning in the "worlds" being advanced by artists in sight and sound? Each medium has its own integrity, its own principles. Yet if the two media are not completely antithetical, or eternally separate, is there some common ground both in medium and therefore in message whereby Shakespeare can be translated to the cinema? Can the "essence" of the play be transformed with proper respect shown to the cinema? Is the philosophy of the theater, as I have defined it, antithetical to the philosophy inherent in the cinema? If we would admit the possibility that the cinema celebrates not just the eye but the mind, not just the here and now, but things that ultimately have a cerebral, even metaphysical dimension, then I would think that the movement of Shakespeare from stage to screen is not impossible.

I would submit, first of all, that the camera's eye is never realistic. It is by definition an abstracting instrument no less so than the brain and its verbal counterpart. The camera's eye is itself a technological abstraction. Besides, the vision it gives is caught in time, the ultimate in philosophical abstractions. We seem to see things happening on screen, but of course they are not happening. We are watching only a record of something that once was, a dead world staged for the camera's benefit.

Our own eye is an abstracting instrument. We can all take in the same image—ten people can simultaneously see a tree. Yet depending on our own feelings about trees, our mood at the time, our sense of priorities (are trees more valuable growing than as kindling wood?), we cannot "see" the same object. It cannot have the same meaning for all of us.

Now the physical present tense of the theater is, we know, a fakery; only an unsophisticated spectator would race up on stage and urge Hamlet to follow through with his speculations about killing Claudius as the king kneels at his prayers. The "reality" of the cinema is one already thrice removed from a Platonic truth by the three eyes of the camera, the director, and the spectator. If the so-called realism of the cinema is itself an abstraction, and if words in Shakespeare *are* abstractions, do we not have the first possibility of some common meeting ground?

When a stage actor calls up an image, no matter how fast the images flow before us, do we not form a physical picture in the mind? Surely the mind can work as fast or faster than the actor's speed of delivery. Often Shakespeare's images, or image clusters, are gradual, as in Macbeth's extraordinary picture of the killing of the king viewed by angels pleading "trumpet-tongu'd" against him. The deed itself is atomized, with its particles infecting the eyes of universal beholders, and the eyes thus irritated pouring down a death-bringing flood on the agent of his "taking off" (1.7.16–25). But even a sudden image, Macbeth's hand making the "multitudinous seas incarnadine," is not so fast that we delight only in the sounds of "multitudinous" and "incarnadine." Indeed, to prepare us for this, the text clearly indicates that the actor raises his murderer's hand to his face: "What hands are here? Ha! they pluck out mine eyes" (2.2.58). And in case we miss the physical meaning of "multitudinous seas incarnadine," the next line resolves the dilemma: "Making the green one red," a phrase with the simplicity of a child's coloring book (2.2.59–63).

Conversely, does the thing photographed by the camera ever remain simply itself? Can it possibly so remain when it is part of an artifice? Even when birds accidentally flew across camera range and were later incorporated by Welles in the film version of *Othello*, they were, properly, no longer just random birds flying, *or* an accident, but part of a design, part of the meaning. Both media have their imagery and its concomitant in abstraction, whether intellectual or imaginative. In one instance the mind's eye gives form to what is initially verbal (though verbal delivered in time by a live actor), and in the other the "physical image" can never remain merely just that.

Shakespeare, there is no doubt, must be "adjusted" for the cinema, with the amount of dialogue reduced and equivalent imagery found. It would not be aesthetically, perhaps not even financially possible to duplicate his images in their entirety. And screen acting is not stage acting; faces acceptable at the long-distance of the legitimate theater might prove unacceptable on screen. The sad history of Broadway actresses of real ability, such as Helen Hayes, who fared less well on the screen is ample proof of this.

If in part the medium is the message, then part of the message, part of the *essence* of the play, must of necessity be lost in the transformation. The question is: must it be the whole message?

In the Renaissance legitimate theater was the people's equivalent of the coterie's sonnets and prose romances. And today the movies belong to the people in a way that poetry or even novels can never belong. Both media have an extensive technical orientation (the stage, the camera and projector, along with actual theaters) not present in more conservative genres. (In poetry first a quill and then—no great leap—a pen would do.) Are the two not possessed, then, of similarities as well as glaring differences? And might they not come together in their common and, as it were, glorious impurity? Both must be ratified by audiences. Actors playing to an empty playhouse are not, I would think, in a play but only in rehearsal; and a movie droning on without an audience is an eerie proposition. There have been would-be playwrights more overtly intellectual than Shakespeare but not comparable as playwrights. One thinks of Henry James, for example, in his middle period of flirtation with the stage. Is there not in the theater a sense of verbal movement, not to mention physical reality and movement, which is essentially filmic?

If Shakespeare must adapt to the cinema, the cinema, conversely, must adapt to Shakespeare. The impersonal, perfectly square screen championed by purists of the silent cinema might not do. We might consider Peter Brook's suggestion: perhaps the cinema will have to experiment with a multiple screen, with images of various kinds (straight film, cartoons, printing, paintings, slides) projected in concert. If Shakespeare as a straight playwright is not yet ready for the screen, perhaps the screen in its present proportions is not yet ready for Shakespeare. The problems are of course enormous, and there is no guarantee that even the visual elements of Shakespeare would be more easily translated than the verbal. A Shakespearean play thus translated might not on the surface look or sound like the stage play.

Still, the issues rest not on the surface but deeper. Can the essence of the play be translated? Could we say proudly at the end of a viewing: this is just what Shakespeare would have done if he wrote for the screen (and not just wrote but directed as well)? We often hear that cliché: if Shakespeare were alive today he would surely be a screen writer. And this very cliché exposes the prejudice—"screen writer." The fact is that the most successful adapters of Shakespeare have generally been the most complete artists: Welles, even Olivier, Castellani, Kurosawa. Hollywood in the 1940s possessed that sort of man; Harold Hawkes wrote, directed, produced, and acted. In our own day Bergman is similarly catholic. Pure directors, pure theorists of the screen, and pure screen plays are essential for one kind of film, but not necessarily for the filmed Shakespeare I am proposing.

To the objection that at best we would be getting someone else's Shakespeare—a Shakespeare reflecting the will of a particular director saddled by the demands of the cinema medium—I would raise Morris Weitz's objection to the critic's claim to know the true Shakespeare, to "see" Hamlet as the author intended him. After examining the major critical approaches to Hamlet, from Coleridge to Bradley, from Ernest Jones to the new critics, Weitz, a philosopher with no stated personal investment in the play, finds all views both right *and* wrong. Each interpretation, he contends, tells us not about the truth at the heart of the play but rather about the critic's own approach, about what the play means to *him* or *her*, and about the truth of *his* or *her* role as critic.[38] Would a film director alert to the interrelation of sight and sound as they exist within a medium and between media be any more relative in this quest for the "true Shakespeare"? If the novelist or lyric poet is in control of his or her medium, the playwright is subject to additional hands, those of the director, the actors, the audience and its mood on a particular day, the physical theater itself. Without doing serious harm, might we add the film director and his audience to this list of cooks who collectively might spoil, but also might not spoil the product?

The question remains: why do it? Why take Shakespeare from a medium in which he is the certain master and move him? Two quick, but shallow responses come first to mind. It has happened already; prohibition would not work here and so, in face of the facts, we ought to be concerned not with impossibilities but responsibilities. Also, the movies *are* our medium, a way of bringing something good to millions, be it Shakespeare or a screenplay. The people's playwright in his day, Shakespeare will not be so today if confined to that legitimate stage that increasingly means college stage or Shakespeare-festival stage.

But these are at best negative or pragmatic reasons. To the same question of why do it, one might also respond that such translation offers another frontier for this new cinema medium that is breaking frontiers daily. That a Shakespeare play cannot be the same on screen might be a sign for rejoicing, not lamenting; we may be getting "two for the price of one," and two from one. If the film is the metaphor for our time, a technological achievement that now focuses literally and figuratively on our technological world with its potential for tragedy and comedy, then the Shakespeare of all ages deserves no less a medium.

The Renaissance apparently felt no qualms in adapting everything from prose romances (Greene's *Pandosto*, Lodge's *Rosalynde*), histories (Holinshed, Hall), to the latest gossip (surely one of the "sources" for *Love's Labour's Lost*). Ovid and Plutarch once "Englished" also made their way happily into Shakespeare. One hears little about violations of the media from Renaissance critics. The Puritans seemed to have their hands full attacking what was already on stage, rather than the process from nondramatic to dramatic.

Perhaps a pluralistic movement would yield greater returns than one more individualistic. As the increasing sophistication in film aesthetics defines the properties peculiar to that art, and as we move from filmed plays to films in the finest sense of that word, might there not be a complementary "impure" aesthetics, one concerned with the larger relationship and the potential for translation among the arts? Nor should we exempt the legitimate stage from the influx of the cinema. I mentioned earlier the play *Fruit Salad*; Sarah Caldwell in Boston has used slides and footage not just as backdrop but as part of a collage including a modernistic opera. Words are words, and sight is sight; that equation will not, to be sure, work in the same way for the theater and the cinema. And yet it might. Either way we stand to be the winners of an aesthetic that will consider the joint issue. Perhaps there will be directors and audiences who literally would like to consider the product.

IX

An old-time vaudevillian once described for me one of the most popular acts in a show in which he toured during the early 1930s. This particular act would take four nights, a sort of serial designed to lure first-nighters back to the show. On the opening night a well-dressed young man coming forth on a dimly lit, suggestive stage would first introduce himself to the audience and then call for his wife. As the stage light went up, she would appear in a rose arbor back stage, pick out a rose, and then gracefully come forward. The couple would chat amiably for a time, kiss discretely; and then the lady would offer her husband the rose. At length she would make her way backstage. *Blackout*. When the lights were turned on to full brightness, the man would toss the rose into the audience and then reveal the "secret." He was a live actor, but his wife was simply a projection on film. Their conversation, the kiss, the exchange of the rose had all been a careful synchronization between the actor and the film, between legitimate theater and screen. (A rose concealed in his coat pocket would do the trick for the one physical transformation from film to life.) The second night the sequence would be repeated, but this time the secret would be that the lady on stage was real, the man filmed (no rose would be tossed on this occasion). The third night—you may have guessed the variation by now—both parties, man and woman, would be on film; the effect came from a clever synchronization of the images on two separate screens. The last night, aided by subdued stage lighting and by the previous confusion between the film image and the live actor, both man and woman would be live. Word would have made its way among the audience that film had been used on three previous occasions. This time a rose would be tossed by both actors as a sign of appreciation for the audience's indulgence—and money!

Obviously this act appealed to the public's fascination with the new film medium. But crude as the presentation may seem in our time, was there not here a suggestion, most certainly unintentional and hardly academic, about the relationship between film and stage? Might we find in this vaudeville act a crude signpost pointing the way toward a more creative partnership between the most eminent playwright of the Western world and that twentieth-century medium that both threatens and should, I believe, encourage the stage?

CODA

Not only is this article about the drama but, as I mentioned in the Preface, there has been something dramatic in the collaboration itself. I asked one of my former graduate students, Neil Feineman, to share his thoughts with me, to be a coauthor. I asked him not only because of his bright mind but also because of his practical experience in filmmaking. Early in that collaboration I found myself very much influenced by my colleague William Robinson in his argument that the message is the medium and that Shakespeare cannot be translated into the cinema. Feineman was at that point still comfortable in using literary terms, such as symbol, when talking about film. As this happy and dramatic collaboration wore on, we found ourselves switching sides, Feineman coming closer to the Robinson argument, I at least willing to suggest some potential grounds for a merging of the two media.

The result is that the first half of this article (sections one to five) represents a collaboration in the purest sense of that word, a meeting of minds. The second half (sections six to nine) are my own thoughts, literally speculations about some common properties in theater and film and a suggestion for a "new cinema" for Shakespeare. But I cannot and do not want to dismiss Feineman's historical and aesthetic argument against Shakespeare in the movies. And so in *summary* fashion, using his own words or approximations, I present his view. It seems appropriate that this collection ends with the reader forced to do some work. He can take our two arguments, in themselves and within the context of the other eleven pieces in this collection, and decide for himself the place of the visual and nonverbal elements in Shakespeare. To what degree would these elements allow for a successful translation, one finer than we have witnessed hitherto, from stage to screen?

The Feineman argument, abbreviated and recorded in a topical outline, follows:

In the theater all other elements of the play exist to aid dialogue that ultimately must carry the heaviest load. Because the visual and the tactile are hampered by the physical characteristics of the theater, words become more functional and more meaningful on stage than they do in non theatrical situations. And because words are not the force on screen that they are on stage, screen language must be more naturalistic and more banal than stage language.

The filmmaker, then, must realize immediately that he is going to have to change Shakespeare's text. Not intimidated by our reverence for Shakespeare's words, he must take his cue from the dramatists who have been freely adapting the plays for years. Only a handful of stage productions attempt to present the entire, definitive text of a Shakespearean play. The filmmaker must rewrite the dialogue so that it becomes subservient to the visual and must elevate the visual so that it controls the film. If this is not done, despite rewriting efforts the dialogue will still overwhelm the visual and limit that movie's effectiveness. Olivier's movies exemplify this failure of adaptation. Although he realizes that the two media are different, Olivier ultimately fails to emphasize the visual at the expense of Shakespeare's language. Instead, he uses varying degrees of the film's visual potentialities to complement and reinforce the dialogue. Though devoting a great deal of attention to the visual, he still refuses to free it from Shakespeare's words, and thus his movies tend to become showcases for Olivier's talent and virtuosity.

This task of translating Shakespeare's language into visual compositions is greatly complicated by Shakespeare's elevation of language from a tool to a central issue of his plays. Romeo's and Juliet's attempts to create a new, private universe through their unique use of language, for example, is a crucial dimension of that play. Shakespeare has intertwined his meaning with his medium. In the cinema, then, the lovers' concern with language must be rethought as a visual issue. The difficulty of this translation is so formidable that the temptation to ignore the issue must have been irresistible to Zeffirelli. Likewise, in his version of *Taming of the Shrew* he totally avoided any of the implications raised by the unique induction scenes and the character of Christopher Sly. Instead, he made a movie that seems to suggest not only that Shakespeare knew Elizabeth Taylor and Richard Burton, but also that he expressly wrote the play as a chronicle of their well-publicized romance.

Two films that were serious attempts to translate Shakespeare have achieved considerable reputation among film critics and students. Both Orson Welles in *Chimes at Midnight* and Akira Kurosawa in *Throne of Blood* approached Shakespeare visually and intelligently. But neither filmmaker was interested in a complete translation of the play, and although *Throne of Blood* and *Chimes at Midnight* are important movies, they contain less Shakespeare and more Kurosawa and more Welles, respectively.

The fact is that in Shakespeare the theater becomes a vital and complex arena with no clear delineation between the actor and the audience. Through the use of characters like Christopher Sly and through the use of metadrama, dumb show, and dialogue, Shakespeare exploits this confusion. When the onstage actors become audiences watching other actors perform, often in the roles of poor or amateur actors, the paying audience is drawn into a relationship of incredible complexity and ambiguity. Because the plays are both part of and different from the nontheatrical world, the distinction between reality and illusion is blurred. By thus demanding a simultaneous suspension and activation of reason the plays force a continual interplay between reason and imagination. Through the manipulation of these confused roles, Shakespeare draws the "audience" into his / the world, involving them in a venture both cosmic and universal. And so the audience is a visible, active participant in the theatrical experience, a living community (with the actors) of interdependent people. This is no less true, indeed is even more obvious in our day. For example, the audience is as exciting, important, and integral to the impact of a Broadway production such as *Jesus Christ Superstar*, the variable success of a performance of *Hair*, or the spontaneity of the rock theater of Bette Midler as is the performance itself.

Now rather than requiring active participants, the movies appeal to the voyeur in us. Whether I get up or stay, the film will play the same. In a movie house there is no confusion over who the audience is and who the actors are; I am either watching the movie or I am on film as a photographic representation of myself. But I am never unsure of which one I am. This does not mean that the movie cannot engross and involve the spectator deeply, but such involvement results from the viewer's identification with the character or situation in the film. Ultimately, then, the involvement is vicarious and individual.

Filmmakers have been aware of this relationship between the audience and the cinema for a long time. In 1931 the Russian director Vertov made a documentary, *The Man with the Movie Camera*, in which he showed the cameraman, audiences, editors, and projectionists as part of the film. More recently, in Peter Brook's *Marat / Sade* the camera pulls back at the end to reveal the audience at the asylum. A more sustained attempt was Harry Hurwitz's 1969 film, *The Projectionist*, the story of a projectionist who improved on his drab life by living in a movie dream world. As lights in the theater go out, a cartoon begins but soon the film breaks. As the real audience starts screaming, reacting to the blank screen and the ineptitude of our projectionist, the screen becomes smaller; we see a theater and an audience in the movie reacting in the same way we are. This is a most inventive beginning, but like all such techniques it is undercut by drawing attention to itself as just that, a technique. For Chuck the projectionist and probably every film buff, the world may be a film but film is clearly not the world. *MASH* ends with an announcement from a loudspeaker that throughout the movie has announced the schedule of films shown on the Army base, "You have been watching *MASH*." And in the nightclub scene of *Cabaret* actors walk in front of the camera, momentarily obscuring Liza Minnelli and her dancers. But rather than raising levels of ambiguity in the film and inserting provocative implications, all these incidents drawing attention to themselves become merely cute tricks.

And unlike Shakespeare's theater that operates in the present because of the self-renewal resulting from the interaction of audience and actors, the film belongs to the past. Movies date themselves, documenting things that have already happened. By the time it reached the theaters *Easy Rider* was dated; before the picture came out thousands of people had already made Captain America's trip, if not physically, at least mentally. Woodstock was not in the past, but *Woodstock* the movie certainly was. Because the film is the same from day to day, the audience cannot help feeling that they are watching events that have already happened unfold, rather than events that are happening now.

Yet despite these limitations, movies seem to be able to capture the realistic elements of Shakespeare better than the theater. Rather than relying on props, symbolic sets, or abstract devices, the movies can film concrete, elaborate, and realistic sets. What the theater can only suggest, the movies can show. However, because the camera is so faithful in its reproduction of our tangible reality, it is forced to recreate only that tangible reality. In other words, we know we are watching a representation of reality. If it does not look real, it draws attention to itself. Conversely, the theater cannot physically capture every element of our tangible reality. It must deal symbolically with our tangible realities. A tree or a stick on stage is in the play's reality a forest; an open area is a banquet hall or a battlefield. The playgoer must make an initial commitment to use his imagination. In this way, the distinction between reality and illusion will be lost, or at least blurred.

The forest in *A Midsummer Night's Dream*, for example, cannot be translated effectively to film. The forest's ethereal, other-worldly, ambiguous nature is a crucial element that must be conveyed. If the filmmaker translates it into a fantasy world and uses spectacular effects such as mists, surreal sets, and unearthly colors, the audience will know that it is no longer is our tangible reality. The ambiguity and atmosphere of the forest are lost. If the filmmaker films a real forest, he gives us scenic beauty, perhaps, but destroys the play's crucial metaphor. Quite simply, the movies can never capture this intangible, but real nature of imaginary worlds and still remain effective.

The movies can, of course, successfully recreate and then make real an imaginative interior world. In Polanski's *Repulsion*, for example, we are taken into the mind and thus the world of a repressed, insane woman. While her reality is not a cosmic one, it is unique, constrictive, and extremely unambiguous. Yet no matter how much we identify with this world, we know that it is a private vision peopled by a single individual. We are not in the ambiguous, undefined, real, and universal other worlds of Shakespeare. His worlds are real for more than one character; both the audience and the actors exist in them. In the movies, other worlds are reserved for private occupancy.

The movies, then, prove unsuitable for the expansive nature of Shakespeare's plays. His theater becomes a cosmic experience in which one's individuality is submerged into a communal body forced to explore and find meaning in an ever-expanding universe. Movies, on the other hand, cannot be expansive; when they try, they merely call attention to themselves and further distance the viewer. This does not make the movies a less profound medium—just a different one.

If one tries to make a movie of a Shakespeare play and retain the essence of the playwright, he is mixing his media. He can film a performance of the play and make no or minimal concessions to the cinema, as Richardson did in *Hamlet*. He can be more cinematic but remain faithful to the text, as Olivier has. He can contemporize the plot line, as in *West Side Story* or *Forbidden Planet*. He can retain some of the language and the plot, and make popular but vapid movies, as Zeffirelli has done. He can use Shakespeare as an inspiration or a starting point, and make exciting movies like *Throne of Blood*. He may or may not make a good movie; in any case, the film's success or failure will have nothing to do with Shakespeare.

NOTES

1. Cope, "Anti-Form in Renaissance Drama," *The Theater and the Dream* (Baltimore, Md., 1973), pp. 1–13.

2. William Robinson, "The Movies, Too, Will Make You Free," *Man and the Movies* (Baton Rouge, La., 1967), p. 129.

3. Robinson, "The Movies, Too," p. 128.

4. George Barbarow, "*Hamlet* Through a Telescope," *Hudson Review* 2 (1949): 100.

5. *Hamlet Father and Son* (Oxford, 1955), pp. 17–23; reprinted in Charles W. Eckert, ed., *Focus on Shakespearean Films* (Englewood Cliffs, N.J., 1972), pp. 69–70. This valuable anthology provides a catholic array of attitudes toward the issue of filming Shakespeare.

6. Quoted by Roy Walker, "In Fair Verona," *The Twentieth Century* 156 (1954): 464–71; reprinted in Eckert, ed., *Focus*, p. 117.

7. Robert Hatch in *The Nation* (8 January 1955), quoted by Paul A. Jorgensen, "Castellani's *Romeo and Juliet*: Intention and Response," *The Quarterly of Film, Radio, and Television* 10 (1955): 1–10; reprinted in Eckert, ed., *Focus*, p. 109.

8. *Four Screenplays of Ingmar Bergman* (New York, 1960), pp. 17–18.

9. Gavin Lambert, *"Romeo and Juliet," Sight and Wound* 25 (1955): 85–86; reprinted in Eckert, ed., *Focus*, p. 124.

10. *"Macbeth*, or the Magical Depths," *Études Cinématographiques* 24–25 (1963): 86–89; reprinted in translation by Eckert, ed., *Focus*, pp. 73–74.

11. Derek Prouse, *"Othello," Sight and Sound* 26 (1956): 30; reprinted in Eckert, ed., *Focus*, p. 126.

12. Geoffrey Reeves, "Finding Shakespeare on Film: From an Interview with Peter Brook," *Tulane Drama Review* 11 (1966): 117–21; reprinted by Eckert, ed., *Focus*, p. 37.

13. Ian Johnson, "Merely Players," *Films and Filming* (1964), 41–48; reprinted by Eckert, ed., *Focus*, p. 15.

14. Robert Richardson, *Literature and Film* (Bloomington, Ill., 1969), pp. 69–70.

15. Reeves, "Interview with Peter Brook," p. 41 (Eckert).

16. Johnson, "Merely Players," quoting René Clair on p. 11 (Eckert).

17. Jorgensen, "Intention and Response," p. 11 (Eckert).

18. "[Review of] *Othello*," *The New Republic* 133 (1955): 22.

19. Parker Tyler, *"Hamlet* and Documentary," *The Kenyon Review* 11 (1949): 528.

20. Prouse, *"Othello*," p. 127 (Eckert).

21. Allardyce Nicholl, *Film and Theater* (New York, 1936), pp. 175–181; reprinted by Eckert, ed., *Focus*, pp. 45–47.

22. Henri Lemaitre, "Shakespeare, the Imaginary Cinema, and the Precinema," *Études Cinématographiques* 6-7 (1960): 383–96; reprinted and translated by Eckert, ed., *Focus*, pp. 33, 29.

23. Johnson, "Merely Players," p. 17 (Eckert).

24. Richard Watts, Jr., "Films of a Moonstruck World," *The Yale Review* 25 (1935): 311–20; reprinted in Eckert, ed., *Focus*, p. 52. But see Micheál MacLiammoir's account of his experience as an actor in Welles's *Othello*, in *Put Money in Thy Purse* (London, 1952).

25. Mary McCarthy, "A Prince of Shreds and Patches," in *Sights and Sounds* (New York, 1956), pp. 141–45; reprinted in Eckert, ed., *Focus*, p. 65.

26. Jorgensen, "Intentions and Response," p. 115 (Eckert).

27. Constance Brown, "Olivier's *Richard III*—a Reevaluation," *Film Quarterly* 20 (1967): 23–32; reprinted in Eckert, ed., *Focus*, pp. 132, 139.

28. Bosley Crowther, *"Henry V*," *The Great Films: Fifty Years of Motion Pictures* (New York, 1967), pp. 165–68; reprinted in Eckert, ed., *Focus*, p. 58.

29. Sergei Eisenstein, *Film Form* (Cleveland and New York, 1957), pp. 232–33.

30. *A Coat of Many Colours* (London, 1945), pp. 230–31. See the interesting discussion of this precinematic quality in literature in Richardson, *Literature and Film*, pp. 5–16.

31. Johnson, "Merely Players," p. 15 (Eckert).

32. James E. Phillips, *"Julius Caesar*: Shakespeare as a Screen Writer," *The Quarterly of Film, Radio, and Television* 8 (1953): 126.

33. See the account in Richard Wilson, *"Macbeth* on Film," *Theater Arts* 33 (1949): 53–55.

34. See Roy Walker, "Bottled Spider," *The Twentieth Century* 156 (1956): 60.

35. "When the Theater Turns to Itself," *New Literary History* 2 (1971): 407–17.

36. William R. Robinson and Mary McDermott, "'2001' and Literary Sensibility," *The Georgia Review* 26 (1972): 37.

37. George Bernard Shaw, *From Our Theatres in the Nineties*, 3 vols. (London, 1932).

38. Morris Weitz, *Hamlet and the Philosophy of Literary Criticism* (Chicago, 1964). I must also mention that since I wrote this chapter, Jack Jorgens's *Shakespeare on Film* (Bloomington, Ind., 1977) has appeared. This book, the most excellent study of Shakespeare in the movies to appear so far, adopts a similarly flexible attitude on the issue of Shakespeare's adaptability to the cinema.

Notes on Contributors

BERNARD BECKERMAN. Author of *Shakespeare at the Globe, 1599–1609* and *Dynamics of Drama*, along with numerous studies focusing on the theatrical dimension of plays, Professor Beckerman is Brander Matthews Professor of Dramatic Literature at Columbia University.

JAMES L. CALDERWOOD. James Calderwood is Professor of English and Comparative Literature at the University of California, Irvine. He has served as coeditor of several textbooks and editions. His first book, *Shakespearean Metadrama*, was followed by *Metadrama in Shakespeare's Henriad*, published by the University of California Press. The essay printed here is a portion of that study.

MAURICE CHARNEY. With interests that range from the aesthetics of Elizabethan drama to Richard Wright, Maurice Charney is Professor of English at Rutgers University. His influential study of *Shakespeare's Roman Plays* has led to recent books on *Style in "Hamlet"* and *How to Read Shakespeare*.

ALAN C. DESSEN. Professor of English at the University of North Carolina, Alan Dessen has served as editor of *Renaissance Drama* and written widely on Shakespeare, Middleton, Jonson, and morality plays. His study of *Jonson's Moral Comedy* appeared in 1971. The University of North Carolina Press published his *Elizabethan Drama and the Viewer's Eye* in 1977.

ROBERT HAPGOOD. Professor of English at the University of New Hampshire, Robert Hapgood won the English Institute Prize in 1968 for his essay on "Shakespeare and the Included Spectator." His publications include several dozen other articles and theater reviews.

ALFRED HARBAGE. Cabot Professor of English Emeritus of Harvard University, Alfred Harbage brought out, during the years of a distinguished career, such works as *Shakespeare's Audience* (1941), *As They Liked It* (1947), *Shakespeare and the Rival Traditions* (1952), *Shakespeare: A Reader's Guide* (1963), and *Conceptions of Shakespeare* (1966). He took particular pleasure in serving as general editor of the Complete Pelican Shakespeare series. He is deeply missed.

TERENCE HAWKES. Terence Hawkes is Professor of English, University College, Cardiff, Wales; he is also a popular Visiting Professor in this country. His book-length publications include *Shakespeare and the Reason, Metaphor, Shakespeare's Talking Animals,* and, most recently, *Structuralism and Semiotics*. He has also edited *Coleridge on Shakespeare* and served as European Editor for *Language and Style* (Queens College Press).

T. WALTER HERBERT. Distinguished Service Professor of English at the University of Florida, T. Walter Herbert has published, among other essays, three studies that bear on his contribution to this collection: "The Naming of Falstaff," "Sound and Sense in Two Shakespeare Sonnets," and "A Study of Meaning in *Antony and Cleopatra*." His early study of John Wesley for Princeton has been followed by editorship of a volume for the Duke University Press Wesley series. In 1977 the Louisiana State University Press published his *Oberon's Mazéd World: A Judicious Young Elizabethan Contemplates "A Midsummer Night's Dream" with a Mind Shaped by the Learning of Christendom, Modified by the New Naturalist Philosophy, and Excited by the Vision of a Rich, Powerful England*.

BARBARA HODGDON. Barbara Hodgdon is Associate Professor of English at Drake University. Along with her work as contributing editor for *Shakespeare Newsletter*, she is the author of articles and critical reviews of Shakespeare in performance and of Shakespeare in the cinema.

SIDNEY HOMAN. The editor of this collection is the Chairman of the High Honors Program of the University of Florida. Along with many studies of Shakespeare, aesthetics, and the cinema, he has edited *A Midsummer Night's Dream*. Professor Homan also served as Project Director for a theatrical tour of *Waiting for Godot*, that played before prisoners in ten correctional institutions. His study of *When the Theater Turns to Itself: The Aesthetic Metaphor in Shakespeare* is forthcoming from the Bucknell University Press.

W. R. ROBINSON. Author of *Edwin Arlington Robinson: A Poetry of the Act*, numerous articles on the movies, and editor of *Man and the Movies*, the film scholar W. R. Robinson is Professor of English at the University of Florida. At present he is completing a study of Hemingway's *A Farewell to Arms* and a book on the movies to be titled *Man in Motion: the Movies as Narrative Art*.

TOMMY RUTH WALDO. Professor of English at the University of Florida, Professor Waldo has published most often on the Renaissance drama. Her latest book on Shakespeare appeared as a volume in the Salzburg Studies in English. She brings to her studies a double interest in music and computers.

DATE DUE